Afternoon Prayers

Notes following Aliyah, Volume 2

Joseph Zitt

METATRON ARTS AND MEDIA
HERZLIYA, ISRAEL - CLEVELAND, OHIO
2024

To Maricar Ferrer Fuchs,
who, with my family,
(after the events of this book)
saved my life

Contents

Introduction

I moved from America to Israel in November 2017. I moved to seek new opportunities, and to be near family, some of whom lived a few blocks from my eventual apartment, in an assisted living community that we jokingly called The House of a Hundred Grandmothers.

From March through September 2018, I worked in a hotel by the beach. I answered the phones, mostly working from 11 PM to 7 AM, including weekends and holidays. It paid just enough for me to get by. I was able to explore the area on days and nights when I didn't work. In that time, I wrote the online diary that became my previous book, *as if in dreams: Notes Following Aliyah*.

In the middle of September, a new job found me. A small but well-established computer company was looking for an English-speaking technical writer who could also do video. They liked me.

A few days before my sixtieth birthday, I left the hotel job and started the new one, back in my original field. I could walk to work. I consistently worked a standard week, Sundays through Thursdays, during the day. It was a small team with little turnover. Much of the staff had been there for twenty years or more.

I rarely got into the larger city just south of us. I mostly went to work, to shop at the nearby mall and the stores on the main street, and home. I would visit relatives nearby. Sometime later, I started going to performances at a dance center on the far side of the other city.

It was a time of integration. I was learning how to fit into the society, now that I had a reasonable paycheck and a conventional schedule. I had to learn a lot about the language, the government, and the way that society worked. I gradually figured a few of these things out. Many would continue to surprise me.

the time between

(the rest of) 2018

Tuesday, September 18th, 2018

Yom Kippur night: The women's section of the small synagogue within the House of a Hundred Grandmothers is packed. We're still waiting, though, for a tenth man to complete the quorum for prayer.

The young cantor and his two brothers come in, a few minutes late, their sandals and sneakers slapping against the tile floor.

The Yom Kippur service begins, without pomp, but with appropriate ceremony. There is no rabbi (from what I can tell), no sermon, no tickets, no nervous dressing up to prove to others once a year that we do, indeed, care about being Jewish.

The Kol Nidre prayer has a different melody than the one I know. The text is also different. All the same words are there, but the order has changed. The cantor sings the prayer three times. Each time, a couple of men and many of the women echo his singing, with a staggered delay. It sounds as if we are in a far larger room that rings with the upper frequencies of its reverberations.

The service ends after an hour. Most of the congregation walks and rolls upstairs. I head home.

Wednesday, September 19th, 2018

The city streets have little powered traffic tonight: no buses, no taxis, a very few electric bikes. The occasional car creeps along apologetically, perhaps coming home late from being elsewhere during the day.

It's Yom Kippur. Some people go to worship, but everyone seems to be outdoors, walking or riding, on foot or on foot-powered bicycles, rollerblades, and skateboards. Children and their families walk down the middle of the street, clustering on or around traffic circles. One girl, perhaps three years old, putters along, low to the ground, on a plastic tricycle. Looking in front of and behind her, I don't see any obvious parents, but everyone is looking out for everybody else.

I text a friend who is also out walking, but we don't meet up. I am heading toward the crowds and noise. She is avoiding them.

I sit for a while at the heart of the city. The streets sound like a playground. All the shops are closed, even those open on the Sabbath. I see people sitting on the patio of a café, but they're hanging out, not eating. Some sit on tables. Some have tracked down chairs. On a swing at the corner, in a streetlamp's spotlight, two young women embrace.

Friday, September 21st, 2018

The city square is ringed with merchants selling ritual items for the next holiday. Sukkot is coming, just five days after Yom Kippur. This is the only full work day between them.

The supermarket has the same items. I would hope that what the merchants have is fresher and better, but if what I've learned from American markets holds true, they may have the same suppliers.

Across the street, I hear a guitarist play four slow chords repeatedly through layers of delay. I go toward the sound, but only see a loud-speaker. Gradually, I recognize the music as an instrumental by Moby, synced to an animal rights video projected by a group of teenagers on a portable screen.

On the bus home, the hum of the air conditioning hangs on the second note of the guitar's scale. It never resolves.

Tuesday, October 30th, 2018

How we vote here: I show up at the polling place and am identified. They hand me a white envelope and a yellow envelope.

Behind a partition, in the equivalent to a voting booth, slips of paper are neatly laid out. Yellow slips have the names of the mayoral candidates. White slips have the logos of the parties/slates running for city council. (There are also blank slips of each color, possibly for write-ins.)

I put a yellow slip in the yellow envelope and a white slip in the white envelope, and drop them in the blue box.

I ask a poll worker to take my picture with my phone as I vote. I tell them that I'm a new immigrant and that this is my first election. Poll workers say "*Mazal Tov!*" and that they hope that I will return for many more.

Shabbat morning at the House of a Hundred Grandmothers: During the Torah reading, I see something I've never experienced before.

As always, the reader chants from the Torah scroll itself. It has only the letters of the text, without vowels, punctuation, or musical cues. Usually, this requires a daunting amount of memorization.

Here, however, there is a prompter: the reader's brother stands next to him with a conventional, fully notated text. He sings sotto voce, slightly ahead of the reader. With his free hand, he signals the music of the chant. It's akin to the Kodaly signals used in *Close Encounters of the Third Kind*, but each gesture signifies a phrase or type of melodic motion, rather than just a pitch.

An upward sweep (if I recall correctly later) gives the standard start to a verse. Waving repeatedly right to left continues as usual. A chop with the palm held vertically gives a mid-verse pause with its particular phrasing; with the palm down, it ends the verse. Other phrases are triggered by sharp pointing, wiggling the hand in midair, or a sort of diagonal.

The brothers are both quite large, and their backs are to the congregation, so most of the people don't see it. Called up to give the blessings, I have to keep from laughing with glee as I watch them do this.

This is the way things are in worship here. There is rarely a need for a rabbi. People know how to do things themselves.

In the afternoon prayers at my office, any of the men (there are undeniable gender issues) can lead the service. One of three people usually does, but it seems, unless I'm missing planning or signals, to be whichever one starts up as soon as we have a quorum. Different people use slightly different liturgies. People know when to pause to let those who are saying more words catch up.

Left to my own, I usually wouldn't be involved in praying. There's no problem in declining to join. Some men at work stay at their desks and don't participate. That's OK. I feel like it's a sort of team activity, like offices elsewhere that do tai chi together. Ten minutes of fervent low-key group mumbling, supporting mourners and others, then it's back to our desks (usually after a stop through the kitchen for even more coffee).

When this Shabbat service ends, people pack up what they need to and gather just outside the hall for wine and cake. Most return upstairs.

I walk home, heat up some cholent that I'd made and frozen before as a solid lunch, then take a much-needed nap.

(all of) 2019

Sunday, February 3rd, 2019

The supermarket is mobbed with people buying chips and beer.

The cashiers seem baffled. Nattering among themselves in Hebrew, Arabic, and Russian they are shifting around, with the managers jumping from lane to lane, opening checkout counters and voiding errors. Of course, several registers break down.

I have a basket of my usual stuff (cheese, grapefruit juice, sweet potatoes, peanut butter) and didn't expect the mob either.

I realize that almost all of them are speaking English, in North American accents. Right. It's the Super Bowl. People are talking about napping before the game, since kickoff is at 1:30 AM. Now that I've been reminded, I'll try to catch video of the half-time show in the morning.

Saturday, February 16th, 2019

Shabbat at the House of a Hundred Grandmothers: I head there in the early morning in the midst of a sudden hailstorm. I've walked through Texas thunder and Cleveland blizzards. I can handle this.

I'd been told ahead of time that they'd need me to reach the quorum of ten men needed for prayer. I'm a few minutes late when I get there. I'm number eight. Number nine comes in a few minutes later. The prayers start. We get as far as we can without a quorum.

Right when the tenth is needed, a man arrives in a wheelchair, driven by a caregiver. He stares benignly forward, not reacting to his surroundings.

A gentle dispute arises over whether he can be counted. He doesn't respond to questions, and we're unsure whether he knows where he is. The apparent rule of thumb: a man can be counted if he can respond "Amen" to blessings. People try to get him to do so, but he doesn't. We're told that he responds if a member of his family is saying the prayer, but only then.

After several minutes of gentle attempts to communicate with him, we reach a consensus that it won't work. Some men pack up and leave, perhaps to go to other congregations. Some continue with what prayers they can still do solo.

I put my raincoat on and head out. A woman at the door insists on giving me a couple of pieces of cake. I thank her and go back home, back to bed.

Friday, March 22nd, 2019

Friday afternoon at the mall: In the food court, a shabby-looking man carrying an armful of children's books shuffles from table to table. He shows the people at each the front of the top book then the back, which bears his picture, perhaps taken in better days.

A few people buy a book. He autographs it, then, often, after an exchange of subtle gestures with a parent, ceremoniously presents it to a child.

In the produce aisle at the grocery store, a baby abruptly sits on my feet and plays with a fallen pomelo. I gently slide my feet out from under her and continue shopping.

At the bus stop outside, someone has taped a flyer about a lost dog to the sidewalk. Maybe they figure that the people now known as "cell-phone zombies" will actually see it there.

Tuesday, April 9th, 2019

Election Day again: Many people are off from work. Many have flocked to the larger city, swarming downtown.

In the hidden discount room at the CD store, music playing from a small radio by the open window blends with the sound from the bar downstairs. "Love Me Do" mixes surprisingly well with last year's still ubiquitous Eurovision winner. Bubbles float past the window, blown by an exhaust fan on the roof of a building a few doors down.

A woman zooms past the bar on a lime-green scooter, wearing a bikini that matches her tattoos. At least I think that that's a bikini and that those are tattoos.

In the basement of the mall, amateurs are doing folk dances. Some trip and fall over. Most don't. I don't even try.

Trapped in the mall's baffling double-helix structure, it takes me an hour to find the store I was headed to when I came in. I had intended to buy something. I don't.

Escaping to the street, I'm right on time for a bus to carry me home.

Saturday, April 13th, 2019

Sabbath morning at the House of a Hundred Grandmothers: Only nine men show up again. We need ten for the service to continue.

The one boy there is just short of bar mitzvah age. We've been debating whether this is a circumstance in which he can be counted. The consensus is that he can't.

He and his father (who doesn't seem too engaged, and is reading a newspaper tucked behind his prayer book) quickly head out, followed by others. They're walking to the next nearest synagogue, officially called "the congregation of the young." Since few young people worship there either, they refer to it by the name of its street.

On my way home, I see people setting up for a party in the park. A half-ring of folding chairs bends around a pair of picnic tablecloths on the ground. A woman walks up carrying a large bouquet of balloons, looking uncertain where to attach them.

When I walk past again in the evening, only a few of the balloons, semi-deflated, remain. Dogs halfheartedly nose them along the ground until, losing interest, they return to sniffing each other instead.

Sunday, April 14th, 2019

I mistranslate the name of this office as "The Ministry of Faces." It's more like "The Ministry of the Inside." I show up on time, take a number, and only have to wait for four people ahead of me before I am summoned to the worker's cube.

I'm there to get my passport. I have all the right paperwork, and have paid the fee ahead of time online. I can understand most of what the worker is saying, but not all. When I get stuck on a few words, she says them again in English, but we speak Hebrew for most of the encounter.

Some of my trouble understanding her is due to the language. Some is due to the noise. Not only is the chattering of dozens of people ricocheting off of the tile floor and hard plastic partitions, but another person has barged into the cube. He stands behind where I'm sitting and yells over the plexiglass at another worker, often drowning out what I'm trying to hear.

When it's time to take my fingerprint, the worker gestures for me to put my finger on a small scanner. After a moment, she says "Don't –" something, the word obscured by the bellowing behind me. I lift my hand. That's what I wasn't supposed to do. She takes hold of my wrist, puts my finger back on the scanner, and holds it there with her own finger until the scan is done.

With a photo of my face ("Look down – no, not that far down – and take off your glasses"), a scan of a finger on the other hand, and a few more signatures, we're done.

As I wait for the elevator, a man standing next to me says something several times, gesturing back at the room. What he's saying is probably funny, but I can't quite hear him, and can't tell. "Just English?" he finally asks. I nod. "Ok," he says. "Have a nice day."

We ride the elevator down in silence, then head back out into the warm sunlight but a surprisingly chilly breeze.

Friday, April 19th, 2019

The Passover Seder at the House of a Hundred Grandmothers: Fewer people are here than last year. Some are with family (made easier by the holiday landing on the Sabbath this time), but fewer people live at the House now. There's a natural attrition and few are moving in, perhaps drawn away to the newer, glossier houses that are opening in the area.

I sit at the head table with my family, who lead the ceremony. For some reason, only two tables have full seder plates, so I have the task of going from table to table with the bitter herbs and charoset (there's no good English word for charoset) when they're needed.

While we eat, I talk with an old family friend, who had been my nieces' teacher some thirty years ago. I speak my halting Hebrew. She speaks simply, telling me of her arrival here in the 1950s. She knew no Hebrew then. The first words that she learned were "Patience. All will be well."

Most people leave before we finish eating, walking off or being wheeled away by their caregivers. Exactly three men remain for the prologue to the Grace after Meals that requires at least three. The third man leaves when that is done. Four of us finish the seder together.

I walk home, brandishing my audio recorder. Last year, I had heard families singing the traditional songs as I passed their houses. This year, I don't hear them, recording instead the relative silence, with footsteps, traffic signals, dogs, distant televisions, and occasional cars of a typical city Sabbath night.

Wednesday, May 8th, 2019

Moments before the nationwide Memorial Day sirens, I look out of my cube and discover that most of our staff has disappeared. I stand by my office window in silence as the sirens blare.

Across the country, most things stop. Cars pull over and people stand beside them. A few minutes later, I send a text to my team, asking where they went. I'm told that they are at the cemetery next door. I go outside and can hear the voices, but can't easily locate them.

When they return, the boss comes over and, very formally, apologizes on behalf of the company for my not having been told. He then introduces me to his youngest son, a bearded soldier with a gun. He describes my accomplishments in terms that I find hard to recognize, then heads out, taking his son to lunch and then home.

Friday, May 17th, 2019

Friday shopping: Disappointments in the larger city. The record store doesn't have the new disc by a favorite ensemble, but the clerk, when I tell him of it, orders several. He knows that other workers will also dive on it.

I try to find where two shops for coffee gear are, supposedly on the same street, a few doors from each other. Other shopkeepers tell me that both closed years ago. Apparently no one told their webmasters.

Back in my city, I get to a bakery at the last moment to buy challah. They're already mopping down the shop's floor, but a worker sits outside near a rack that is still almost full of freshly baked loaves. He's only doing cash transactions.

I want one challah, but he insists that I buy two at a discount. I shrug, get both, and put one in the freezer when I get home.

Friday, June 14th, 2019

Most places dispense their coffee granitas (just called *"ice café"*) pre-made, from something like Slushie machines. At this place, they make it from scratch. When I order an ice café, the barista asks me what kind.

"Um, large?" I say.

"We have many different kinds," he says, and points to a completely cryptic menu. I stare at it, trying to understand much of anything. "We can also do regular," he finally says.

"Good," I say, relieved. "Just regular."

He goes through the whole ritual: brewing espresso ("Long or short? Weak or strong?") then pouring it, milk, and ice in a blender. After blending, he puts in a to-go cup and asks if I want – um, something – in it. I think he means a straw, and I say "Yes."

He sprays enough whipped cream in the top that it starts to ooze. He hands it to me, and points to where – um, some other noun I don't know – are. I look. Those are the straws.

After the whole performance, the *"ice café"* costs twice as much as I expect. I sit and drink it. I like the cheap ones from the coffee chain better.

Monday, July 15th, 2019

I'm getting a fairly consistent bit of feedback on my new book. Americans are enjoying it. Some are saying it gives them unexpected insight into life here in Israel. Israelis, on the other hand, are shrugging. "You've described life here just as it is. Why would that be interesting?" At least I'm getting a sense of the audience.

Thursday, July 18th, 2019

Walking with a group through Nazareth, I ask our tour guide if his tattoo is indeed the outline of the state of Ohio.

"Yes. But it was not my decision."

Friday, July 19th, 2019

I survived the Great Galilee Cardio Death March. So many stairs, so little time.

Saturday, July 20th, 2019

"You are here to eat or just to look? To look? No! This is business, not museum. Go away. You in the hat, standing there, you are here to eat? Good! You want to sit inside or outside? I tell you, you want to sit outside. Step in here. That is where I cook pancakes. It is hot. Yes, sit outside. You choose well. Now, I bring you menu. We have good Arab food. You choose freekeh? You know what freekeh is? Good! I bring freekeh, salad, the best mint lemonade, and after, I make you something very sweet, special Arab sweet, and coffee. You will like it. Good!"

Saturday, July 27th, 2019

Shabbat morning at the House of a Hundred Grandmothers: As I enter the synagogue, a bit late, I hear a voice from the pulpit, chanting, an octave higher than usual. A boy, just three weeks past his bar mitzvah, is leading the service.

He moves through it smoothly and confidently. His father, sitting nearby, nods in appreciation and occasionally dozes off.

When the boy reads from the Torah, he makes a few mistakes (even for a native Hebrew speaker, reading from the scroll without vowels, punctuation, or musical cues is hard) but members of the congregation call out corrections. When he stumbles over one phrase then recovers, the usual reader, standing next to him, gives him a thumbs-up.

As I walk home through the park, a blue bird, practicing low-altitude maneuvers, zooms past my knees, loops under the brim of a trashcan, then flies past me again into a bush. It pauses briefly, then launches into another test run.

Sunday, July 28th, 2019

The afternoon prayers at the office get started more or less on time today, as a tenth man is reluctantly pulled into the conference room.

Today, fortunately, the coworker with the best voice is leading the service. It has its usual lumpy structure: people murmur prayers, beginning in unison but continuing at different speeds. When the leader hears that many of the men are done with a prayer, he sings the ending and begins the next.

The longest stretch is actually a group of eighteen different prayers run together. Almost everyone else has been saying them several times a day in their native language for decades. They get done about twice as quickly as I do.

Usually, the leader picks up again while I'm still in the middle. This time, he waits for me as others shuffle their feet in annoyance.

Later, I tell him that I know that I'm slower than everyone else, and that he can continue if I'm not done yet. It turns out that he's a stickler for the rules, and insists that he can't go on until at least ten congregants are done – and since we had exactly ten, he had to wait.

So now I have to hope that we get not just ten men each day but eleven, so enough will finish before me. Or maybe I'll just hit the high points and leapfrog to the end.

Thursday, August 1st, 2019

When I get to the conference room for afternoon worship, a coworker is laying out cookies and soft drinks.

I first guess that he's decided that you can attract more worshipers with munchies than with badgering, but there's more to it. Today, because it's the eleven-month anniversary of his father's death, he will stop saying Kaddish at each service. A sign next to the cookies says "For the elevation of the soul of (whomever) son of (whomever)." Apparently, each prayer said with each item eaten helps propel his father's soul into the World to Come.

I tell him that I hadn't encountered that custom before (though later, I realize that I had, at the House of a Hundred Grandmothers).

He says "That is good. I hope you never have to do this."

He leads the service himself, zooming through it, loud and staccato, like an auctioneer. Within moments after the end of worship, all the cookies have been consumed.

Thursday, August 15th, 2019

A man walks in, dragging carpet samples, through the office's open doors. He gets as far as the conference room, looks at the men standing around, and is confused. We look back at him.

"Is this the furniture company?"

"No, that's down the hall. We figured you were here for afternoon prayers."

"You're doing them? May I?"

"Of course! Just drop your samples anywhere. You're the tenth man."

The leader launches into the service. At the end of the long silent prayer, we have to wait for the visitor. He's praying even more slowly than I do, though not through lack of practice. He's completely involved in doing them, with dramatic hand motions and facial expressions as he bobs back and forth.

When we're done, he holds a fervent pose for a moment, then turns and picks up his samples. "So, the furniture office?"

"Out the door and dead ahead."

"Thanks. Be blessed."

"Be well," today's leader replies.

The visitor heads back into the hall. We get back to work.

Saturday, August 17th, 2019

Shabbat morning at the House of a Hundred Grandmothers: Partway through the Torah reading, the leader says prayers for people who are ill. (Usually, we identify people by their name and their father's name; for these prayers, we use their mother's name.)

Today, a name that's been on the list for a while is missing. A man sitting behind me calls out "You forgot David."

There's a moment's pause. Someone else says, "David passed away."

"What? No! When?"

Other voices say "Monday? Tuesday?"

Another silence. The man behind me quietly repeats "Oh. Oh. Oh. Oh. Oh." A woman who can see him tells me later that he looks like he's been punched.

We wait until he falls silent. Then the leader looks back at his texts and resumes praying for the health of the others who had been named.

Friday, August 23rd, 2019

This burger joint is better than I'd feared.

I had been here once before, and the burger then was a disaster, a gray puck drowned in so much mayonnaise that when I bit down, the wilted lettuce and tomato shot out of the bun and onto my lap. That was just a few days after the place opened, though, and I know that it often takes a week or so for an eatery to find its legs.

The burger this time is quite good – not at a steakhouse level, but better than most fast food. And the other stuff in the bun is in a near-perfect balance.

The patio is packed. Right outside the door, four older women with South African accents (I think) are talking and laughing. At the table next to mine, a younger couple quietly eats and smokes. Their cell phone streams soft-rock hits, heavy on the Alan Parsons.

A little girl in a floral dress skips back and forth, sometimes trying for distance on each stride, sometimes going for height. As she nears the curb, a soldier, holding a mushroom burger with one hand, reaches back with the other and, without looking, snares the girl before she risks crashing into a turning bus. The girl laughs and runs back to her parents. Her mother calls out, "Thank you." The soldier nods and munches on his sweet potato fries.

Monday, September 2nd, 2019

The shofar is strikingly loud in the conference room, especially since I'm not expecting it. In the month preceding the New Year, some communities blow the ram's horn every day at the morning service. My boss has decided that, since many of us who gather in the afternoon don't attend services in the morning, he will do it now.

He has been holding the shofar inconspicuously throughout the service. At what would usually be the end, he makes a brief announcement that I don't quite understand, then lets loose with the traditional blasts: one long tone, three shorter ones, nine staccato blips, then another, even longer than the first. Its tone hits the resonant frequency of the room and bounces around, even louder than usual, before stopping. We then say one additional psalm, and the leader and mourners recite the Kaddish prayer for the fourth time in the fifteen-minute service.

The shofar is supposed to awaken us, at least metaphorically, when it is heard. I have started to doze at the end of the service in the crowded room when the sound rings out. It works.

Tuesday, September 3rd, 2019

The little girl in line in front of me at the supermarket is pulling on her hair (long, brunette, with blond highlights at the edges) while tapping a complex rhythm on her forehead. In the midst of checking out, her mother says, "Oh!" and runs off into the depths of the store. This happens a lot – usually, I think, here in the Fast Checkout aisle.

The cashier sighs and raises his eyebrows and hands. The last remnants of curly white hair form a fuzzy crown on his otherwise bald head, making him look like Ben Gurion or an earthly incarnation of the shrug emoji. He might be able to suspend their transaction, move on to other customers, then resume it, but if it's anywhere near as complicated a process as it was when I was a cashier, it's probably easier just to deal with the grumbling of the other waiting customers.

The mother meanders back, not carrying any merchandise, and finishes checking out as if nothing had happened. The girl wraps her arms around her, pleased that she has finally returned.

Thursday, September 5th, 2019

The choreographer (I presume) leaps onto the stage from the theatre floor, joins hands with the dancer farthest to the right, and leads the troupe forward for another curtain call. Some members of the audience stand and cheer. Others feel immediately compelled to check their phones. The rest applaud. The applause syncs into a steady pulse, at two beats per second. The house lights come up. The clapping fades.

The audience gradually rises and streams down the steps, through the lobby, and out to the open square.

A man on a stone bench by the exit plays classical guitar. To his left, another man with a multicolored hat spins to the music, his tzitzit spreading out like woolen spokes from beneath his shirt. The guitarist glances at him in annoyance, but smiles and nods as people drop coins in the open case at his feet.

I follow the crowd east along the cobblestones, past the artists' galleries, now closed for the night, and the crowded high-end gelato shops, returning to the city's too-bright asphalt streets to catch a late bus home.

Tuesday, September 17th, 2019

A postcard on my doorstep tells me, just in time, that my polling place has changed.

As I approach the school, a couple of blocks from my house, a voice with an Australian accent calls out "Hello, Cleveland!" A man waves from a booth for my party, just outside the boundary. Apparently he recognized my Cuyahoga t-shirt.

In a classroom, I hand the poll watchers the postcard and my ID. They hand me a blue envelope. I step behind a cardboard barrier, slip a piece of paper with my party's initials inside it, then drop the sealed envelope in a box where the poll watchers can see it.

Moments later, a block away from the school, I arbitrarily catch a passing bus into the larger city. Its card reader is disabled. On Election day, a legal holiday, buses are free.

I hop off the bus at the square where five streets meet. In the center, a white-haired woman, portly and joyous with pink sunglasses, a guitar case with loose change open at her feet, sits in a lawn chair surrounded by plastic flowers and sings popular, religious, and patriotic songs. A large crowd dances and sings along.

When she stops to swap the karaoke disc in her player, she orders the crowd to vote. "I don't care who you vote for – well, I do care, but I won't say – but if you haven't voted yet, go vote, and then come back!" A few men start a chant of "Bibi! Bibi!" but it fades quickly.

A gaunt woman of African descent, bent over and without teeth, approaches the singer, her palm out. The singer takes a coin from a plastic bag and gives it to her, then announces, "This woman has nothing. I have started her off with ten shekels. Who will add more to help her live?"

The bowed woman moves among the crowd. The white-haired woman sings again. I stay with the crowd, listening, filming, and singing, until sunset.

Thursday, September 19th, 2019

The shopkeeper makes the affogato in reverse, at least compared to other places that I've ordered it. First, she draws a shot of espresso into a wide paper cup. Once that's ready, she plops the scoop of cinnamon gelato that I've requested onto the center.

"A good choice," she says. "Cinnamon complements coffee well." She speaks to me in Hebrew-accented English, as she does to all the customers and to all the other workers. When not speaking to her, the workers talk among themselves in Hebrew and Arabic, and the shopkeeper switches to fluent Hebrew if a customer insists. But it's her shop, she's the boss, and apparently she likes English best.

I sit outside, alone, at the one unoccupied table. A woman with a pistachio cone sits on a bench a meter or so away, deftly catching the drips before they can hit her elegant clothes. I gesture to her, inviting her to join me, but she declines. Once I get up, though, she dives onto the table's other chair, grabbing a napkin from the dispenser and nabbing a blob of gelato as it falls.

I nod at her and smile. Now that I'm leaving, she smiles back.

Thursday, September 26th, 2019

As he cuts my hair, the barber sings along to a trip-hop remix of "Helplessly Hoping." The shop is quiet now, though it will be mobbed in the afternoon.

He shuttles back and forth between another customer and me. He is coloring her hair, applying a butterscotch-beige paste with a broad paintbrush, then working it in with the pointy end of a comb and a cotton swab.

Passing by his shop this morning on my way from Hebrew class to work, I had stopped in. Since only the coloring session was scheduled for now, and that involved a lot of waiting, he offered to handle us both at once.

The other customer was late, so he had called her. She was circling, looking for a parking spot. One had just opened up outside the shop, so he picked up a wicker chair, ran down to the street, and put the chair down in the spot to reserve it. The customer carried the chair back in when she arrived.

Now, as he guides a razor down the path of my sideburns, I tell him that I hadn't planned to drop in but did so spontaneously.

"You're becoming a local," he says. "You see that when going from there to there you can also go here and here, and you do it. For two years, you've been like an airplane, circling the city. Now, you know how things fit together, and you're coming in to land."

Sunday, September 29th, 2019

It's going to be a big Rosh Hashanah for barbecue. The temperature hasn't dropped much from the peak of summer, but at least it isn't painfully hot.

In front of the market, down the square from where I'm enjoying a plate of hummus, a display holds a dozen black bags. Each bears a drawing of a fire pit and, in bold white and yellow letters, the words "Umm Al-Fahem BBQ Charcoal."

Between the shop and me, a little boy runs after pigeons. They fly away just as he reaches them. I worry that if he falls, his finger may go farther up his nose than he intended. A girl not much older than he is stands nearby. Her t-shirt reads, both normally and as if reflected below a dotted blue line, "Heartbreak Hotel, E.29th & Broadway, NYC."

Across the intersection at the center of town, young people talk with others at a stand with a well-made sign: "A sandwich for whoever needs one." In Hebrew, it rhymes.

Tuesday, October 1st, 2019

The Tashlich ceremony at the House of a Hundred Grandmothers is held indoors. A sculpted fountain with running water in the lobby is enough like a stream to qualify. We don't toss crumbs or other objects into it, though, since there are no fish or ducks to eat them, and they would just clog the plumbing.

Once again, I'm asked to say Kiddush in the acute care area. I bless the wine. My sister, who has come in with me, explains the ritual foods on the table. Once again, the prayer for having sustained us and kept us alive through this moment seems more meaningful here.

Afterward, I join the family in the dining hall for supper. The servers recognize me and load up my plate with goose, vegetables, and fragrant rice. It's as if they worry that I haven't eaten since I joined them last at Passover.

The synagogue space was full for the morning service, but is emptier now that it's evening. On the way past, I'm dragged in to be the emergency tenth man.

It's good to see some people who hadn't been there in a while. Some have been in poor health and are now much less mobile, but the congregation does what we need to so everyone can play his part. No one's in charge, and no one is officially coordinating things, but when the community acts together, it works.

Friday, October 4th, 2019

In the next town over, in the center of town, I hear music from behind a pillar to my left. Walking around it, I see a man with an electronic keyboard playing something soft, somewhat like jazz. Handwritten signs say "Official organist," "Welcoming committee," and "I am organic."

A block further down, a man sits on a bench by the curb, brandishing a violin bow. When someone notices him, he lifts the violin and plays a few bars of something Eastern European, but then puts it back down.

Outside the mall at the other end of the bus lines, the man who usually plays amplified banjo is playing violin, riffing on American folk tunes. Occasionally people notice and toss coins in his case. He nods and keeps playing. His smile says that he's found his place in the universe.

Sunday, October 6th, 2019

Traffic on this street is slower than a funeral and not as happy. Three cars ahead of us, a street sweeper is following a trash truck. Arrows on its back are blinking, suggesting that we go around it, but there are cars parked on one side and a median strip on the other. Drivers will hop curbs to park on sidewalks, but the strip along here is too narrow.

I got the next-to-last seat on this express bus. People in the aisles wobble and lurch each time the bus inches forward. A soldier's gun bangs into the metal pole near the exit steps. People on either side of me are listening to loud music on their phones. The high-frequency percussion that leaks from their earbuds is almost, but not quite, in sync.

I can see that the person one row ahead of me, across the aisle, is listening to a gentle track from *Electric Ladyland*. Good idea. I'm squeezed tight against the cargo pants of the person next to me, but if I could get my phone out of my pocket, I would listen to it too. Until then, I close my eyes and try to appreciate the sounds and scents around me.

Wednesday, October 9th, 2019

Yom Kippur afternoon: The street is crowded with children on tricycles and skateboards. There's almost no traffic.

Two police cars creep down the road toward each other. When they meet, the drivers get out and talk. An ambulance, lights blazing, moves silently but more swiftly around a corner. People get out of the way.

I expect the center of town to be more crowded than the streets further out, but it isn't. Electric bicycles roll past the storefronts, pedaled, not powered. Traffic signals follow their usual patterns of clicks and colors. Everyone ignores them.

TV stations are off the air, showing a silent image with a holiday greeting and a note saying when they'll be back. I sit downtown for a while, outside the Great Synagogue.

When evening services begin, though, I decide not to go in. Tired and with a headache from fasting and walking, I head home.

Monday, October 14th, 2019

On the night of the full moon, I sit on a bench on a city street. A gimbal holds my phone, keeping it steady while filming. A monopod beneath it keeps it at an even height. Some people look at me curiously. Most ignore me.

In front of me, more or less centered in the camera view, five traffic lights cycle through their patterns, about two minutes long. The moon appears steady in the sky above them, its diameter the same as those of the lights. Clouds pass in front of it. It isn't as clear as I'd like, but I can't control that.

Lower in the frame, cars and motorcycles pass, straight across the horizontal on the street that crosses mine, on a diagonal here on the road where I sit. On the sidewalk, people stroll with or without families. All the adults are on foot, while many children are on bicycles, tricycles, skateboards, and roller skates. Dogs also pass, with people tethered to them. Cats wander about, rarely in straight lines. They glance at the cars, the people, the lights, and the moon, shrug, and carry on.

Tuesday, October 15th, 2019

The birds in the noise tree may be invisible. I've heard them chattering, shrieking, and singing since I moved here, but, even when the branches are more bare, I haven't seen them.

Tonight, the air is cooler than it has been. This afternoon, rain fell for the first time since spring. Now, after dark, the birds are performing for each other and the people below.

I stand quietly beneath the tree with a stereo recorder. Above me, the sound of the birds shifts between left, center, and right, as if a conductor were triggering scattered choirs overhead. The deeper roars and rumbles of traffic contrast with their song, providing an unstable bass line closer to the ground. The voices of people passing start and stop, filling in the middle range.

I see little of this happening as I focus on the recorder's meters. Backing away when I'm done, I collide with the wall of what had been a café behind me. I turn and look inside. The shop is dark, its floor completely clear except for the chairs still stacked against the glass. Images of people, bikes, and buses pass through the reflected light. I still see no birds.

Thursday, October 17th, 2019

In the square at the heart of the city, there's a traffic jam of wheelchairs and baby carriages.

A holiday celebration has drawn a small crowd. There should be plenty of room to get around the makeshift stage and rows of plastic chairs, but two canopied urban go-carts have been parked and abandoned in the worst possible place. Only two people at a time can squeeze past them, and only one person who is on wheels.

As I stand to the side, I see people jam the bottleneck, trying to roll through it in opposing directions at the same time. If a wheelchair and a baby carriage conflict, the wheelchair usually wins. Respect for the aged is so ingrained in people here that it tames even arrogant drivers. If two wheelchairs face one another, the caregivers guiding them quickly reach agreements. If two baby carriages meet, though, the mothers stand their ground, each waiting for the other to back up. That takes longer.

Once, I see an old woman stand and shove the carriage nearer to her out of the way. Otherwise, one of the mothers eventually yields, with a deep sigh signaling to the heavens that the universe is once again being particularly unfair to her.

Onstage, a drummer and a singing guitarist work their way through medleys of the usual popular religious songs. When they pause, they announce community singing later in the evening. I'm too tired to stick around.

Wednesday, November 6th, 2019

I get to the dance center much earlier than I'd planned. An unexpected pedestrian path leads me from work to an express bus, and I walk efficiently from the bus to the center without getting lost.

I sit for a while outside, checking my email. The classical guitarist is there again, playing a version of the Moonlight Sonata. I remember to toss some shekels into his case this time before I wander on.

A larger plaza awaits on the other side of the center. At a restaurant at a far corner, recorded crooners serenade well-dressed customers with songs that seem to have hung in the air there for decades.

Beyond the tall windows of a studio next door, two men run at each other, crash, swing each other into the air, then back up and do it again.

Just past the studio, a white-haired woman sings a song about water to a little girl. She holds both the child's hands as she helps her learn to walk, splashing in a stream that runs through a carefully laid gap in the cobblestones. Two boys, only slightly older, kick a soccer ball past them and around the other people standing outside.

A pedestrian street heads away from the plaza. Rather than the usual bollard, an ice cream cone, as tall as I am, stands where the road starts. The gelato shop just past it looks tempting, but I'm still full from the shawarma I ate while walking here. Maybe I'll stop there after the show.

Thursday, November 7th, 2019

I lean against a wall across from the shop, carefully eating a cup of gelato. The flavor has no name. The sign stuck in the tray says "Ask us." When I requested a cup of whatever it was, the server asked if I was OK with hazelnuts. Apparently, some people aren't.

The sign on the wall above me says I'm on Pines Street, but "Pines" is pronounced as if the vowels were in Italian. Around me, people chatter in French, German, Dutch, and in English with several different accents. I only hear one couple speaking Hebrew.

Taxis roll slowly down the streets that cross here, waiting for people to get out of the way. At the intersection, they alternate going through, as if at a stop sign. The drivers aren't known for their patience, but here they have no choice.

Across the other street from me, men hop off a cart and load it with scooters that have been left lying around. They talk loudly in Arabic. Everyone ignores them. When they're done, they drive down the sidewalk as far as they can, then shift onto the street and away from us, down toward the sea.

Tuesday, November 12th, 2019

It's only a little quieter than usual at work today. In towns where
the rocket sirens have blared, schools and some businesses are closed.
Several of my coworkers with kids are staying home with them. At the
House of a Hundred Grandmothers, the Arab workers were delayed but
eventually arrived.

I see that the dance center has canceled tonight's performance. I'm at
work, but a window on my computer is tracking a liveblog of relevant
news. Text message chains go around with information, misinforma-
tion, fact checking, and jokes. We wait to see who might be called for
reserve duty.

People ask me if this is the first of these situations I've been through.
It is. They tell me not to worry. My family tells me that we are only
halfway to an emergency. Everyone tries to shrug it off. But there are
more people than usual at the afternoon prayers.

Wednesday, November 13th, 2019

No one I've spoken to today has mentioned the rockets. From the
news feeds, it looks like things might be getting worse. but no one I've
seen is visibly bothered.

Schools and businesses are open again. Work continues. On my walk
home, everything seems to be as it has been. The city square smells of
good pipe tobacco. Somewhere on the pedestrian street, someone is
trying to play "Für Elise" too quickly.

The new kitten in our yard runs up to me when I get home and briefly
tolerates being petted. I kick fallen grapefruit and oranges out of my
way in an impromptu game of solitaire soccer fruit bocce before I head
inside.

Thursday, November 14th, 2019

The dance center is almost full tonight. I think an announcer said
that the performance was sold out, but I'm not sure. It's the first of three
evenings of a festival of premieres. I don't know any of the artists.

I'm in the second row of the balcony, on the end. I like having an
escape route. The row in front of me is full of teenage girls, possibly
dance students. The first five in the row are all wearing cropped tops,

shorts, and knitted sweaters, in a riot of colors. Several brought bouquets of flowers and don't know where to put them during the show. I hope they don't mean to throw them onto the stage. We're pretty far back, and they would just hurt someone in the audience below.

Another teenager down the row from me asks me something. I have trouble hearing and understanding her. After several repetitions, I catch "Can I see your –" and see that she's pointing at my program. Certainly. And now I know the word for "program," though I may forget it by morning.

Wednesday, November 20th, 2019

A sign on the counter at the all-day breakfast joint says "Are you drinking enough water? Help yourself to some." A large decanter and a stack of plastic cups sit next to it.

It's supposed to be the rainy season, but we've only had brief showers on three days so far. The TV says the humidity is at ten percent.

The New York Breakfast at this place consists of two slices of whole wheat toast, one with what may be a sort of cheese or may be egg whites, and the other with smoked salmon, tomatoes, and onion. I eat them as a sandwich but, toward the end, realize that they're probably meant to be eaten independently. There's a green salad on the side.

I do everything in Hebrew, hoping that I'll be pleasantly surprised by what I don't understand about what I've ordered. When I'm almost done, the waiter asks "Would you like some –" and says a word I don't understand. I repeat the word, and he pegs me as an English speaker. "Dessert?" he asks. He speaks to me in English from then on.

The food is good, and about the same price as McDonald's. But I think I'll order something else next time.

Thursday, November 21st, 2019

An older wine-and-cheese audience wanders in clumps through the dance center lobby. They maneuver around pillars, stanchions, and tables covered with plastic goblets and trays of fruit. There is no cheese.

I think I hear a soprano, but it's the sound of a handpan someone's playing at one end of the space, filtered through the crowd noise and echoing off the stone ceiling and walls.

Down near the street, the usual guitarist plays for tips, just far enough away that his music and the handpan don't clash.

Across the plaza, a German shepherd, his leash held loosely by a woman who is typing on her phone with one thumb, nudges fallen grapefruit with his nose, as if trying to get them to form a meaningful constellation.

Uptown, later, another crowd, several blocks long, marches silently down a main street, bearing white balloons and placards. It's too dark to read their signs.

Sunday, November 24th, 2019

As I approach the office lobby from the outside, a little girl tries to push the door open from within. I stand just out of view and slowly pull on the handle so that the girl thinks that she is opening the door herself. Her mother, pushing an empty stroller, nods at me and smiles.

Slices of chocolate cake with white frosting crowd the edge of the guard's desk, lined up on paper plates with plastic forks. The slices and forks all point in exactly the same direction.

One of the people standing around the desk is singing "And I Love Her." The lyrics are only approximate. I hum along as the elevator doors close and I rise toward the office.

Thursday, December 5th, 2019

A statue on the far side of the plaza turns out to be a real person. She sits even more quietly than I do, backlit by a spotlight, then rises, gathers some objects that I can't identify, and walks toward and past me into the dance center.

I'm out here later than usual. The show won't start until ten. As I listen, I hear birds, distant traffic, and water running on both sides of me. They are gradually drowned out by human voices, footsteps and the sound of hand luggage being dragged across time-smoothed stone. I stand. It's time to go in.

Friday, December 6th, 2019

Friday shopping: "You want only one challah? Here, they are seven shekel for one, but now four for twenty!"

I only want one. As it is, I always end up throwing out what's left of the previous week's when I get a new one.

"And you want only one donut?"

I do. This is donut season, but I try to eat no more than one a day.

"This one has no strawberry jam. You want strawberry jam? I get you with strawberry jam."

The baker disappears from behind the counter and reappears with what I guess is a different donut. They look the same to me.

Outside, a flock of pigeons tears apart a challah someone set out for them.

Around the corner, a pillar bears a half dozen death notices. Other signs on it announce that a new Torah scroll will be inaugurated at a synagogue down the street, and that a hummus joint that I've never tried has lost its kosher certification.

Two chassidim pack up a table a few meters away where they've been trying to get men to put on tefillin. Shops start to close. Shabbat is almost here.

Sunday, December 8th, 2019

All the snails are out tonight. Today, we've had the first steady rain since spring. It's the first time I've seen more than a couple of tiny ones sneak out from under the bushes onto the walkways.

The pedestrian street is now a minefield of mollusks. I have to be careful to step around them while trying not to slip on the wet stones. Occasional dogs and cats walk up to them, sniff, and wander off. Maybe they don't like the scent. Maybe they're looking for a snack that's not quite so crunchy.

If I stare at each snail for a while, I can tell that it's moving, though not in any consistent direction.

I know that by morning they'll be gone. Hunkered down in the shadows, they'll wait for the next rain to summon them to patrol.

Friday, December 13th, 2019

Ordering breakfast has too many variables. How would you like your eggs? What kind of bread? Green salad or Israeli? Avocado?

I stumble through the interrogation, understanding what I can and guessing at the rest.

The server is stumbling too. Partway through, she says "English?"

I nod.

She looks relieved. "Good. Let's start again." Her accent seems Israeli, but, like me, she is from elsewhere. English is her second language, Hebrew her third.

The breakfast is sumptuous and not too expensive. What I hear as "eggs like eyes" are indeed sunny side up. With the bread basket (good whole wheat bread; they are out of multigrain) and the coffee mug taking up space, the plate, with eggs in the left compartment, salad to the right, and scoops of tuna, avocado, and some sort of cheese in the center, is too large for the tray.

I balance it all carefully as I carry it from the counter to my seat. A man in a wheelchair backs up abruptly into my path, but I see him in time. Nothing spills. Nothing falls.

I sit down, shift the complimentary chocolate away from the coffee cup so that it doesn't melt, and begin to eat.

Sunday, December 15th, 2019

A little girl in a bright pink parka sings the Hallelujah Chorus, swinging an umbrella wildly about in rhythm with the song. I wonder if she's singing in Hebrew or English. She loops back to the beginning before she runs out of Hallelujahs, so there's no way to tell.

Other people on the sidewalk duck around her and the umbrella. She almost jabs it between a bicycle's spokes. The rider starts to curse but, seeing how small she is, thinks better of it.

A large dog, lying under a table at its human's feet, growls as she approaches, then whimpers as the end of the umbrella bounces off its head. The dog looks up at the human, who says something calming, then rests its head on its paws and goes back to sleep.

When I get to the cinema entrance, a man inside opens the door just enough to say "No admittance for fifteen more minutes." I shrug and lean against the wall outside.

A moment later he returns, rolling a cart of 3D glasses to the ticket stand. He opens the door wider this time. "But since you're already here, welcome."

He takes my ticket, tears it, and hands me the stub and a pair of glasses. "Theater 2."

I'm the first one in the theater. I find my seat, though the diagram online was completely wrong. I'm halfway up, on the aisle, which I like.

From my seat, I am surrounded by a muted chorus of air conditioning systems. A maze of hisses and pitches comes from in front of me and from the sides. Some are so soft that they seem to pulse in rhythm with my heartbeat in my ears. Soundtracks from the movies in adjacent theaters pop and rumble at a similar level, playing an unpredictable bass line under the whisper of the machines.

When the rest of the audience arrives, they're preceded by the strong scent of popcorn. Only a couple of dozen people come in. Many are excited. Some have been waiting for this moment for 42 years. A moving picture pops into view, followed by sound. Time for commercials, trailers, reminders, and, finally, the movie.

(the beginning of) 2020

Sunday, January 19th, 2020

The waiting room at the Dental Imaging Centre is small but reasonably cheerful, painted bright white and a muted yellow-green.

An embellished photo of Jerusalem hangs behind the counter. The Western Wall is speckled with flecks of gold. Signs on other surfaces praise Rabbi Nachman. One offers books from his Breslov sect for sale. The boss wears a Chabad yarmulke.

As I sit down, a text comes to my phone: "Waiting for your turn? Click this link for children's games and information about dental health."

A customer and two workers, the man in black and white with a wide-brimmed hat and the women in colorful kerchiefs, discuss their sects' stances toward television. One's allows it. One's bans it. The third's allows religious broadcasts, National Geographic, and kosher cooking shows.

They speak among themselves and with me in Hebrew, but when another customer, a Black man with a North American accent, comes in, they switch to English. They know him from before. He sits down next to me. We silently flip through magazines as we wait for them to take our X-rays.

Thursday, January 23rd, 2020

The cart in the ER waiting room is out of sandwiches. They seemed to have had plenty when they arrived, but I got called away, so nurses could draw my blood for a fourth time.

I've been X-rayed, scanned, had a couple of people listen to my heart and lungs, and had two ECGs since this morning. The doctor has scolded me: "When your chest feels like that, don't wait a week for an appointment. Head right to the hospital."

I've been in and out of offices and exam rooms for the past eight hours. It looks like they'll keep me overnight. Maybe by then they'll have a better idea what's happening, though they don't think it was a heart attack.

The man to my left is saying evening prayers under his breath, reading the texts from his phone. To my right, a doctor barks at an older couple: "I know you've been here since ten, but I'm running to a patient who is between life and death. You will wait."

I sit here, dozing off and on, listening for my name and to the conversations in many languages that swirl around me.

Monday, March 2ⁿᵈ, 2020

Voting is straightforward, once I figure out which of the labyrinthine cluster of classrooms is my polling place. There are about a dozen different ones here, identified by apparently random numbers.

Once I find the room, I present my government ID. They hand me a blue envelope. I go behind a partition, put the slip of paper representing my party in the envelope, then step out and drop it through a slot into a cardboard box.

Outside, two boys are playing a hybrid sport on a ping-pong table, knocking a soccer ball back and forth with their heads.

At lunch, I sit with six other English speakers, meeting most for the first time. Many of them have been in the country for years. Some have never learned much Hebrew. "I still can't remember if my name begins with the 6 or with the hat."

It's a good group. I'm the only man. One jokes that the restaurant staff will think they're my harem. I shrug and smile.

the year of the mask

(the rest of) March, 2020

Monday, March 9th, 2020

A white mask covers my bus driver's nose and mouth. Many children on the bus and on the street also wear masks, but they're of cartoon characters and princesses. Purim is this evening. More people than usual are wearing tutus or carrying flimsy swords.

The front row of the bus is blocked off with cloth-like tubing. By order of the Transportation Ministry, no one may sit or stand close to the driver. On my previous bus, toilet paper was draped and taped across the front seats, serving well enough as a barrier.

In the office and on the street, most of the jokes that I hear have the virus as a punchline. People can still laugh. One patient is four degrees of separation from me: his child is the classmate of a child of one of my coworkers. I've stocked up with enough supplies to get me through a two-week quarantine, should that be needed.

On the bus and in the stores, people wish each other a happy Purim. For many, a day of serious drinking is ahead.

Tuesday, March 10th, 2020

The House of a Hundred Grandmothers is under quarantine. No one but residents and workers may enter. I won't be visiting for a while.

Work today is quiet, because of the holiday, not the virus. We don't officially have the day off, but most of the more religious workers have taken a vacation day to celebrate.

Those of us at the office are even more relaxed than usual. Gossip swirls through the air about whether one worker has been quarantined and whether we should be concerned that two others were in Thailand a month ago. We don't reach a consensus.

Few of the hamantaschen that I bring in are eaten. Though the bakery where I got them makes excellent challah, these are disappointing, overly dry and with a flavorless chocolate filling.

At ten to two, I set things up for afternoon prayers as usual and wait for others to arrive. No one else does. I'm not surprised. I wait for ten minutes, until the time that the service usually ends, then shut off the conference room lights, close the doors, and return to my desk.

Wednesday, March 11th, 2020

The counter in the kitchen at work is full of small wrapped candies, a result of the holiday yesterday. Like trick-or-treating run backwards, people visit friends and neighbors, sometimes in costumes, and give them gifts of food. It's supposed to be a real meal, but candy happens.

In the office, we're preparing to work remotely, installing the needed software on each computer and making sure that everyone can video chat. We don't need to yet, but we may. The government just banned gatherings of more than a hundred people. We only have two dozen in our office, but it's time to plan.

A worker who has been out sick with flu symptoms may be going through a battery of tests. Or he may not. His text messages are cryptic, even to native speakers.

In the men's room, I find that we're out of paper towels again. I wash my hands for twenty seconds, singing the chorus to "Jolene," shake them around till they're not too wet, then finish drying them in the kitchen.

Thursday, March 12th, 2020

Fierce winds are blowing through the city. Branches are down in my backyard. Some relatives have lost power. Word has it that hard rain will follow, through tomorrow night.

News is flying around more swiftly than the blowing leaves. The House of a Hundred Grandmothers isn't completely in quarantine. People from outside can't come in, but people from inside can go out. Still, the birthday party that we had planned for tomorrow is canceled. For a person in several risk categories, meeting at a restaurant feels too dangerous.

Schools are closed after today for at least a month. Further away, I'm told that all the churches have closed in Rome. Close to midnight, I haven't yet heard any rain. The wind whistles and screams at times, but then falls silent. I still have power in my apartment. But if it goes, I know that I can find my bed by moonlight.

The mall is usually far busier on Fridays than it is today. All the stores are open, though signs on the revolving doors tell us that, because of the virus, everything but the supermarket and pharmacy will be closing early until further notice.

Inside the supermarket, a rack of challahs sits mostly untouched. I start to take one, using a plastic bread bag to grasp it, but it is still too hot to hold. I decide to come back at the end of shopping.

I do more stocking up just in case. I get a one-kilo box of matzohs, even though Passover isn't for another month. They are often much cheaper just before the holiday but, since people who tend to take vacations on Passover will be staying home, there may be a shortage.

At the pop-up Shabbat food vendor's table, I get items at the end-of-the-day prices. The veggie cholent and the beef and rice stew will freeze well.

At the registers, the young North American dudes from the business college are buying six-packs of Corona beer. I think that's the thing that they call "irony."

Saturday, March 14th, 2020

Three other parties are sitting in the café. On the Sabbath, I usually visit relatives at the House of a Hundred Grandmothers, but no one other than residents and workers are allowed in. I didn't want to miss a day seeing other people in person while it's still allowed, so I'm here, at the only place that's open.

At one table, two old men are arguing politics over tea with mint. At another, four people chat in Hebrew and English. Their tiny black dog keeps jumping from the floor onto a woman's lap and then onto the table. In front of me, a couple shares an Israeli breakfast. Each man ceremoniously scoops up various dips with bread and feeds it to the other, often closing the action with a brief kiss.

At one point, they and the other men at the table sing something in unison, so softly that I can't tell what language it's in. Their interjections, called out with laughter, are clearly in Hebrew, though some words sound like Arabic.

I get through most of the ordering process in Hebrew. When I hesitate, the server explains in English what she can tell that I didn't understand, then switches back to Hebrew. This is better than before.

Usually, when people switch to English, they stay in English, but she can tell that my Hebrew is getting good enough that I can get through most of it without translation.

The breakfast is excellent. Later, I hear the Prime Minister announce that all restaurants are to close. I'm glad to have gotten there one last time.

Sunday, March 15th, 2020

The power goes out in our office building right at the end of the afternoon prayers. The ten men we have scrounged together are praying in an open hallway rather than the conference room, keeping two meters away from one another, more or less.

Just as the prayer leader finishes the mourners' kaddish, the lights go out. At first, we think someone has bumped into a light switch again. Then we realize that neither the refrigerator nor, more critically, the computers in the server room are humming. And it's not just us. Looking at the other hallways through the central atrium, we see that there's no power to the whole building. A series of cell phone calls confirms that no one knows why.

Most of us retire to our cubes. Without anything to do, I fall asleep.

I'm awakened by music. A support tech is strumming his acoustic guitar down the aisle from me. I wander over, as do most of the rest of the staff. He and others play and sing several songs by Led Zeppelin and Shlomo Carlebach.

Eventually the lights go on, and the computers boot back up. I've only lost a little work. We're supposed to start working at home, but if our systems won't stay up, we won't be able to connect to them remotely.

I start moving my project onto the cloud. Despite the health warnings, it looks like I'll be back in the office tomorrow, at least.

Monday, March 16th, 2020

The line at the small computer shop stretches out the door. Some people have carried chairs outside to sit in while they wait.

On most evenings, the shop has the same number of customers, all standing and sitting inside. They form an invisible queue. Customers, coming in, call out "Who is last?" and declare themselves to be in line behind whoever answers. Tonight, though, everyone is trying to stay two meters apart, so the crowd has spread out, like dots painted on an expanding balloon.

When it's my turn, I stand at a spot marked in white tape about a meter away from the service desk. The store has the Ethernet and HDMI cables that I need. The worker asks for my phone number to look up my customer record. When he hears me say it slowly (I still am unsure when it comes to numbers), he says "Let's do English. It will be faster."

He isn't touching credit cards. The customers before me read him their names, numbers, and expiration dates. It takes a long time. I pay cash, stepping forward and placing a hundred-shekel note on the desk, then picking up the change that he places on the receipt. We wish each other a good evening as he rubs a large blob of sanitizer on his hands.

Tuesday, March 17th, 2020

The rain starts, of course, as I'm walking home from work. I'd figured that it might. I often catch a bus in this weather, but transit has gotten unpredictable. After tonight, they won't be running in the evening anyway, and they may have already started skipping most stops.

On Tuesdays, I usually walk to the mall while listening to my favorite weekly podcast. But the mall is closed, and the park that I walk through to it may be closed too. I know that it will be as of tomorrow.

Along the main street, the larger restaurants are closed. Some storefront eateries are still open, but with only outdoor seating.

The doors are open at my usual shawarma joint, but everything is shut down inside. The usual array of condiments and add-ons is gone, and the grill, deep fryer, and shawarma spit are pulled away from the wall, possibly for cleaning.

I stop into a cheap coffee shop and pick up a prefab pasta plate to take home. It costs less than two US dollars and is quite good. At home, I curl up in front of the big screen. I would love to shelter in place, but, at my boss's request, I'll be back at the office tomorrow.

Wednesday, March 18th, 2020

A barrier of caution tape surrounds my office building's security desk. The guard is wearing a mask. So are half the people in the supermarket on the ground floor.

The masks are getting fancier. Some are more shaped and textured than the simple coverings I saw a few days ago. Some have multiple colors, mostly black and red, and scientific looking outcroppings and doodads.

The store is only a little more crowded than usual. I can get down all the aisles easily, except for the one with paper goods. They've overstocked on toilet paper, prepared for a panic that hasn't happened yet. Some of it is on sale. A few people in the cashiers' lines have packages of it, but I don't know if there are more than usual. I'd never thought to notice how much toilet paper other people were buying before.

Someone sends me a message about a protest happening tomorrow. Unfortunately, the person in the video is speaking really quickly, and the text is a graphic that I can't drop into a translation program. I'm usually up for a good protest. But it helps to know what they're protesting against.

Thursday, March 19th, 2020

Most of the eateries that were open with outdoor seating yesterday are closed. That's not due to any new edict, though. It's been raining and chilly. Few people want to hang out outside. Those who are walking do a dance of avoidance, trying to keep two meters between themselves and the people they pass.

Traffic is a little slower than before. The buses that lumber past are nearly empty. To my right, a tall teenager skips down the middle of a side street, her long hair waving behind her with each bounce.

Bulletin boards along the way, usually covered with posters for upcoming events, bear random scraps and staples where people have torn down the signs for shows that now won't happen.

A massive dog, off leash, blocks the end of the pedestrian street, watching me as I walk toward him, a block away. I watch him, too, alert to his stance and movement. If he were to charge, I wouldn't be able to either outrun or fight him. But I sense that he is calm. After a while, he turns and trots back toward the yard where I had seen him patrolling before. I pass where he had stood and reach my house moments before the rain returns.

Friday, March 20th, 2020

The park between my house and the House of a Hundred Grandmothers should be closed, but the gates are open. I go through. No one else is there.

When I reach the House, I wave at the guard through the glass doors. He comes to a window that I hadn't noticed before, dressed in a mask and scrubs, and opens it. I hand him my package and tell him who it's for and that it's a birthday present. I send them a text message. Their caregiver comes down and gets it.

At the bakery at the heart of town, the racks are full of challahs, as usual on a Friday, but rather than sitting there open to the air, each is in an individual bag.

The cheap coffee shop next door is open again, for takeout only. I get a coffee and a cheese burekas and sit at a bench by the curb eating them. A man whom I don't know passes by. He wishes me the Hebrew equivalent of "*Bon appetit*" and a good Shabbat.

I get a hummus plate to go at the usual place and bring it home to eat. Once home, I see that my robot vacuum cleaner has finished its job, but is stuck in a loop trying to park, repeatedly tracing the same triangular path. I move it closer to its docking station and settle down at my desk.

It's only midday, but I don't have anywhere else to go. And close to nothing, not even my usual Shabbat café, will be open tomorrow.

Saturday, March 21st, 2020

I'm told that it's been a nice day outside. I haven't looked out the door at all, and the windows are too high in this basement apartment for me to see much. I heard rain this morning.

I haven't seen another person since lunchtime yesterday. I spoke to one relative on the phone this morning and to another by video chat in the evening, but to no one in person.

I'm monkeying around a lot with inanimate objects. My two computers and my TV are now happily networked. I've cleaned out the innards of the vacuum robot. This is where we are now, not seeing other humans much.

Back in the 80s, back before many of my friends were born, after another friend quietly died alone, a group of us swore that we wouldn't let a day go by without encountering another person, even if it was to go downstairs to a deli (we all lived in New York City at the time) and get a coffee at the counter. I'd only missed two days since then, once when I was sick at home, and on a Christmas in Cleveland, when everyone else in my house was elsewhere, and I saw no one on a long walk through town.

I'll be back among people tomorrow, going to work and to get groceries. But Shabbat is going to be very quiet for a while.

Sunday, March 22nd, 2020

The laundry man waves and calls out to me as I pass his shop. He's shutting down his storefront, so he won't have walk-in customers, but if l want the usual pickup next Sunday, I should just send him a text message.

Traffic is slow, with maybe a half-dozen cars passing each minute on a usually traffic-jammed street.

Soon after I reach the office, we hear lushly orchestrated pop music fade in, gradually getting louder until it is overwhelming. It isn't anyone's phone or computer: a truck is slowly rolling past, four stories below us, with large loudspeakers blasting the sound. Someone jokes that it is "in honor of the Feast of Corona."

At the supermarket, the cashiers are wearing something like flimsy helmets: a sheet of transparent plastic, like the ones once used for overhead projectors, covers their faces, attached to a headband labeled "antivirus" in caution-tape yellow and black.

Last week, the store replaced their register keyboards with touchscreens, which appear harder to use, especially when the cashiers are wearing latex gloves. The second screens, which customers can see, are harder to read. I have to assume that they're charging the right prices. I only know for sure when I see the receipt.

Monday, March 23rd, 2020

My landlady is in the front yard as I head out in the morning. She asks if I'm going to work. I am. "Good," she says. "That's good."

As I enter the office, I hear, "Joe, I'm glad you're here. We need your smile."

We manage to get enough people together for afternoon prayers today, though we hadn't yesterday. Or was that on Thursday? The days are blurring together.

Tuesday, March 24th, 2020

At ten minutes to two, I set out stacks of yarmulkes and prayer books on our front desk, next to the hand sanitizer. A single guest shows up for afternoon prayers. He uses the sanitizer, then takes a photo of the bottle. He likes the scent.

Fifteen minutes later, only a few other people have shown up. Almost all the offices other than ours are closed. Since there are fewer than ten men, they leave. I carry the stacks back to the conference room and return to my cube.

At 4:30, I go to the ground floor for a snack. The café to the left of the main doors bears two new handwritten signs, each saying "A cup of orange or carrot juice: 7 shekels." It is closed and dark.

In the supermarket to the left, plexiglas shields, a meter square, are now attached to the back of the touchscreens, between the cashiers and the customers. I have to stand off to one side to pay and get my change.

Decals on the floor, two meters apart, now show us where to stand in line. We would usually unload our bags or carts onto the conveyor belt while the customers before us were getting scanned out, but we stand too far apart for that now. Since the store is nearly empty, it doesn't slow us down as much as it might.

Ducking around a child and a dog as I leave, I crash into one of several large outdoor displays of toilet paper. The rolls yield upon impact. Neither they nor I fall.

Wednesday, March 25th, 2020

A knife and part of a lemon usually rest on a cutting board in the office kitchen. We drink a lot of tea at work, so people slice off bits of the communal lemon, finishing one every day.

I haven't seen a lemon there at all this week. We've had fewer people in the office, and I suspect that, due to worries about the virus, people haven't wanted to share. It hasn't affected me, though I usually have a cup of tea after lunch. The salad that I tend to get contains a wedge of lemon that I never use, so I take it out, wipe the tuna off of it, and use it for my tea.

Downstairs, the café is open for takeout again, though it may not be tomorrow. Strict rules as of tonight allow restaurants only to do deliveries.

At the supermarket, the workers now wear vests of fashionable black and yellow. Large letters on the back say, "We are staying at work on your behalf." When I go there in mid-afternoon, people enter freely.

By evening, after the new rules hit, a line forms outside. When one customer leaves, they let another in.

I get produce for tonight in a small market that I've passed twice a day but never entered. It's clean, the produce and prices seem good, and the cashier is reasonably friendly. I'll be back.

Thursday, March 26th, 2020

I stand in line outside the supermarket, waiting. The guard, who has often appeared to be dozing before, has snapped into action, glorying in actually having something to do. When one person leaves, he lets another person in. When two people leave, he lets two people in.

He won't let a mother and her teenage son enter together when only one other person has left. The son must wait. I am behind him.

A couple leaves a moment later. The son and I enter.

"Stop," the guard says to me imperiously. "Sir, you shall not pass." (That doesn't sound as daunting in Hebrew, and I doubt he knows who Gandalf is.)

The guy behind me says "Look there – two people left." To our right, the couple are heading away. The man is much larger than the woman, and possibly blocked her from the guard's view.

The guard looks and nods. "You are correct." He makes a grand gesture. "Welcome, sir."

I enter. Once inside, I feel like I have to shop quickly, since each moment that I take delays someone else in line. There are few people at the meat counter, but I still have to wait.

When the butcher gestures at me, I step forward. "Two meters!" he barks.

I step back. I tell him what I want. He pulls some chicken out of the case, wraps it, and steps far back from the counter. I step forward and take it. It's not what I wanted. I probably got the name wrong. I get it anyway. I buy more groceries than I expected, and feel guilty when I realize that I'm getting twelve items in the ten-items-or-less line. The cashier doesn't seem to mind as she chatters endlessly at me in Ethiopian (I think)-accented Hebrew that I can't understand at all. I step to the right of the plexiglass, pay, and leave.

Of course, as I step outside again, it starts to rain.

Friday, March 27th, 2020

The park that I walk through toward the House of a Hundred Grand-mothers is locked. It doesn't matter, though, since I can't visit there anyway. Their quarantine has gotten more strict. Even the caregivers can't leave the grounds.

I detour around the park on my way to the supermarket – not the one below my office, but a much smaller one owned by the same company. It has the same plexiglass shields at the registers and the same decals on the floor. They aren't limiting the number of the people in the store, though. It is packed with shoppers.

In each aisle, I have to squeeze past other customers. I don't go down the aisle of cleaning supplies, since it is blocked by a man in a mask and gloves, one hand in the air, dancing alone quite well to the Justin Bieber song playing overhead. It would be a shame to interrupt him.

I only find a few of the things that I want. They are out of challah, but I'll make do with what remains from last week's. I get toilet paper, since I actually am running low. I don't need a pack of 32 rolls, which would last me close to a year, but that's all they have. I only notice when I get outside that the paper is bright pink. So be it.

Walking home, there is little traffic. An ambulance zooms silently past me, lights flashing. Children cluster close to the ground on a dead-end street, drawing in chalk on the bricks. Their mothers stand a dis-tance away, apart from each other, each with her own baby carriage, talking.

My landlord is cleaning up our yard. When I get home, he is standing with a hose on the stairs to my apartment, spraying down the bricks. He steps back as I enter. I see that some of the water from when he washed the door has leaked into my kitchen. It reminds me that I should wash the floor sometime. But I probably won't get around to it soon.

Saturday, March 28th, 2020

Some of the mixture of barley, rice, and red lentils has stuck to the bottom of the pot, but not as much as I'd feared. I don't know how to time it, since I'm used to using a rice cooker with a timer, but I caught it before it could scorch.

In my kitchen, space limits what I can do. I have a toaster oven rather than a full-size one, and a two-burner hot plate instead of a stove. It's sufficient. I make what I can.

Ordering lunch at work has become erratic. I'm back to making lunches as I did when I worked at the bookstore.

It's time for the return of the JoeBowl. I didn't name it. I don't remember who did. But it was enough of a consistent thing that it grew a name. It's easy to make on a weekend and freeze.

I build it in layers, making five or six bowls at a time in microwave-safe containers. First: the grains and lentils. On top of that, in order: black beans, tahini, spinach, walnuts, slivered almonds, pomegranate seeds, and sliced strawberries. At least that's what I'm making now. Elements differ.

In the States, I would use berries rather than pomegranate seeds, but things are much more seasonal here. I'm told that I can get frozen berries, but I haven't found them yet. There, I prepared the tahini with soy sauce and water, but I just use it straight here. And I used to use kale or chard or another leafy green, but I've only found spinach here.

When everything is layered, I put a lid on each bowl and freeze it. I bring one to work each day, where I microwave it. Tomorrow I'll eat my first JoeBowl in a new land. There may be a blessing for that.

Sunday, March 29th, 2020

The communal lemon has returned. In deference to the current crises, whoever put it out in the office kitchen has done it differently today. It's already been sliced. The pieces are laid out on a paper plate, with a toothpick in each. Near it on the counter, larger plates hold three different kinds of cookies and a homemade Nutella cake. A message on the office WhatsApp channel shows a photo of the cookies and the caption "In honor of these difficult times."

The cookies and cake disappear quickly. At the end of the day, most of the lemon slices remain. Our tea drinkers are not coming in.

On the way home, I see few people on the road. More joggers than usual trot past me, alone or in carefully distanced packs.

I stop into the produce shop again to buy some apples. The worker, probably the owner, finishes sweeping up as I approach the counter. He strips off and discards the gloves that he had been wearing and puts on another pair. After ringing me up and taking my cash, he strips off and discards those gloves. I don't see whether he immediately puts on a third pair.

When I get home, I see my bag of laundry sitting outside, right where I had left it in the morning. I wonder whether the delivery person had forgotten the pickup. It has happened before. Looking more closely, though, I see that the clothes are neatly folded and there's a receipt on the outside. It usually takes three or four days to get my laundry back. This time, they have cleaned and returned it the same day. Without walk-up and drop-off business, they were able to get my clothes done quickly. That's good news for me, but not for them.

I remind myself again of how lucky I am right now, and that many others are not.

Monday, March 30th, 2020

On my way to work, I see a handwritten sign on an electrical tower, blurred by rain. In large letters, it says "Ay yi yi yi. The world is happy. The world is shining. The world forgets." Or maybe the middle phrase is "The world is screaming." The handwriting is odd. I show people a photo of it. Each has a different reading. Below that, smaller letters, possibly written by someone else, say "Everything will be OK." On the next block, three cardboard boxes rest on a brick wall. Each bears a sign, drawn by a child. The sign in the center, surrounded by colorful diamonds, says "You will be healthy and happy." To the left: "Don't worry. It will be OK." To the right, again, "It will be OK."

At the office, the man in the cube across from mine is moving slowly. He admits that he isn't feeling well. Much of the rest of the team (not the bosses, who aren't there yet) surround him and order him to go home. He does.

Another worker disinfects everything the man touched. He didn't have symptoms I recognize as the virus, but everyone is being careful.

My hands are dry and itching from all the handwashing. I've left my skin lotion at home. I go down to the near-empty supermarket and get another tube of it, which I'll keep in my desk drawer. The café across from the market is dark, but a new handwritten sign says that they are now delivering.

On my way home, I see a large banner suspended from the porch of an apartment above a silent traffic circle. It, too, looks like it was made by children. It, too, has bright letters and a rainbow. It, too, says "Everything will be OK."

Tuesday, March 31ˢᵗ, 2020

I crouch close to the ground to read another sign, posted on a gate, drawn by another child. Surrounding a black and yellow blur that may either be a smiley face or the sun, large letters read "This too shall pass."

Closer to work, I see books abandoned on the street. A haphazard group of texts in Hebrew and, I think, Dutch are stacked on a bench.

Nearby, on a low wall surrounding a communal trash area, someone has left a handsome multi-volume bible, profusely illustrated with a commentary by someone whose name I don't recognize. Some volumes have fallen into the pile of empty boxes and broken furniture next to them. It's rare to see bibles in or near the trash. There are traditions about dealing with and discarding them. I don't rescue the books, but hope that someone else will.

At work, we're told that each of us will have to submit a document each morning stating their temperature and that they haven't tested positive. The Ministry of Health tells us that we all should wear some sort of mask when going out.

Most masks don't do much, but they're better than nothing. Our bosses handed them out last week, one to each worker. I've had mine in the pocket of my hoodie ever since. I put it on for the first time as I head out of the office. I feel conspicuous, but see that about half the people on the street are wearing them.

On the way home, I listen to two episodes of my favorite podcast for learning Hebrew. The host, traveling the world, is quarantined in Shanghai and recording the show in his hotel. The key words for these episodes are "thermometer" and "isolation."

Near the traffic circle, a couple passes me, silently chatting in sign language. Their hands, in bright blue gloves, fly in rapid formations in front of their black t-shirts and white masks.

When I get home, I have more trouble than I expect trying to untie my mask. My hair is tangled in the strings. I had been meaning to get a haircut about a month ago, but waited too long. All the barber shops have shut down. I wonder how long my hair will get before they reopen. With all the other changes, we may be heading into a much shaggier world.

April 2020

Wednesday, April 1ˢᵗ, 2020

On the pale bricks, a quilted pattern of multi-colored chalk forms words I frequently hear and see: "This too shall pass." They span most of the width of the pedestrian street. At the center, much smaller, in black, is the tag "#COVID19." This must have been drawn in the early morning. It wasn't affected by the rain that fell just before dawn, knocking out my internet access and, briefly, electricity.

On the way to work, I only see two boxes on the wall. I look behind them to see if the third has fallen and to put it back up if it is there, but it isn't.

Heading home after work, I pass few people. Some keep a careful distance from others. Some cluster together. Outside the produce store, three young women embrace then walk away from one another. A teenage girl sits on the steps to an apartment house near the wall with the boxes. A boy sits on the sidewalk in front of her, their feet touching.

I pass a few more pieces of paper taped to poles, low to the ground. It has gotten too dark for me to read them. On the pedestrian street, I see that the chalk art is gone.

Thursday, April 2ⁿᵈ, 2020

More chalk writing covers the square of bricks where the pedestrian street and my street cross. It looks like several children took quite a while making it. I see both Hebrew and English, but as I arrive home it's too dark once again to read them. I hope it's still there in the morning when I wander out to get groceries. I don't think it's supposed to rain tonight.

Nothing of note has happened today: no new government decrees, no surprises at work, no word of people whom I know personally having fallen ill. Numbers on news pages continue to rise, showing those who have the virus, those whom the virus has taken, and, on some sites, those who have recovered.

I keep hearing of musicians around the world, more or less well known, that we've lost. I wear my mask consistently when I go out, usually cursing while I put it on as the straps and my fingers get tangled in my hair.

I haven't gone into the supermarket today or noticed anything about the café. I have spent all day at my desk, working on projects that are deemed essential but seem far removed from the crisis. I remember that an old friend is now a nurse in New York. I resolve to write to her this evening, though I don't know if she'll have time to respond.

Friday, April 3rd, 2020

The guard at the nearest large supermarket won't let anyone in without a mask. I'm wearing one. I get in easily. The guy behind me has a young daughter and a rolling cart, but not a mask. He can't come in.

In the produce department, a woman wearing non-skid rubber gloves tears clear plastic bags off a roll and easily opens them. The next customer, with slippery clear gloves, can't open his. After several attempts, he looks over to the woman and asks "Possible?" She takes his bag and opens it. The customer behind her gestures with her bag. The woman takes that, too, and opens it for her. A third, without gloves, raises his hand to his mouth but, with the mask in place, can't moisten his fingers. He approaches the woman with his bag and says "Ma'am?" I walk away, but when I glance back from the other end of the aisle, she is still opening bags for people.

The store is scruffy and chaotic. The prices are higher than I've seen elsewhere. They do have the frozen berries that I had sought for the JoeBowl, but not some of the cleaning supplies that I want. I remember why I only shop there once a year or so.

As I exit, the guard is rationing the number of people he lets in. The woman in front of me heads out with a small girl. "One," the guard intones. Two people try to enter. "One," he says again.

The man points to the girl. "But…"

Apparently she doesn't count. "One."

I speak up from behind him. "I'm leaving." I head out. The guard declares, "Another one." The couple enters.

I see about a dozen people outside the store, lined up, widely spaced, waiting. No one else was in line when I went in. I got there just in time.

Saturday, April 4th, 2020

My landlord is whistling outside my window. At least I think it's my landlord. I haven't looked outside yet.

It's an indoor day. If I want, I can wander one hundred meters from my house. I have a map showing me how far that is: to my nearest bus stop, down to the traffic circle at the corner and back, then about one block down the pedestrian street. But I stay inside, cleaning and organizing.

I finally go through four large containers that I had brought with me over two years ago but hadn't looked at much. I put the VHS tapes on a shelf, the electronic gear in a cabinet, the vintage t-shirts in my closet, and the rest, including a complete collection of my bookstore's teddy bears, back into a single bin.

The bins nest easily. The whole set, which had been almost as tall as I am, now is only half a meter high. The item I am looking for, an old webcam, is, of course, at the bottom of the last bin. After some confusion and a few odd failures, I hook it up to my Mac.

I listen to some new music as well as some older music that I once listened to frequently but had forgotten. Tomorrow: shopping, work, and much more walking. At least it will be a short week.

Sunday, April 5th, 2020

Most of the people on the main street are wearing masks. Almost no one on the smaller streets is. People are keeping an appropriate distance from one another, though some cluster in pairs.

The straps on my mask have broken from overuse, so I'll have to go without until I find or make more. All the articles and videos I find on making them depend on items that everyone supposedly has, but I don't: bandannas, kitchen towels, hair ties, rubber bands, or a stapler.

In the supermarket, I only look for a few items. It takes me a while before I find what I think is raw horseradish. I enter the word on the label above it into a translation program. The word means either "you're back" or "the mumps." Another program tells me that it is indeed horseradish. The words are spelled the same way when you leave out the vowels.

People are panicking over a reported shortage of eggs. Two customers crouch at the egg case, carefully going through the packages there to avoid any broken ones. A line forms behind each of them. When I get up to the case, I have no trouble getting a couple of dozen. I usually don't eat many, but I'm headed into a week of making matzoh brei for breakfast.

Outside a shuttered kindergarten, I see a bulletin board that had been covered with the shredded remnants of posters for shows that had been cancelled. It now bears one large homemade sign. The corners and edges have short phrases wishing us strength and a good holiday. Letters at the center spell two colorful words in biblical Hebrew: "Your souls shall rejoice." Or maybe it says, "Watch yourselves." Beneath the dim streetlamp filtered through trees, it's hard to tell.

Monday, April 6th, 2020

Sometimes my boss walks around the office in the late afternoon offering cookies or fruit. Today, he has a large bowl with wedges of cabbage. I don't recognize what they are at first. At a glance, each looks like a stack of layers of thin wafers. I ask him what they are. He hands me one. "It's good. Take it. Eat some." I do. It's quite good, and more healthy than the snack that I had planned.

As usual, I'm one of the last people to leave the office. I put on my new mask, which I got in a trade: several masks and some hand sanitizer for some of the raw horseradish I got yesterday. The new mask goes on more easily than the last one. It has elastic rather than strings. I don't have to tie knots behind my head.

On the way home, I see a woman jumping rope in front of an apartment house. I saw her in the same spot yesterday, rolling out a yoga mat on the rough cement.

At the produce market, the wall phone rings while I'm shopping. The man at the counter, answering, just says "Vegetables." The store has half the produce that it did on my previous trips. I hear him say that the supply chain is breaking down. Some stuff never arrives. Some is delivered at 7 AM and gone by 8:30. I find what I need.

In the evening, I see the Prime Minister announce that there will be a complete lockdown on the first night of Passover. Last year, walking home from the House of a Hundred Grandmothers, I had heard large families singing from within their houses. I planned to walk around and record them from the street this year. But there will be no large gatherings for the seder. I hope to get together with other members of my family online, at least, and do what we can.

Tuesday, April 7th, 2020

I get on the elevator together with a coworker. We're both wearing masks. He is wearing clear plastic gloves. "This is my first time wearing these. I feel stupid, like my hands are in sandwich bags. But I'm wearing them."

The office orders pizzas for lunch. Seven of us are here today. We sit in the conference room, widely separated. Three workers who speak Spanish explain some nuances of the language to the rest of us in Hebrew.

On the way home, I see a handwritten sign at a tiny market: "Rolls for Passover." It's still open. I look everywhere for the rolls then ask the shopkeeper.

She points to a single bag on top of the ice cream case. "This is all there is. The last. We got a lot this morning. They're all gone."

It's just what I need. I buy them and a canned iced coffee. "All will be well," she says. "This will pass. This will pass."

Two soldiers and two police walk past us. They tell a man sitting on a park bench that he can't be there. He works at one of the shops and had stepped out for a smoke.

The cashier runs out of the store to catch up with the soldiers. She asks them details about tomorrow's curfew. I walk away and don't hear their response.

When I try to enter a pharmacy, a man with a thermometer scans my forehead and my wrist. My body temperature tends to be low. He thinks he's not getting a proper reading. After several attempts get the same result, he lets me in. Apparently I am still alive.

Wednesday, April 8th, 2020

Five people from four generations in three households on two continents: this one seder works pretty well.

There are a few glitches, both technological and liturgical, the result of new technology and mismatched texts. Still, most of us get through it. The toddler needs to go to bed halfway through and her father falls asleep with her. The rest of us reach the end just before the leader's phone battery runs out.

We don't have the usual massive meal. We aren't a big gathering in a single place. I have some salmon, broccoli and a sweet potato. Others have chicken with eggplant. On the American side, It's just after lunchtime, though there is grape juice there for the blessings over wine.

There is only one seder here each year, not two. The smaller meal means quicker cleanup. Tonight, we put away the ritual items when we're done. Next year, we hope, more of us will be together, if not yet in Jerusalem.

Thursday, April 9th, 2020

Another day where nothing happens: hours pass, but in no particular order. I eat. I sleep. I watch videos. I continue with my endless hobby of tagging and organizing media files.

It's a holiday, so an internal calendar tells me that I should at least try to go to synagogue. Then I remember that no synagogues are open, and that the building containing mine is under quarantine.

I disassemble some empty boxes that have been sitting here for months. Tomorrow, perhaps, I'll take them out to the neighborhood junk pile.

Friday, April 10th, 2020

I'm almost at the clinic when I see someone wearing a mask and realize that I forgot mine.

I've been having a problem with the skin on my hands, something like a bad sunburn. Two days ago, I spoke to a doctor. He said he was filing a prescription. I headed straight to the pharmacy, but they had no record of it.

Today, a friend from work phones me first thing in the morning and nudges me to call my health plan. I do. It takes several tries to get someone who speaks English. She tells me to call my clinic, which is open today. I do. They tell me that they don't have anyone who can help, but to go to the central clinic in my city, where there is a dermatologist on duty. I do. (I realize now that the problem started soon after that strange man accosted me on the street and kept saying "der-ma-to-lo-gist".)

I arrive at the clinic only to find that the dermatologist didn't show up today. The nurse at the entrance takes my temperature, then hands me a mask and a pair of gloves.

I go to the fourth floor, as she suggests. No one there can do anything, but they make me an appointment for Sunday morning.

I ask a pharmacist downstairs for a suggestion. He sells me some ointment and a box of gloves. Another customer butts in with a recommendation. She's speaking English, but I don't know what she means. I thank her for the information.

I stop at a produce shop on the way home and get some peppers and persimmons. The persimmons are a bit overripe, but I can eat them with a spoon. The cashier looks at them critically. "These are very soft. You are sure that you want them?" I nod. "Then I will only charge you half price."

Little else is open. One shop is selling cosmetics and handbags. An ice cream joint that stays open on Shabbat is selling desserts through the doorway, without letting customers enter. A handwritten sign on another small market offers KN95 masks for over eight dollars apiece, with ten for almost seventy. The simpler masks that I have are sufficient.

A line snakes out from another larger market. Seven people stand two meters apart. I think of stopping in there, then walk away. I have what I need.

Saturday, April 11th, 2020

I only step outside once today, in the early evening. The laundry man is coming in the morning. I place my bagged-up clothes on the upstairs porch, far enough in to avoid the rain.

No other humans are outside. I had heard them earlier. Some children were in the yard before I awoke. Now that it's dark, everyone is gone.

The seeds that had been on a ledge by my stairs have finally disappeared. An orange had fallen there in the autumn. Over the months, I saw it turn from bright orange to moldy white, then fall in on itself. The rind dropped away, then the fruit itself, until all that remained were those seeds. They rested there for a couple of more months. Now they've either blown away or been carried off by more mobile creatures.

Several of the house's cats are upstairs when I bring my laundry outside. My landlord maintains a set of cardboard boxes, laid out in a precise line, as a home for them. They come out each morning to feast on the clusters of dry food that he sets out in mounds around the yard.

When I come back down, one of the cats is sitting by my open door. She surveys what she sees, but has no interest in coming in. I step over her and close the door slowly. She scampers away as I turn off the outside light.

Sunday, April 12th, 2020

Every other chair in the dermatologist's lobby has two paper signs, one on the back and one on the seat. Each sign asks patients to leave an empty chair between them. No one else is there. I don't know whether we're supposed to sit on the chairs with the signs or the ones without them. I sit on an unmarked seat to leave the most signs visible.

The dermatologist is one of the best around. We have a mutual friend, who used to walk her beagles. She looks at my hands and asks me what happened. I hope she can tell me. It looks like I've been suntanning at Chernobyl.

She prescribes some cream and a cortisone shot. I need to go downstairs, buy them at the pharmacy on the ground floor, and bring them back up. The shot costs one shekel, about 28 US cents.

I vaguely recall having had trouble with topical cortisone in the past. The nurse tells me that the topical and injected cortisone work differently. I should wait there for half an hour after the shot. If I'm still breathing then, I should be OK. I am.

Since the shot will suppress my immune system, I have to stay home, other than for a followup appointment. I'm prepared. I have the technology to work from home. I stocked up on two weeks' supplies a month ago.

I pass cheerful signs as I walk back. One sign, posted by the city government on an empty pillar that's usually covered with flyers, says "We should only be healthy." Another similar one says, in foot-tall letters, "It will be OK." Our neighborhood graffitist, the one who keeps scrawling cryptic messages about "fourteen commandments" on bus stops, has written under it "only after people stop ignoring the Torah." A large poster of the Rebbe says "Healing and rescue and he will redeem us."

I think of stopping at a produce shop for fresh fruit but decide against it. I head straight home. I can really use some coffee.

Monday, April 13th, 2020

A day spent juggling technology. Working with others from our homes is trickier than it seems. Lots of different programs claim to do everything, but we end up using one program for screen sharing, another for taking notes, a third for text messages, and a fourth for working remotely on machines in the office. After trying several tools for teleconferencing and talking, with and without video, we speak on the phone.

On my own network, I juggle a patchwork of operating systems and devices. I thought I had revived my Linux box. I hadn't. It's unusable. Something keeps injecting streams of periods into the typing buffer. Someone knocked it off a table years ago at New York ComicCon. I don't think it ever recovered.

I step outside for under a minute to retrieve my laundry from the porch. None of the cats are there.

I spend some time researching food delivery from restaurants. The market is large, but has abruptly shifted. Rather than delivering to busy offices, they need to get the food to homes where people work alone.

The Industrial Zone is probably a ghost town. It once held factories and processing plants, but is now filled with shiny towers with tech logos. When I first got here, I interviewed in interchangeable offices in the Zone. They all tried to be quirky and distinctive in pretty much the same way.

Shops and restaurants there usually cater to those who work in the towers. Now, I suspect, most of the traffic consists of people on motorcycles, delivering food from the eateries to people elsewhere. The services look quite good. Some even have free delivery and discounts off the listed prices. This may change. There are fewer economies of scale when the meals go to more widely separated places. I immediately want to try everything. I hold off, at least until after Passover. There will be plenty of time to try things then.

Tuesday, April 14th, 2020

The dermatologist is running a little late. That's OK. I'm in no hurry. I have nowhere better to be.

More patients are here than before. I find an empty seat. We all sit on chairs between the signs, not the chairs with them. I don't know if that's the rule or if everyone followed the lead of the first person who sat down.

The electronic displays show the current appointment number for each doctor. Simple animations beside them advertise a children's health app ("Dr. Gadget"), alternative medicine (including "the Chinese doctor"), and over-the-counter medications (mostly Maalox Plus).

A man speaks to the receptionist in equally broken Hebrew and English, then wanders around the lobby singing "*Besame Mucho.*"

The dermatologist says that my hands are looking better, but that I should be using a lot more of the cream. So be it. She also prescribes a less potent ointment for points on my face. I'm to stay in "the same kind of isolation as the rest of us," but, as an essential worker, can return to the office on Sunday.

The pharmacist downstairs sees that the doctor has written "body" and "face" in English on my prescription and also writes the words on the boxes.

I stop into a produce market and quickly stock up on some missing items. As I arrive home, my landlord is quietly watering his garden. My internet cable runs underneath it. I may be off-line for much of the rest of the day.

Wednesday, April 15th, 2020

My robot is happy. On the last day of Passover, it's wandering around the living room hoovering up matzoh crumbs. I listen for where it is and where it gets stuck. I know that I have to lift a clothing rack off the floor. The robot gets wedged under it so tightly that it can't back out. And I have to flip my bathrobe on its hook so that the robot doesn't try to eat its belt.

I haven't been outside today. There's been no reason to venture out. No one is around, and nothing is being delivered. Tomorrow was supposed to be another holiday, with parties in parks. That won't be happening either. Today, I'm staying in and continuing to wrestle with technology. It gives me something to do.

Thursday, April 16th, 2020

Overhead, as I shop, the announcer's voice blasts from the supermarket speakers between "Take on Me" and "Funkytown." It used to shout about sales and bargains. Now, it warns us that the Ministry of Health demands that we all wear masks and stand two meters apart. In the overly bright light, it feels less like a dystopian future that we might have envisioned a few months ago and more like those seen in British science fiction of the sixties.

Almost everyone I see outdoors has a mask. Many people let them dangle below their chins, rapidly pulling them up over their faces when others approach. Some wear gloves. I don't. Gloves stop my hands from healing.

On the way home, I take an illustrated book of our city's history from the top of a recycling bin. Two white-haired men raise the hood of a car on the side of the road and place a battery inside. A cat yowls as I pass it, but neither approaches nor runs away.

Children play on a grassy lot across from my house. Their parents sit on a picnic blanket, watching them. One toddler throws a ball at another. It bounces off his head. He doesn't seem to notice. The ball rolls down the street toward me. I stop it with my foot and try to kick it toward them. It drifts vaguely away. I bend over and give it a more definite swat with the book. The girl waits for the ball to reach her, grabbing it when it does.

The parents call out their thanks. I smile, but realize that they can't see that through the mask. I wonder if they'll sanitize the ball now that a strange man's shoes have touched it.

Friday, April 17th, 2020

The door to my favorite shawarma joint is open. A sign outside, taped to the propped-up lid of a styrofoam cooler, says that they are only doing deliveries.

The owner sees me pass and calls out "Hi! Shawarma? But don't come inside." A line of chairs blocks the entrance. He and the other worker put the shawarma together, asking if I want each of the ingredients, skipping those that they remember that I don't get.

As I wait, a young man, his mask dangling below his beard, vaults over the chairs and heads straight into the restroom. The other worker shrugs. She shrugs again when he runs out and away.

She brings the shawarma, carefully packaged, to where I stand, puts it on a chair, and takes my credit card. We wish each other a good Sabbath when she returns with it.

Turning, I see that a couple of more people have lined up behind me. The larger shawarma joint, two doors down, and another falafel joint, far down the street, have longer lines. The food may be better, but I like the people here.

Most of the food stores downtown are open, though they have few customers. Most of the other stores are closed. I look into a new kitchen-ware shop at the Heart of the City. The items there are too high-end for impulse buys. I get a challah and some pita at a bakery, waiting outside until they beckon me in.

When I get home, the shawarma is still hot.

Saturday, April 18ᵗʰ, 2020

The Heart of the City is silent. I'm not surprised. All of its shops are closed on the Sabbath. Still, small groups of people usually sit around or drift through the mall's open space.

Today, I only see one person at a time. A round man with a surgical mask wanders past a broken set of escalators. A boy with a helmet on a foot-powered scooter keeps one hand on a wall to keep from falling. A solitary pigeon feasts on a piece of bread that it has found. A child's pink tricycle sits alone by the ledge where free newspapers appear on Fridays. I haven't looked at one of those in a while. I wonder if the loss of advertising is hitting them as badly as the newspapers in the States.

I hear almost-melodic screaming from the square outside the Great Synagogue across the street. I imagine that children are exploring the echoes of the empty outdoor spaces. As I get closer, I see a single boy lying on the ground, having a meltdown. A man stands next to him, watching patiently until it passes. I continue filming signs and buildings on the street. I don't photograph the child, but I do get a good recording of his keening. I might be able to use the sound.

Sunday, April 19ᵗʰ, 2020

The first bus stop that I pass on my walk to work is roped off. Some-one has placed bricks on each of its seats. I wonder if this is so that fewer people will ride the buses. As I get closer, I see that it is under construction. The bricks have been pried up from underneath it. A hole reaches deep into the sand where they were.

A few doors down, across from the produce market and the laundry, a small truck blocks the entrance to the road. A man in a yellow vest sits in the intersection on a folding chair.

Other than that, I think that everything looks normal. Then I realize that I'm not noticing the minimal traffic, the people in masks and gloves, and the dances of avoidance that keep passersby far enough apart.

A few more people than before are at work. A small pack of masks sits on the reception desk. We don't wear them in the office, but some people take them when they leave.

To my surprise, no line has formed at the supermarket in the evening. The door is unguarded. I go in and get a few things, partly to restock what I used from my quarantine stash in my week at home. The guard is back when I leave, taking people's temperatures before he lets them in.

I pass a family on a narrow shortcut between two larger streets. As they approach, without masks, they fill the width of the path. Seeing me, they shift into a straight line against the bushes on their side as I press against the wall on mine. I look back after they pass and see them form again into a shapeless cluster as they walk.

Monday, April 20th, 2020

I'm surprised when a group gathers for afternoon prayers. We hadn't tried yesterday, since there were too few men in the office. Now, an insurance man from down the hall has appeared, as well as a dentist from downstairs. One of our regulars who had been working from home is here. Another worker who joins in if we need the numbers comes over.

I get the prayer books and yarmulkes and put them at the entrance to the office. We gather just outside, in the hallway. We count the men without using numbers. There's a taboo about that. We have nine of the needed ten. People call others who sometimes join us, but none of them are around.

As we're about to give up, a young man with a close-cropped beard emerges from the restroom, carrying a box of cleaning supplies. "Brother!" someone calls out. "Afternoon prayers!" The man frowns. Someone else says, "Just stand here with us for five minutes, OK? We have people who need to say the mourners' kaddish." He nods and puts down the box. Someone gets him a prayer book and yarmulke.

We move through the prayers quickly, as usual. In this slightly different space, after a week away, I find that my rhythms are off. When we're done, the young man picks up his box and wanders away. Most of us head back into the office. Looking around, we don't know if there will be enough of us again tomorrow.

Tuesday, April 21ˢᵗ, 2020

The sirens sound as I walk to work. I hear four or five of them, surrounding me. I don't know how many are echoes.

An old couple stands in their yard, waiting for them. Those of us who have been walking stop. The one car that is moving down the street pauses. It doesn't pull over. The driver gets out and stands beside it.

The pitch rises over the first few seconds, then remains steady. Against it, I hear other sounds more clearly than against traffic or silence. Several different birds are singing. One dog barks, then another, and another. A dog far in the distance howls briefly, as if trying to sing along. A child is calling to its mother, who doesn't respond.

Down the street, I see that the three cardboard boxes have reappeared on the wall. New crayon drawings are pasted to them.

Holocaust Remembrance Day events appear online, small ceremonies from the state and the city, produced for livestreams. The news shows cars on the highways stopping for the sirens. Last year, they had been in traffic jams. This year the roads are more empty.

When the sirens end, we resume walking. The street seems even quieter than before.

Wednesday, April 22ⁿᵈ, 2020

One of the elevators at the office is broken. As I wait for another on our floor, it rings out a two-note motif. The doors don't open. I hear a calm voice from inside repeat, "The elevator is descending. The elevator is descending."

I take a different one down to the lobby. The broken elevator is behaving the same way there, as if it were present and waiting for us behind its closed doors. Two people get on the one that I had ridden, heading to underground parking. More wait for the next. Other than families, no more than two people ride in elevators together.

I head into the supermarket for some quick shopping: an afternoon snack of yogurt with nuts and a clementine, plus cheese and peppers and a pack of foil baking pans. The pans that I had gotten yesterday were too big for my toaster oven. I get the next smaller size.

The non-foods aisle still overflows with packs of toilet paper. The bright red dots near the checkout lines that had marked where people should stand have either worn off or been removed. Vague strips of white tape act as spacers now.

Two large men stand equidistant from the first register. I ask who is the last in line. Each growls, "He is," and glares at the other. I get in a different line.

More people are outdoors this evening as I walk home. I pass several pairs of runners. Four boys sit on a ledge outside a grocery store eating ice cream. The athletic woman lies on her yoga mat on the cement in the space outside her apartment complex. I don't understand the exercises that she is doing with her legs, or how they are possible.

When I get home, I try to fit the baking pans in the toaster oven. These, too, are too large. I put them aside for a relative who bakes, assuming we'll get together if the virus ever lets up. I measure the inside of the toaster oven: thirty centimeters wide by twenty deep.

Too tired for inventive cooking, I microwave some cheese in a pita, wash a pepper and an apple, and sit down to see what's online.

Thursday, April 23rd, 2020

At work, the bosses serve ice cream pops and talk about the virus. More people are there today. Some stay behind closed doors in the offices of people who are working from home. The rest of us mill about, working in individual cubes and keeping a proper distance.

The whole talk is in Hebrew. I understand most of it, as I now understand most of the conversations about our work. Later, I ask my boss about one point that I couldn't follow.

On the way home, I once again see pairs of runners and children with cones and ice cream sandwiches. An electric scooter, the first I've seen in a month, zooms past me on a small street. Two boys on foot-powered scooters follow, rolling down the center of the road.

Another person has joined the athletic woman in doing implausible exercises. A large dog, off-leash, trots up to me and sniffs my hands, then runs back to its human.

I see one new sign along the way. Inch-tall letters, drawn in black crayon on white paper, spell out English words: "Here comes the sun."

Friday, April 24th, 2020

The take-out counter at the local café is open. I order a salad.

The worker frowns. "No. No kitchen. Just coffee. Hot or iced." I ask for an espresso. "Double? Long? Short?" Double. "Eight shekels." I pay him.

He says something that I don't quite catch. He pauses, repeats the phrase, then, seeing that I still don't react, says it in English: "Go to the back. He brings it to you."

I walk around to the parking lot behind the café, just beyond the trash area and the restroom. Several people are already waiting, standing around in no perceptible order. Another man opens the back door and brings drinks to two of them. He remembers who is getting what. I would easily get that wrong.

On his third trip out, he hands me my espresso. I walk to a safe distance away from everyone else. Balancing my cup on the edge of a planter, I pour in the sweetener that I had gotten up front. I pull down my mask and slowly sip my drink. It's the first espresso I have had in a month. It is good.

Saturday, April 25th, 2020

I finally take the trash out in the late afternoon. I'm almost at the gate when I realize that I've forgotten my mask. I think for a moment about gambling on going without it, but there are children playing outside. I don't want to set a bad example. I go back inside then return, wearing the mask.

My landlord has set up a large flag at the gate and is hanging a row of smaller ones along the fence. Independence Day is coming. I see that others have hung flags, too.

A burst of purple flowers has erupted on a wall on the pedestrian street. Around the corner, the fence at a construction site is gone. I stop and look. So do other people. The apartment building has the same blocky construction as most of the others, but the exterior isn't the usual white cement. This one has what looks like wood paneling. It's a pleasant change.

A man with twin toddlers starts to set out a blanket on a patch of grass, then stops. He walks over to a dispenser near the sidewalk, pulls out a black plastic bag, then returns and picks up a lump of dog droppings with it. He deposits it in a trash can near the dispenser. He and the boys set out the blanket and sit down.

Two women holding children and balloons stand by a car. One opens the door to get in and lets go of her balloon. It rises out of sight. The child in her arms waves goodbye.

Sunday, April 26th, 2020

Lunch arrives during afternoon prayers. The bosses have ordered it from the best shawarma joint in town, two doors down from the friendly one that I go to.

We come in from the hallway. I pause to gather up the prayer books and yarmulkes and put them away.

The food is in the conference room. Usually we sit around the table, each of us with a falafel or shawarma, serving ourselves relishes, vegetables, sauces, and fries from containers arrayed down the center.

Today, too many of us are at the office to sit in there with proper distancing. Instead, we stand at the doorway. Two workers inside put together plates that they hand out to us. We sit at our desks to eat.

I check the news for any new loosening or tightening of rules. I see that hair salons are open. I resolve to stop by mine after work to see if I can get an appointment.

I send a photo to my family of the prayer books and yarmulkes sitting next to a box of masks, hand sanitizer, and a thermometer. I write a liturgical phrase in Hebrew as a caption: "Healing for the spirit, healing for the body." A message comes back: "Exactly." I nod and get back to my work.

Monday, April 27th, 2020

A man waves a bouquet of flowers above his head. He is talking on his phone, too quietly for me to eavesdrop. I follow his gaze. Three floors up, someone waves at him from a porch, also talking on the phone.

Two girls on pink bicycles with matching helmets, one with training wheels, one without, roll between the man and me. Another child comes toward us with her mother, keeping one hand on a stroller. The child takes a step with her right foot, hops in the air with her left, then repeats. I don't know if she is still learning to walk or just finds moving like that fun.

I'm surprised to see that the produce shop is closed, then remember that it's Monday. Many small stores close here on Monday afternoons. I'm told that's when they do store-to-store business.

I have a hard time remembering what day it is. They aren't blurring together as they did when I was stuck at home, but the rhythms of the week are off. Several of the TV shows that I follow are preempted or in reruns until they can finish new episodes. We've had two of the three past Wednesdays and one of the Thursdays off for the beginning and end of Passover. This Wednesday, we'll have another for Independence Day. The Sabbath still comes each week, as usual, but other days feel random. I realize that I'm lucky, at least, that they don't all feel the same.

Tuesday, April 28ᵗʰ, 2020

The sirens sound at 11 AM. All conversations in the office stop. Those of us who are standing around remain in place, heads bowed. Those who are sitting stand. A worker in the aisle takes a few more steps and puts his coffee down on the wall of the nearest cube.

I hear at least three distinct sirens this time. All the sound comes in through one open window, so I don't have a sense of location, but it pulses with beats caused by not quite identical pitches.

Last year on Memorial Day, the staff went to a ceremony at the grave-yard next door. I missed it. I had been in the restroom when everyone left. No one realized that I wouldn't know where they were going.

Today, there is no ceremony. We stay in the office. Civilian cemeteries are open, but we're asked not to cluster together in them.

We all leave work by 5 PM. After that, no one may travel between cities. Last year, I filmed the crowds at the evening's celebrations downtown. Tonight, I will go home. I will eat a hamburger. I will watch TV.

Wednesday, April 29ᵗʰ, 2020

I think I hear fighter jets zooming overhead. They are supposed to fly through the country sometime today, tracing a path over hospitals as an Independence Day salute. Maybe I'm hearing them now. In the morning, I heard what seemed to be a sound truck several blocks away, playing festive music. Last night, I thought I heard fireworks. Maybe I did. Maybe they had them, without crowds, for people to see from their porches or windows. I haven't gone out to look at any of those.

I should shower and get dressed sometime, but with nowhere to go and no one to meet, I probably won't.

Late in the day, I cook a new set of JoeBowls. I run out of regular tahini, so I use some that is mixed with honey. I hope it doesn't overwhelm the other flavors.

I don't have leafy greens, so I sauté some broccoli instead. I stop stirring for a moment and close my eyes. I'm at the dance center, sitting outside, seeing people walk past me, waiting for a performance to begin. Then I smell the broccoli starting to catch. I open my eyes. I'm back at home. I should clean my kitchen sometime.

Thursday, April 30th, 2020

Leaving the supermarket, I wonder for a moment how many of the people there had worn masks. I hadn't noticed. Then I realize that everyone would have had them. We can't go in without them. After a few weeks, though, it has become unremarkable, except when viewed against memories of what seems like a long time ago.

Metal fences surround the entrance. People walk in through gaps in them, one at a time. Three bikes are chained to the furthest fence. A backpack is chained to each.

This still surprises me. When I first worked here, over thirty years ago, an unattended package might be handled by the bomb squad. Someone once had left a bag at a bus stop near my office. Police cleared the buildings for a block in every direction. A robot or something like it blew the bag up. I remember my father telling me about it. Now, people leave bags on benches and at bus stops containing things they are giving away.

The backpacks outside the supermarket are not a problem. The guard may or may not be keeping an eye on them. He used to sit by the entrance, vaguely nodding as people went in. Now he is busy scanning customers' temperature. We've always lived with a steady state of vigilance and an undertone of fear. Over the years, what we watch and why we worry seems to continually change.

May, 2020

Friday, May 1st, 2020

The streetcorner violinist is back. He is wearing his mask under his chin, smoking a cigarette as he plays. Backing tracks sound from a speaker at his feet. I've seen him play a banjo, too, here and outside the mall. He's sticking to violin today.

I listen to him as I order a falafel at my favorite place. The worker cooks up a fresh batch of the falafel balls. She packs more of them into the pita than should be possible. Thinking about them, I can't remember the English word for chickpeas. I cycle through words in Hebrew, Spanish, Arabic, and Yiddish before it comes back to me.

My boss walks by, calls my name, and wishes me a good Sabbath.

Most shops are open. The bookstore and cinematheque remain closed. A new shop offers Middle Eastern pastries. I think of getting something, but I'm not sure what is what. The tiny space that had sold transit cards is becoming a new café.

The ice cream shop is open for the first time since the lockdown began. I go in and order, in Hebrew, a cup of dulce de leche and cinnamon. The worker repeats my order in English and serves it up. I sit on a bench to eat it, away from other people.

When I'm done, I step into the bakery and pick out a challah. The worker tells me that it is a sweet challah, including a word that I don't know. At dinner, I feel and taste raisins in it, but have forgotten the Hebrew word.

Saturday, May 2nd, 2020

On the grassy lot across from my house, a woman presses a selfie stick into the ground. Once it stands on its own, she points her phone at a picnic basket and a child beyond it. She scurries forward and places a soccer ball in line with the basket and child. Coming back, she slides the phone a little higher and takes the shot.

Close to the center of town, clothes are scattered near a dumpster and a Give-and-Take box. Whoever left them may have placed them neatly, but someone or something has thrown them about. I think of pulling them together into a coherent pile. I don't. I worry whether that would be safe with the virus going around.

I look at what else is in the box: a brightly colored remote, a Hebrew translation of *Oedipus the King*, and what might be part of a blender. I don't take anything.

At the Heart of the City, I follow a deep repeating gurgling sound. It's the call of an unusually large baritone pigeon. The bird sees me coming toward it and waddles away.

Most of the stores here have handwritten signs. Each says how many customers may be in the store at one time and that everyone must wear masks. Few are open today.

Children on scooters roll through the space. One girl has a matching helmet and tutu.

At a stone table, two old men play backgammon. They may be closer together than the rules allow. They look as if they've been there together for their whole lives. They're not going to stop now.

Sunday, May 3rd, 2020

I sit on a bench outside the barber shop until the person before me is done. Only one customer may be in the shop at a time. I had scheduled this appointment last Sunday, when hair salons reopened. The first available slot was today, in the late afternoon. The barber's schedule is already full for the coming week.

When he's ready, he steps outside and calls me in. He is wearing both a mask and a transparent shield over his face, as well as black gloves that match the rest of his clothes. "Your hair is getting lighter," he tells me. "You are getting surfer hair." He doesn't mention that my hair is also getting thinner.

He asks about my family. He knows some of them. Otherwise, he's less talkative than usual. No music is playing in the shop. All I can see of his face are his eyes, but they look tired. When he cuts the hair around my ears, he moves the elastic from my mask off of them, first on one side and then the other. The mask stays in place. A five o'clock shadow has its uses.

Afterwards, I head back to the office. I pass odd objects on the side-walk: a coffee pot, a propane grill, and a nicely upholstered chair. A bulletin board has what looks like new posters. They announce concerts a month ago that didn't happen. I wonder why I hadn't noticed them before.

Monday, May 4th, 2020

I buy more than I mean to get at the supermarket today. Everything fits in my cloth shopping bag, but it's heavy. I hope the handles don't come off. It mostly holds the usual things: green apples, red peppers, white cheese, peanut butter, rice pudding, and a loaf of bread. I also buy low-calorie snack bars to restock my quarantine stash and coconut milk to make chicken curry. At least I think it's coconut milk. The container says, in English, "coconut cream." Only real milk is called milk here. Soy milk is vaguely labeled "soy beverage."

I try not to spend more than a hundred shekels on any one grocery trip. This purchase rings up at 99.51. I used to watch a game show where almost guessing the cost of something but not going over the real price was a big win. I guess I won. There's no glamorous model in an overwrought evening gown, though, to give me a car. That's probably good. Gas is expensive, and I wouldn't have anywhere to park it. But at least I would be able to drive these heavy groceries home.

Tuesday, May 5th, 2020

Just as I'm about to leave the office, another worker peeks over the wall of my cube. Can I proofread a PPT that has to go out tonight? Sure. I wonder, though, what a PPT is. Personal Protective Trenchcoat? An email arrives. It's a Powerpoint presentation. Oh.

I get to work on it, spotting inconsistent capitalizations, bullet points that aren't lined up, semicolons that should be colons, and the like. If it were to go out as it was, I doubt that anyone would notice, but it's my job to be finicky. I send my notes back after about an hour and head out.

It's dark when I leave, which hasn't happened in a month or so. The rain has stopped. The cars have their headlights on, which makes things a little more abstract. Smaller lights shoot past me, mounted on bicycles or the helmets of people on scooters. I find that my peripheral vision doesn't work well at night when I'm wearing a mask. I don't actually see the mask, except for just below the lower edge of my glasses. It shouldn't affect my vision, but it does.

Outside the supermarket, two boys bump elbows, spin, duck down, and bump them again. It's a secret handshake, adapted for the time of the virus.

A black double-wide baby carriage comes toward me out of the darkness. I have to step out into the street to avoid it. Cats fade in and out of shadows. A raven swoops down from beyond a streetlamp, lands on a fence, and caws at me. I caw back. It just stares. I'm betrayed by my American accent, once again.

Wednesday, May 6th, 2020

My phone buzzes as I reach the end of the pedestrian street. It's a message from the postal system. A package has arrived for me. The neighborhood pickup point is a small grocery store a block ahead of me. I head over.

I am so close to the store when the notification arrives that the shop-keeper is still unloading the same box of packages when I walk in. He's at a table in the back. I tell him that I have a package waiting and give him the notification code. He pulls it out of the box and asks me for my government ID number. He tells me to sign on the screen with my finger. I do. He hands me the package. His facial expression never changes. It seems to be permanently stuck at a setting halfway between deadpan and grumpy.

I glance about to see if I want to buy anything. I don't. I wonder once again how having the mail drop in his store works financially. Does the post office pay him for doing it? Does he have it in hopes that customers will buy things at the store? I haven't asked him. I don't have the Hebrew vocabulary for it, and he doesn't seem interested in conversation.

The package, as usual, contains a book. I had forgotten that I had ordered it from a site in England about a month ago. Apparently the virus hasn't made the postal system any slower. I put the book in my shoulder bag. It barely fits. The last two books that I had ordered are still in there, unread. I tell myself that I'll get to them sometime. Maybe I will.

Thursday, May 7th, 2020

The bus stop that I pass on the way to work is gone. A few weeks ago, it seemed to be under construction. The bricks under it were torn up. Some were placed on its seats. Now it has disappeared completely. The bricks are back in place, set so smoothly that I'm not sure precisely where the bus stop was.

Its side of the street is closed off in the mornings. A vehicle blocks the lane. A person in a yellow hazard vest sits in a chair beside it. I don't know why. I don't see any construction near it.

The street is clear and in use in the evenings. The bus stop on the other side is still active. I've never taken the bus that had stopped there. I haven't taken any buses in a couple of months now. I don't know if the line has been rerouted, either just in the mornings or all the time. The website is cryptic. I hear that more bus lines are coming back.

I think of going to the mall after work. It's reopening today. I might be able to take a bus home. That's not a good idea, though. Many more people will be swarming toward it today. There would be a long line to get in. The food court is still closed as, I think, the rest of the eateries are. I know that there's nowhere to sit down and eat. I suppose that I should wait until the initial frenzy ends.

I grew up in New Jersey, so shopping malls are my native habitat. Someday soon, I will wander among the stores, most of which are full of things I would never buy. I will ride the buses home. But not today. Today I walk: to work, to the supermarket, down quiet streets and pedestrian alleys, past runners, children, cats and dogs, and home.

Friday, May 8th, 2020

The coffee shop with the excellent burekas also has masks for sale. I go in and ask about them. We start off in Hebrew. I use the wrong plural form for "masks," masculine rather than feminine. The worker corrects me and switches to English. They are just what I want: fifty surgical masks with comfortable elastic ear pieces for one hundred shekels, less than sixty US cents each. A lot of people on the street today are wearing stylish black masks. Many have a Nike logo. I have no idea where they get them.

Downtown is busy. Most shops have lines outside. They have to limit the number of people who can come in.

At the produce shop, I see leafy greens that I don't recognize. Their stalks come together at a common base. I snap off enough to fill a small bag. As I detach the last one, I see a head of cauliflower at the center. I don't care for cauliflower. I bring the bag of stalks to the register, as well as sweet potatoes and loquats. The cashier asks if I really want just the greens. I do. I plan to sauté them. She doesn't charge me for them.

My favorite shawarma joint doesn't have a line. The owner rests against the refrigerator. His eyes are closed. He snaps to attention when I say hello.

I get a falafel there and a granita from the cheap coffee chain. I sit down to eat them on a bench away from the crowd, across from where I got the masks. Children roll past on bikes and scooters. A group of three boys and a girl circle around four times before they head into the toy store. They leave their bicycles by the door, inside the gates. A large German shepherd rests next to a baby carriage. A cat wanders over and stretches out by its side. They watch two pigeons nearby pecking at a piece of bread. I watch them too. It's still early in the afternoon. None of us have to be anywhere else.

Saturday, May 9th, 2020

Several parties are in progress in my neighborhood. Loud music blasts from behind stone walls, mixed with multiple voices. I smell at least two barbecues. Hickory smoke drifts from the one near my house, though not the one closer to downtown.

I stop into an ice cream joint, one of the few places open on the Sabbath. I get a cone with one scoop of Snickers gelato. The temperature outdoors is a few degrees warmer than it was last time I got ice cream. By the time I find a bench and sit down, much of the gelato has melted and run down my hand. Time to switch to cups rather than cones. When I try to eat some of it, it collides with my mask. I've forgotten that I'm wearing one.

A religious family with two baby carriages and more children that I can count is across the square from me. A few meters away, a toddler walks unsteadily along the brick wall of a long planter. His mother holds his hand and speaks to him in something like Russian. When he reaches the corner, he looks down and around, uncertain how to proceed. His mother lifts him in the air, turns him ninety degrees, and puts him back down. He continues walking.

Two cats, one black and white and one orange, wander past them. A black cat darts in from the side. It runs up to the orange cat and puts its paws on its back. The orange cat, startled, leaps straight up into the air. The black cat flips over and lands upside down. They both recover and stand in place. Neither seems sure what just happened, They run off in opposite directions.

The Give-and-Take box on my way home is covered with clothes and books. I don't look at the clothes. Most of the books are for children. I take one cookbook: "Salads of the World." It's in Hebrew, but the words probably stick to a small domain of knowledge. I think I can hack my way through it.

Sunday, May 10th, 2020

I get to the hallway for the afternoon prayers then stop, return to my desk, and put on my mask. When I get back, the building manager is talking to one of my coworkers. The coworker asks me, in English, if I've noticed a smell in the men's room. I have. I tell him that for weeks now, one spot in there has smelled like a subway. He tells the manager, in Hebrew, that it smells like the Central Bus Station. That apparently means the same thing. I've been there. I can believe it. I don't remember a smell in the station, but I may have been too confused by the architecture. The building manager trots down the hall to the men's room to check it out.

By the time he gets back, we have ten men. We start the prayers. Almost everyone is back in the office. One programmer who is over seventy now works from home. So do a few people whose young children haven't returned to school yet. The rest are here. Students are back at the elementary school that I pass on the way home from work. Children play in its yard, behind a high fence. Nothing keeps them a proper distance apart from each other. That may be impossible.

I come home early to make a video call. It's Mother's Day in the States. I call my mother, brother, and sister simultaneously. The call connects without much hassle. My sister and I are in our apartments. My mother is sitting out on her porch. My brother is several meters away on her lawn. Their phones echo and feed back on each other, but we make it work. Next time, it should be easier.

Monday, May 11th, 2020

At the end of the pedestrian street, a pale pink flower falls from a tree. It gets wedged beneath an old truck's wiper blades. Branches with purple flowers cover a garbage heap. Discarded masks and gloves lie around them.

On a narrow path, a man with an orange vest, protective earphones, and cargo shorts trims a tall bush with a chainsaw. He is facing east as I approach from the west. He can neither see nor hear me. There isn't room for me to safely walk by. I toss a twig with yellow flowers at him. It hits him in the leg. He turns, sees me, and shuts off the chainsaw. I walk past him and nod. He nods back, waits until I'm at a safe distance, and switches the saw back on.

Traffic cones block the street where the bus stop had been. The usual vehicle and the worker in the chair aren't there today. Down the block, what had been a large pile of books is smaller now. The children's books are gone. Translations of foreign bestsellers remain: *The Secret*, something by Paulo Coelho, and John Clavell's *Shogun.* A tiny pair of girl's jeans with embroidered patches is draped across a bench. It has been there for about a week. Someone has taken the pair that had been next to it.

Around the corner, a porcelain seder plate rests on a low stone wall. I think about taking it. I don't. Other passersby might need and treasure it more.

Tuesday, May 12th, 2020

I ride the southeast elevator up to my office. I don't have a good internal compass. I only know it's southeast because we face in that direction when we pray toward Jerusalem.

When the doors open, I see a wooden path leading from the elevator to an office far away on our floor. I walk on the boards as far as the restroom. Each plank is slightly warped, with the center raised. Each step makes three sounds, not two. My heel hits the wood with a hollow pop. The wood clicks against the tiles when it flattens under my weight. The ball of my foot taps the board more softly, with a higher pitch.

When I head out for the night, I see that the elevator has also been lined with wood. Riding down alone, I tap patterns on the walls. The boards with the open spaces around the elevator buttons sound richer than those fastened flat against the other walls.

On my way home, two brightly colored trucks blast loud music as they roll past me down the road. Today is a minor holiday, though gatherings and the traditional bonfires have been banned. After the second truck goes by, I hear something like a bullroarer, punctuated by an even tick. I look to my left. The athletic woman is in her yard, jumping rope so rapidly that the rope whirs through the air.

Teenagers zoom past on scooters. Each has a mask with a different colorful pattern. What once were emblems of fear have now become fashion.

Wednesday, May 13th, 2020

The drugstore is nearly empty when I come in. The man at the door scans my forehead with a thermometer and nods. I head straight for the back. No one is in line.

I approach the counter. The pharmacist doesn't look up from his phone. "You need a number." I go to the machine, take a number, and return to wait at the line marked on the floor. "OK."

I walk up and slide the number and my health system ID through the slot in the plexiglass divider. It wasn't there the last time I was in the store. He scans the card. "What do you need?" I mention one drug, but I should get refills on everything. "Anything else?"

I try to answer in Hebrew. I fail. The words I need leave my mind for the moment. I ask if he speaks English. "Sure," he says. He has a dense Arabic accent, but each of us understands what the other is saying.

He runs down the list of my medications. I say yes to each one. He goes and gets them and brings them back. He doesn't need to count out or label anything. Everything comes in boxes of blister packs.

"So where do you live?" Here, in the same town.

"You don't sound Israeli. Where are you from?" The US. But that's never enough of an answer.

"Where?" I rattle off where I've lived: New Jersey, DC, Ohio, Texas, California. Oh, and Brooklyn.

"Brooklyn," he repeats. People seem to think it's the largest place in America.

"You're in tech." I nod.

"Where do you work here?" Also in the same town.

"Still in tech?" Yes.

"Still working?" Yes.

"Wow. Respect."

I slide my credit card under the plexiglass and pay. He slides the boxes of pills, an empty bag, and the card back to me. "If you need to know anything about the medications, just ask."

I know enough. I've been taking most of them for a long time.

I think of getting more things while I'm there. A long line has now formed at the registers up front. I decide against it. I maneuver around the other people and head out.

The shawarma joint across the street is closed. The ice cream parlor two doors down is open. I'm tempted, but I haven't eaten dinner yet. I grudgingly convince myself not to stop in. I take my earbuds out of my pocket, select another podcast, and wander on.

Thursday, May 14th, 2020

Walking to the mall from work takes longer than I expect. I usually cut through an athletes' park, around basketball and tennis courts, soccer fields, and a skating rink. The park is closed. I don't know why I didn't think that it would be.

The path around the outside isn't all that much longer. The streets have good sidewalks. I'm still annoyed.

Nothing at the mall looks any different as I approach, other than that there are spaces open in the parking lot. The usual guard sits at the entrance. In theory, the mall can only let a limited number of people in. He doesn't seem to be keeping count. I don't know how they could do so, since the mall has multiple entrances. He scans my temperature and waves me in without looking inside my shoulder bag.

About half the shops in the mall are open. Most of the clothing stores are closed. They might find dealing with people trying on clothes to be too much of a hassle. The cinema is closed. The restaurants are closed. Seating in the food court is roped off, but several of the eateries are open for to-go orders.

I stop into the natural food store where I get my favorite soap. I look for a small bottle of it that I can carry around, but they don't have them. I ask if they carry small empty bottles designed for that. They don't. They suggest the drug store down the hall. I get a larger bottle of the soap for my quarantine stash. It would last about a year. At that point I probably would have starved to death, but I'd leave behind a clean body.

I get a couple of inexpensive items at the computer store. I do it all in Hebrew until the worker sees my name on my credit card and switches to English. I wish she had switched earlier. She had had trouble fitting the larger item in the bag after she put the smaller one in. Putting the larger one in first would have been easier. I couldn't put the Hebrew words together to say that.

I leave the computer store and swing quickly through the supermarket. I go back to the food court and pick up dinner. I have fifteen minutes to cross the traffic circle between the mall and the bus stop and to catch the last bus. No problem – except that they have put high fences all around this side of the mall. The whole street is closed while they put in electric tracks to the train station a block away.

I walk along the other side of the road, trying to get across to where I expect the buses to run. Giving up, I walk back toward work.

I pause at the bus stop outside the cemetery next door to the office. I don't think there will be any buses. I have heard that they were supposed to end a few minutes earlier, with no more buses until Sunday. My transit app says that there will be one more. I sit and wait. There is.

Friday, May 15th, 2020

I sit outside the Heart of the City, drinking a coffee granita. I'm surprised to see buses go past. I had heard that, as in previous weeks, they would not be running on Fridays. The report was wrong. Or out of date. Or confused. So it goes with so much of the news.

The sidewalks are less busy than last week. The novelty of shopping again has worn off. It's also getting hot. It's not bad now, about ninety degrees Fahrenheit, but it'll be hotter in the next few days.

I get my usual challah at the bakery and falafel at the shawarma joint. At the store for nuts and berries, I get a kilogram of Colombian coffee, coarsely ground for cold brew. That's more than the dispenser contains.

The worker hops up and places one sandaled foot on the ledge below the coffee and the other on the counter across from it. He gradually rises to standing, a meter or so above the ground. He's more agile than I would have thought. He reaches up to the top shelf, near the ceiling, and pulls several large bags of coffee out from behind a display. He puts most on the shelf below it. He places the remaining bag next to the grinder. Bending over, he puts his hands on the ledge and the counter, in front of his feet. He slides his feet inward, over the empty space between them, balancing on his hands. He lowers himself to the ground and proceeds to grind the coffee. I am impressed.

I also buy some organic peanut butter. I keep hoping that I'll find the good stuff somewhere. I get some hummus to go from my usual place on the square. They remember how I like it, and include all the added elements in separate containers.

When I headed downtown, the Give-and-Take box held a large pile of men's shoes. When I pass it on my way home, they're gone. A bag of stuffed toys is in their place. Pikachu sits alone on the bench, looking off into the distance.

I get home and put most of the groceries away. I sit down at my desk and fall asleep for several hours. When I wake up, the falafel is still on the kitchen table. I think of eating it, but it's been out for a long time. It spent some of that time in the heat outdoors. I throw it away. I don't want to take any chances. I tell myself that I helped a friendly business by buying it. But I would have liked to have eaten it, too.

Saturday, May 16th, 2020

I don't even try to go outside today. The weather reports call for high temperatures. By mid-afternoon, it's gone up to 105 degrees Fahrenheit. I don't know how useful taking the temperature of people entering malls can be today. The air itself has a fever.

When I find where I'd left my water bottle, it's still full of water from sometime last year. I empty it, clean it out, then fill it with boiling water for a while. I'll have it with me this week.

I don't think I'll enjoy walking to work as much as usual. Reports tell us that the weather will be about the same. At least we can look forward to rain sometime around October.

The temperature hasn't bothered me at home today. I live in a hole in the ground, surrounded by insulation. I wear a sweatshirt all day.

For lunch, I have the last of the cholent that I made and froze months ago. This batch was disappointing. Barbecue sauce helps. For dinner, I have a hamburger with hummus in a pita. I make the latest version of JoeBowls as lunches for the week: brown rice, fava beans, tahini, swiss chard, cranberries, and walnuts. Then I get back to battling my computer network and, eventually, sleep.

Sunday, May 17th, 2020

A playing card lies face down at the start of the pedestrian path. I can't resist flipping it over. It's the Queen of Diamonds. If I were one to believe in random oracles, I might look up what it would mean. But I'm not, so I don't. I wonder whether I might have exposed myself to the virus by touching the card's smooth surface. There's no way to know. I decide not to worry about it.

Early in the afternoon, my boss announces that it's 43 degrees outside. That's about 110 Fahrenheit. "Aren't you glad that we work indoors?" Right then, the building's air conditioning shuts off. Again. It comes back on quickly. Our office has few windows. It doesn't get hot.

As usual, the afternoon prayers are in the hallway. Tall windows there look down on a central court. I lean against the glass to my right and almost burn my arm. I stand straighter during the rest of the prayers. My concentration also improves.

I head home at seven. It isn't oppressively hot by then. A man on a bicycle zigzags between houses on the pedestrian street, stuffing flyers behind door knobs or dropping them on the houses' front steps.

I come up behind a large dog and a man. I stay two meters away. The dog keeps looking back at me. When they pause, I make a wide loop around them and continue walking. When I step into shadows, I can see their reflection in my glasses. The dog, at least, seems happier when I remain in view.

Monday, May 18th, 2020

On the street where I get my mail, a young woman picks up leaves from the ground and puts them in a blue shopping bag. At first I think it's some sort of clean-up effort. Then I see that she is only saving one out of every eight or nine leaves. She drops the rest back on the ground. Maybe it's an art project. I can't tell, from several meters away, why she chooses the ones that she does.

Workers are finally digging up spots on the street where the bus stop had been. They are tearing up bricks from the pavement and holes in the road. I guess that they are a construction team rather than archaeologists. You never know, though, when people will stumble across something like a Phoenician temple around here.

It's hot again in the morning, but it doesn't get nearly as bad as yesterday. We're told that the temperature will rise above 100 degrees

Fahrenheit for six straight days this week. It's like I'm back living in Dallas. But at least 100 is better than 110.

I work late into the evening, rewriting marketing materials with my boss. We have different writing styles, but we make it work. I groove on collaboration. And I know when to let the wookiee win.

I'm surprised to see fallen grapefruit and oranges in my yard when I get home. I thought they had all come down a month ago. These last few must have needed to be more thoroughly convinced that winter is finally done.

Tuesday, May 19th, 2020

For the first time in weeks, I'm not wearing a mask as I walk to work. The Health Ministry has declared that we don't have to wear them outside for the next few days. While it's this hot, some people are having trouble breathing while wearing them. The Ministry has told people in high risk groups to stay indoors. The House of a Hundred Grandmothers had set up a table outside, where residents could meet with their families. That's not happening now.

Schools in my town are closed again. Having this plague of heat at the same time as the virus isn't fair. Even in Exodus, the plagues were sequential, not simultaneous. I decide to lodge a complaint during the afternoon prayers.

I put my mask on as I step into my office building. This seems backwards, but makes sense. The chance of catching the virus in an enclosed space such as our lobby is greater than outdoors.

When it's time for the afternoon prayers, a new person wanders up the hall to join us. He's a friend of a regular member. Unafraid of the virus, they embrace.

He asks me for a prayer book. I offer him two different versions. He chooses the larger one. I use the smaller. He is nervous, unsure of which prayer is said when. Others coach him through it. The prayer he most needs, the Mourner's Kaddish, is printed on the back cover. I had never noticed that before. When it's time, he reads it from there, along with the other mourners. It goes well. He'll probably be back.

Wednesday, May 20th, 2020

In the early morning, a friend on Twitter tells me the name of the trees with the purple flowers: jacaranda. As I pass the flowers on the way to work, the word rattles around in my head like a mantra. Jacaranda. Jacaranda. They call the trees Jacaranda.

When I get to work, I look up the word in Hebrew. It's the same. And that tells me that the J is pronounced as "Joseph" is in English, not as J might be in Spanish or French or German. I don't remember if I've ever seen a J in Italian, or how it would be pronounced.

I walk to work a little earlier than usual. A notice had appeared, taped to our mailbox, a week ago. Whoever is in charge of electricity would be shutting off the power to our neighborhood for a few hours today. Fortunately I work in a place with good air conditioning. I worry about people who might be stuck in their homes in this heat.

During afternoon prayers, the door lock on the office next to ours beeps randomly. None of us are good enough at Morse code to know if it is beeping out the prayers. We wonder if it would count for the quorum if it were. Since more than enough of us have gathered, though, the question is moot.

When I come home, it looks like no one actually cut the power. My alarm clock shows the right time. When there's a power glitch, it restarts and counts the time beginning from when it comes back on. I switch on the devices that I had shut down in the morning and watch them catch up with whatever else had happened today.

Thursday, May 21st, 2020

Down the aisle from me, someone speaks quietly on the phone in a language that I can't identify. The pitch of his voice is close to the resonant frequency of our cement-walled cubes. The sound pulses like an electrical hum. Its volume changes along with its pitch.

A text message breaks my attention. My health plan is finally offering home delivery of medications. There's a small charge, but it's free if you're over 75.

On the way to work, I see that the building under construction is close to complete. A crane lowers bundles of what look like paving bricks into its front yard. On my way home, the crane is gone. The stacks of bricks are taller than I am, hiding the building from view.

In the produce store, no one else, even the shopkeeper, is wearing a mask. I splurge on items for next week's JoeBowls: fresh spinach, cherries, and dried cranberries. I still need to get more fava beans and rice. I could save money if I ordered lunch from work, but these are a pleasant break.

At the register, the shopkeeper rings me up then frowns. He takes what he's already tallied out of the shopping bag and starts again. This time it comes to fifteen shekels more. I can't complain. I know that he's actually rung some things up for less than the marked prices.

When I get home, I put the air conditioner on just long enough to air out the room. The air is pleasantly cool. Tomorrow, it should be cooler outdoors.

Friday, May 22nd, 2020

I start coughing when I take my mask off in the square downtown. Someone has smoked something noxious nearby. I often like the scent of tobacco and other herbs. This smells more like someone lit a trash bin on fire. Maybe someone did.

I do my usual Friday morning rounds: a challah at the bakery, espresso at the cheap coffee chain, falafel at my favorite shawarma joint.

A delivery person pulls up to the doorway of the shawarma place on a powered scooter just before I get there. He's picking up five varied falafels for a family on my street. I hear the address, but not the name. The shop had gotten the order earlier. Falafel should be fresh, so they hold off on making it until someone is actually there to pick it up. I have to wait. That's OK.

They make them one at a time. They label the bags that they put them in so that people can tell them apart.

I admire the rider's mask. It's more rigid than most. It looks like it was designed for the contours of his face, and blends well with his black helmet.

Downtown, only one in ten people or so are wearing masks. Fewer are wearing them in my neighborhood. People in my generation seem to be more likely to wear them. Of those whom I hear speaking English, no one else with a North American accent has one on.

I know that the rules were lifted for the heatwave. I'm told that they might continue through today, even though it's cooled down. I'm not sure, so I wear mine anyway, except when I'm eating.

I get a large jar of pure peanut butter at the nuts and berries store. The small jar that I got there last week was the best I've found. It's still not as good as the fresh-ground stuff I got in the states. I don't put any in the quarantine stash. The commercial peanut butter, laden as it is with preservatives and other goo, is less likely to break down over time. Maybe my next JoeBowls will use a peanut sauce rather than tahini. I have a recipe. I head back to the square to eat my falafel.

When I find a bench, I sit down, take off my mask, and start coughing. I get up and move to another bench a few meters away. The air is better there.

Saturday, May 23rd, 2020

I haven't been on this street in a year or so. I'm running an errand for my family. I lived here when I first moved to this city. I haven't been to this neighborhood much since, though I'm often within a few blocks of it.

Most of what I see is the same. There's an endless array of effectively identical apartment houses, built as if inattentive giants dropped cinder blocks from above. The newest building is different enough that it stands out. When I lived nearby, the lot was a hole in the ground behind a fence. Another apartment house is there now. The facade for the ground floor is paneled with something that looks like dark wood. A driveway from the street descends to underground parking. The upper floors are the usual grayish-white stone. They haven't yet developed the stains and weathering that mark its neighbors. They will, in time.

I'm out earlier than usual on a Saturday morning. In the city square, seven women, my age or older, sit around a low table. They pour coffee from thermoses and eat snacks from open containers that they have put out. Some wear masks below their chins as they lean in close to one another and chat.

Outside an open sweet shop, seven men sit in chairs and drink black coffee. They laugh and talk loudly in what sounds like Arabic.

At the corner of the main street and the street where I lived, seven more men stand and talk. They are dressed for worship in suits and prayer shawls. They may be coming from the Sabbath morning service. They may even have prayed outdoors, near where they now stand. I wonder why each group that I passed has exactly seven members. If I were to make a film with them in it, I would have to either randomize those numbers or assign them some meaning.

I arrive at my old apartment. I help in moving objects down from there to the street level. I manage to go up and down the four flights of stairs four times before my knees give out.

Slightly after noon, I head home. More people are on the street. On the corner where the men in suits had stood, two boys chase each other around with squirt guns. I stop at the ice cream shop and get a cup of something good. Later on, I can't remember what it was.

I sit in the city square where the women had been, eat the ice cream, and fall asleep. My phone and wallet are secure, safe from pickpockets, though I've never knowingly seen any. When I awaken, I get up and walk home, where I fall asleep again.

Sunday, May 24th, 2020

A cat lies on an uneven pile of boards in our backyard. I imagine that lying there would be uncomfortable. Wouldn't it prefer the piece of smooth cardboard a few steps away? Maybe it thinks this is fun. Maybe this is what counts as excitement in its life.

I see fresh posters on the bulletin board close to work. They stand out, red and yellow against the off-white shreds beneath them. They seem to say that a religious community is holding a raffle for the holiday later this week. I'm not entirely sure what is going on.

Outside my office building, about a dozen massive cloth bags with handles sit by the curb, filled with smooth pebbles. During afternoon prayers, I see that some of the stones have been spread on top of the plastic runners in the court at the center of the building. Someone there tells us that they're putting in a pool. He's probably kidding. The space was left unfinished when the virus hit. This is the first work that I've seen done down there since then.

On the way home, I see three identical shoe boxes lined up on a wall. The first two contain shoes. The third holds a cat. It could be the same one. It's getting dark. It's hard to tell.

Monday, May 25th, 2020

As I walk past my landlord's porch, I see a large white bag waiting for me. My laundry person has returned the clothes that I put out yesterday. I pick it up, turn around, and bring it back down to my apartment. I'll unpack it in the evening.

As I carry it, a nonsense phrase loops in my head: "Buffalo Gals, put the laundry outside." It sticks with me until another earworm drives it out.

On the way to work, on a narrow path, I suddenly hear a motorcycle come up behind me, slightly to my left. I instinctively shift and crash into the hedge to my right. The branches scrape my arm. The sound of the motorcycle passes me, but I don't see it. I then realize that it had been in the driveway next door, on the other side of the other hedge.

A few minutes later, when I check my phone, I see that my hand has been bleeding a bit. I wash it off in the restroom at work, though I can't use the soap there. I hope the alcohol gel next to the prayer books on the reception desk helps.

When I step into the company kitchen to get coffee, one of my coworkers turns to me and says, "Joe, in Yiddish, it's a *brokh*, right?" I have no idea what he's talking about. I shrug. "But it is a *brokh?*" I don't know. My Yiddish is worse than my Hebrew, other than what I picked up from my father and from Leo Rosten books as a kid. I guess that a *brokh* has something to do with blessings, but I don't know for sure. I make my coffee and wander off, muttering vaguely.

Later, I look the word up. It means a wreck. Or a failure. Or a curse. Or something. I still don't know what he was talking about.

Tuesday, May 26th, 2020

At lunchtime, I duck around the swarming workers at the café downstairs. I've stepped in to get something to go. The café is fully reopening tomorrow. It's been open for takeout for the past few weeks and for delivery for a while longer. I've seen people sitting on the built-in benches that ring its patio, drinking coffee. But now they're setting everything up there, under the awning, in the shade outside.

The order from our usual lunch place didn't happen today, and I hadn't brought my own, so here I am. Inside the café, takeaway sandwiches are lined up within a display case. I ask the cashier for the salmon sandwich, in Hebrew. "Anything else?" I ask for a Coke Zero. She switches to English, with an accent close to mine. "They're in the fridge, behind you." No matter what I do, I end up saying "Coke Zero" like an American. It's my tell.

I turn, get one, and come back to the counter. I look down at the sandwich. It's smaller than I thought. She reads my mind, or at least my face, even through the mask. "Yeah, they aren't really enough for a lunch. I'd go for the tuna or avocado." I get the tuna.

"You want me to open the Coke?" She's holding a bottle opener. I don't know if we have one in the office. I nod. She opens it.

On my way out, I almost walk into a worker carrying a stack of chairs. They've put most of the tables in place while I've been inside. Most have chairs on top of them. From what I understand, they'll only be able to use some of the tables. I guess the rest will still have chairs, or some other marker, on them. I'll see tomorrow.

Wednesday, May 27th, 2020

I've been looking forward to this Israeli breakfast for a while. I should be eating dinner now. I don't care. Neither does the cashier. He takes my order, asking for all the variables. I get through the whole thing without getting stuck.

I wait for them to call my name at the counter, standing behind the line that others ignore. I pick up my tray and bring it to my table when It's ready. There have been some substitutions: whole wheat bread rather than multi-grain, and some sort of shredded cheese rather than avocado. That's OK.

While we need to wear masks to enter the mall, fewer than half the people inside are wearing them properly. No one working in the café is. Most have them down below their chins. Some cover their mouths but not their noses, or pull them down to speak. They seem to wear them as talismans, there to magically protect them from harm rather than to have any concrete function.

The driver on the bus home seems to think of its brakes the same way. As long as he steps on the pedal somewhere near an intersection, regardless of exactly when or how hard, he'll be protected from harm. The same isn't true for the passengers, who slam into the seats in front of them or cry out when we almost hit a bicycle. But he isn't bothered by these details.

At least the buses are running again, at their usual stops and something like their usual schedules, assuming that by "usual" we mean that traffic is once again terrifying. I guess it's a start.

Thursday, May 28th, 2020

It's been a compressed day. There's a holiday tonight and tomorrow.

Unlike before the Sabbath, though, we don't officially have the day off. The support team and I come in for about half the day. I finally escape from an interminable meeting at about 2 PM.

I immediately head over to the House of Hundred Grandmothers. They're still under quarantine. I get to speak to one family member and transfer some items through a ground floor window.

On the way home, I walk by a father and two small boys washing an SUV. I barely avoid getting splashed and sprayed as I pass them on the narrow sidewalk. One of the boys laughs as I do a goofy dance move, ducking under a hose that spirals down from the top of a fence.

Once home, I sit and try to figure out what I'll do with the next two days. I did the usual Thursday night and Friday shopping last night, since stores are closed tonight and tomorrow. I didn't get a challah, but I'll survive without it. I have other things to do that I've put off until this weekend. Maybe I'll get started on some of them.

Friday, May 29th, 2020

I don't get outside at all today. I don't have or make any particular plans to do so. It's a holiday. Little is open.

Instead, after a bout of relaxation and procrastination, I get back to work on a film project. I've been recomposing the music. In a sense, I've been continually composing the same piece for forty years or so. This is the latest version.

Stepping away from that, I look through some of the footage that I've shot, mostly last year, to see what I might use. Several films and clips that I've watched recently are changing my mind about what I want to do visually. I'm also getting ideas from what I experience while falling asleep in front of the TV.

I listen to some of the spoken word elements that I've recorded for it, as well as to the field recordings. Something new is coming together. I just have to look and listen to what I experience, both within and outside of my head, to learn what it is.

Saturday, May 30th, 2020

I'm not sure if the café is open. From a distance, I don't see anyone there. It's usually crowded on Sabbath afternoons.

As I approach it, a few people come into view, seated at widely separated tables. Two parties are on the patio. One couple is indoors. None of the customers appear to have masks on their faces, so I take mine off as I sit at a small table outdoors.

A server comes up to me. She ceremoniously scans my forehead with a thermometer and says several things in rapid Hebrew that I barely understand. One of them involves masks. Looking around, I see that the other customers do have masks, but have tucked them under their chins. I put mine back on and do the same.

She nods and leaves me a paper menu. It's smaller than the usual one. They don't appear to be serving breakfast in the afternoon anymore. I stare at it for a while and figure out what I want.

The server returns and asks me. I order from the menu, stumbling over a few words. "Where are you from?" she asks in English. The US. "New York?" I've lived there. "You have the same accent as my aunt. She lives in Riverdale, New York." I've been there twice. One time I visited someone I'd met online. I remember walking down an endless rabbit warren of hallways, far up in a high-rise, to reach his apartment. I don't remember why I was there the second time. I may have been speaking to a class about something. Close to forty years later, the memory is vague.

After a few minutes, another server brings my cappuccino. She is taller than the first. She walks as if she's on a tightrope, trying not to spill the overfilled cup. My sandwich appears a little later with an American-style salad.

More people arrive as I sit, eat, and read the book that I brought with me. Several smoke, but they're all downwind. Two women arrive without masks and appear to insist that the rules are only for other people. The server steps into the back and returns with generic surgical masks for each of them. They roll their eyes and tuck the masks under their chins.

I check my phone briefly. Friends of friends in America are facing tear gas, pepper spray, and fires. If I were in their city or one of many others over there, I would be with them, though I would try to document and support what they're doing at a distance from the front lines. All I can do from here is stay in touch.

My server brings me the check. I take out my credit card. "Would you like to put a tip on the card? What percentage?" I tell her. She is surprised. I had forgotten that people tip much less here. It's OK. The service was good. Here in the quiet Middle East, it's been a pleasant afternoon.

Few people in the supermarket are wearing masks today. The guard is. As I come in, he dutifully scans my forehead. But many of the workers and most of the customers either have taken them off or are wearing them below their chins. Many who are covering their mouths aren't covering their noses.

People in charge have warned us about getting complacent. It doesn't look like the people on the street are listening. A lot more joggers than usual are out tonight. It's neither too hot nor too cool to run. Some of them have masks on. Some do not.

About a block away from me on the pedestrian street, a small long-tailed rodent emerges from the bushes. I see it in silhouette. I don't know what it is.

It suddenly stops in the middle of the road. Two joggers are headed toward it from opposite directions. It turns toward one, then the other, then looks ahead again to where it had been headed. A cat has appeared there, watching it. It spins around and heads back into the bushes. The cat doesn't move. The joggers nod as they pass each other and continue on their way.

June 2020

Monday, June 1ˢᵗ, 2020

I pass my landlord on the path through our front yard. As we say "Good morning" to each other, I crash into glass wind chimes hanging from a tree. I hadn't noticed them before. The wind chimes are much louder than I would have guessed from their size. They continue to clatter and ring for at least a minute.

I exit the yard, pet the cat that enjoys riding the swinging gate, and put on my earbuds. I don't know for how much longer the wind chimes continue to ring.

At the end of the day, a woman riding the southeast elevator with me drops her keys. They, too, are louder than I expect. The elevator is still lined with wood. The sound resonates differently and for longer than it would have in the other elevators made of metal and plastic.

On my way home, I see that the door to my favorite shawarma joint is open. They had been closing much earlier during the lockdown. Inside, it looks like they may be done for the day.

I start to leave, but the owner emerges from the back. He tells me that they still have shawarma, if I want it. I do. He brings a container of the meat back out and puts it on the grill. He cuts open a pita and puts hummus and other elements in it that haven't yet been put away.

I sit at a table outside. As I eat, he picks up other tables and chairs and carries them into the shop. I stand, looking to get out of the way and finish the shawarma elsewhere, but he waves and shakes his head. "No, no, sit and eat. There is still time."

When I'm done, I wave to him. We each say "Good evening." I wander off to the bus stop.

I get home quickly. The cat sees me coming and hops up on the gate to take a ride. I check the wind chimes as I pass them. Nothing is broken. I tap them gently. They continue to clatter and ring as I step inside.

Tuesday, June 2ⁿᵈ, 2020

An operatic baritone, singing in Russian, booms forth from the office under construction down the hall. Before I notice how good the voice is, I remember that loud singing is more likely to spread the virus than simply breathing would be.

In the elevator down from work, a large woman riding with me breathes quickly and heavily. She had been running. She managed to dive in before the doors closed. She places one hand on the wall to steady herself. When we reach the ground floor, she heads toward the medical clinic to our right. I go out, to the left.

The park on the way to the mall is open again. The usual number of people are playing basketball and soccer and zooming around on skateboards and rollerblades, but everything seems hushed, quieter.

At the mall, the tables in the food court have reopened. Fewer may be out there than before. I'm not sure. Low barriers divide some of the walkways. They may be designed to control the traffic flow, but I don't see any logic to them.

Signs on each open shop on the mall show how many customers may be in the store at the same time. Some clothing shops that I pass can accept three, five, and eight customers. The supermarket can hold 135. The aisles inside it are chaotic, but workers are trying to neaten things.

At the bus stop, two teenage boys spin something made of fabric in the air. It looks like a bandana on a square wooden frame. They twirl it like a pizza, tossing it back and forth. When the bus pulls up, one of them tosses it high in the air and catches it behind his back. Both of them hop on board.

Wednesday, June 3ʳᵈ, 2020

As I pass the school, a torrent of children barrels out of a side door and into the fenced-in yard. The first two girls to emerge hide behind a massive trash bin. When most of the rest are outside, they jump up and yell. The other kids scream. The girls laugh and join them.

At the other end of the schoolyard, a dozen kids stand in a straight line. Their teacher stands with them. The girl in front runs to a post a few meters ahead of them, then back. She hands something like a baton to the boy who had been behind her, then heads to the end of the line as he runs to the post and back.

At the entrance to the supermarket, three old men sit in folding chairs, not talking. I stand in front of them until one gets up and scans my forehead. It isn't the one that I expected.

An old woman comes out with a small shopping cart. Another of the men stands and picks up his cane. They walk away together.

While I wait for the elevator at the end of the day, a man, woman, and boy emerge from the dermatologist's office. The elevator nearest them opens. I step toward it, but they get in first. I step back. I don't need to squeeze in with them.

They see me and realize that I'd been waiting for the elevator before them. The woman apologizes. I tell them it's OK. They step out and hold the door open for me. I get in and smile at them. I don't know if they know that I did. Smiles get lost when we wear our masks.

Thursday, June 4th, 2020

It starts to rain as I'm walking home. At first, I think something like an air conditioner is dripping on me, but it continues as I walk down the street. If a drone large enough to carry an air conditioner were following me, I probably would hear it.

Other people look up and around, trying to figure out what's happening. It doesn't rain here in June. Some small cloud may have been blown far off course.

The rain gives up quickly. In the warmth of summer, the cloud didn't have a chance. I'm surprised at how sad I feel for the cloud, considering that it probably didn't exist.

Outside the Heart of the City and across the street from it, dueling buskers play unrelated music. Their sounds blend and clash as I approach them, but each is loud enough that when I get close to one, I can't hear the other.

The accordionist is playing an old-time Italian tune. The violinist has paused to smoke. His boombox is playing what sounds like a karaoke version of Leonard Cohen's "Hallelujah." As I pass him, he picks up his violin and plays along. I have guessed correctly.

When I get home, I'm surprised to see a large sofa on our lawn. The cats who usually lie on our yard's stone path are stretched out on it, lounging in luxury. My landlady texts me to ask if I would want it. I'm tempted, but it wouldn't work in this small apartment. I text back my thanks, but have to decline.

"No. I can't accept that." The worker at the hummus joint looks down at the money I am holding out. "Imagine if I were to give that as change to a customer."

I look at the money myself. Much of the twenty shekel note, usually red, is brown. It looks burnt to me, but it might be a stain. If it is, I don't want to know what stained it and how. I hadn't noticed that before. I must have gotten it as change but I don't know when or where. I put the note back in my wallet and count out coins. A handwritten sign says that on Fridays they only accept cash. Between one-shekel and half-shekel coins, I have enough money.

It's my first time sitting down to eat hummus here since the lockdown started. What I've been served now is a little different from what I'd gotten for the same order from the same worker before. There's a lot more paprika and more of a green herb that I can't identify. But it's good.

As I sit alone, a guy wanders up to me and tries to sell me random items from a bag: Chanel-branded cologne, an electric massager, and other odd objects. I keep saying no. I can't recall how to say anything more forceful. He doesn't leave until he's gone through the entire contents of the bag.

Once I'm done eating, I make my usual rounds. I get a challah at the bakery and a double espresso at the cheap coffee chain next door. A new kitchenware outlet has opened within the Heart of the City mall. I get two spatulas, red for meat and blue for dairy.

At the international foods store, I look at spices, dried fruit, noodles, and other items, mostly from Asia. They do a lot of business with foreign workers. The shopkeeper speaks fluent English. As I recall, he has a son in Los Angeles. Still, I do the whole transaction in Hebrew. I hadn't able to do that before.

At the produce shop, I get sweet potatoes, yellow peppers, and green apples. As I wait in what loosely resembles a line, the cashier reaches into a bin and hands a fistful of fresh basil to the customer behind me. The scent as it passes me is overpowering, but not in a bad way.

I head home past the hummus joint. When I was there earlier, the line had been five or six people long, stretching back from the counter. It now holds about twenty people and bends to the left. The ones in back will have to wait. Today is one of the longest Fridays of the year.

There will be plenty of time before they close for the Sabbath.

Saturday, June 6th, 2020

Pods from the giraffe tree litter the ground in the park on the way to the House of a Hundred Grandmothers. None of the pods appear to have split or sprouted. Maybe those that did have been taken away.

It's been more than three months since I've come through here. It's been that long since I've been inside the House. The building has been under strict quarantine. It's been tough for the people there, but it has worked. Unlike many such places, in all that time, no one has caught the virus.

I come in and ride the elevator up several floors. The lights inside it are brighter than I remember.

As usual, my family is in their small apartment. Just after I enter, the caregiver leaves for her first day off since the lockdown began. Had things gone as intended, she would be returning right now from her wedding in the Philippines. That's been delayed, as have so many things in so much of the world.

I sit across the room from my family, our masks still on. I'm wearing a generic surgical mask. It fits precisely enough that they tell me they can see my lips move through it. They can tell when I smile.

I have dinner with them, masks off for the moment. We sit in a different order than usual. I sit farthest from the most fragile of us.

When we are done, I turn and toss the trash from dinner in the garbage bin. The plastic chair I'm sitting in isn't used to someone of my size twisting in it like that. The back legs snap off. I crash to the ground. I'm not hurt, but I can't move. Someone else has to pull the fragments of the chair out from under me, so I can get the leverage to stand up.

We go back and sit in the living room. When it's time for me to go, we step toward each other for the usual hug. We stop before we make contact, step back, and wave at each other.

I take the other elevator down to the exit. The lights inside it are equally bright. In the hall, I look at the large fish tank, wondering if my favorite fish are still there. They aren't. I realize that it's been several months since I last touched another person.

Sunday, June 7th, 2020

I'm surprised that the wrapper on my burger says "vegan." After a couple of bites, I realize why. The mushroom burger isn't a burger with added mushrooms. It's made of mushrooms, shaped into a breaded patty. I like it. It's better than the regular burgers that I've had at this place.

Ordering is confusing. I have trouble understanding what the worker at the counter mumbles through her mask, even when she switches from Hebrew to English. At least she is wearing a mask. People who work restaurant counters rarely do, even though they speak to customers face to face at close range.

I sit down outside with my soda to wait for my order. A religious family is sitting two tables away. That's unexpected. This burger joint doesn't keep kosher. Signs advertise their cheeseburgers. They're not hiding it. I look more closely and see that the family is eating pizza. That explains that. This place shares a patio with the Pizza Hut next door, which is kosher.

As I eat, I start to read a new book on film editing that arrived for me this morning. I quickly give up. I'm too tired to juggle both a burger and a paperback. I focus on the food. The fries are uninspiring. I remember too late that I had liked the sweet potato fries last time. I'll get them when I come back. I'll know to order the mushroom burger again.

Monday, June 8th, 2020

The guard waves me in to the supermarket. No line, no thermometer: he's back to just sitting there and nodding.

We're getting contradictory news about the virus. Performance halls can open soon for crowds of up to 250. That might include the dance center, if they limit tickets to the main space or close off the balcony. Their website isn't saying yet.

Trains were supposed to start tomorrow, but now it looks like they won't. No one has figured out how to limit crowding on them. They may be starting up more enforcement on buses. Schools have opened, but some have had clusters of positive tests and are closing again. Headlines tell us that smokers are at a greater risk, but nicotine might prevent some symptoms. We've hit a stasis of low-level confusion.

In my kitchen, as I prepare to cook more JoeBowls, the first cockroach of the season emerges from beneath my refrigerator and runs onto my foot. I kick it away. It flies involuntarily into a wall. I get a paper towel to pick it up and drop it outside. When I turn back to get it, it's gone. It will be back, or another one just like it. Summer is almost here.

Tuesday, June 9th, 2020

The display on the front of the bus is scrambled. I can't make out which line it is or where it's headed. As it passes me, I see from the display on the side that it is the line that I need. I chase after it for a couple of meters, waving my transit card in the air. I stop as it heads into the traffic circle. I put my card back in my pocket, rest my bag of groceries on the ground, and sigh. Chasing the bus never works. I will have to wait for another half an hour.

I walk back to the stop and sit on the bench. A moment later, I see a bus for the same line come off the traffic circle and head down the divided road in the other direction. I watch as it passes. The lines end at the train station a block away. Buses often pause there before beginning another run.

At the train station, the bus loops around and comes back toward me. I see the scrambled display on the front. It's the same bus. It stops where I'm sitting and opens its back door. I hop on and call out my thanks to the driver. There are no transit card scanners toward the back, so I stumble forward as the bus heads around the circle again. "It's OK," the driver says. "Sit. Sit. Nothing's working."

I notice that none of the interior lights are on. The display up front does show the stops. The recorded announcer calls them out. A few more people get on the bus along the way. He tells each of them to sit down. The ride is free. When my stop appears, I press the buzzer and get off. I don't have to wait for traffic to pass. In our yard, I see that the sofa is gone, but my laundry has returned. I juggle the laundry and my groceries as I fumble for my key.

As I open the door, a cockroach who has been waiting on the step for me runs inside, disappearing into the darkness. Maybe I'll find it later. Maybe I won't.

Wednesday, June 10th, 2020

I wait in line at the small grocery store to pick up my packages. I had been there yesterday, but the postal terminal froze with a Blue

Screen of Death. The shopkeeper, grumpy as always, said I would have to wait for fifteen or twenty minutes. I had to go to work.

I'm back now. I have gotten phone alerts that two more packages have arrived. I have never gotten more than one at a time. When it's my turn, I tell the shopkeeper that I have three packages. "Yes, thank you for telling me." He says it with an exaggerated politeness that suggests that I have done something dumb.

He picks up the first package. "ID Number?" I tell him. He types it in. "Sign there, Joseph." He has never called me by my name before. I didn't think he knew it. I sign on the screen with the tip of my finger. I look on my phone for the codes for the other two packages.

"Joseph?" he asks, then again, a bit louder, "Joseph?" I look up. He is already holding the other two packages. "Here. You're done." I had thought that I would have to tell him their codes and sign for them again. Apparently not. I take them from him and thank him. "Next?" he says.

I head out to the recycling box and open the packages. Each contains a separate order from the same shop in England: a new biography of Ornette Coleman, a recent book of poetry by Ron Silliman, and a beautiful small edition of Thoreau.

I stuff the packaging into the recycling box. I stuff the books into my shoulder bag. That takes longer. With all the other things in there, including my tablet, its keyboard, and my lunch, they barely fit.

I head on to work. I would rather just get some coffee, sit on the bench outside the shop, and read.

Thursday, June 11th, 2020

At first, I don't notice who the person walking past me is. I do notice immediately that a word on his t-shirt is misspelled. I don't catch what the word or the error are, though I do know that it was toward the end of the top word on a stack of three lines of text.

A few minutes later, he comes past me again. The word is "Manhatten", spelled with an "e". I tell him. "That's intentional. I wear a shirt with a misspelled word, so people spot it and feel smart."

I'm dubious. I tell him that I notice things like that. I can tell that there's a problem with spelling or punctuation before I consciously register what it is. "That's your Old City kicking in." I don't know what he means. A few minutes later, I realize that he said "OCD." My ears don't debug text as quickly as my eyes.

Much of my job is fixing other people's English. It's hard to convince them of some things. Adjectives in English sound wrong when they're out of order. English does weird things with singulars and plurals: We say "book store" not "books store." Sometimes the people fix what they write. Sometimes they don't. I do what I can.

Friday, June 12th, 2020

The arch of balloons, red, white, and black, rises from wooden stanchions, a couple of meters from the counter at the mall café. It looks like a random decoration at first. After a moment, I realize that it guides the line of customers. I stand beneath it until the previous person is done.

When I reach the counter, I order my usual Israeli breakfast. I do OK until the worker asks "Anything in addition?" This puts me off balance. I'm usually asked that later in the process. I ask her for a large iced coffee. She frowns.

"You speak English?" I nod. She continues in English. "You can have tuna, soft cheese, and avocado, or tuna, soft cheese, and Bulgarian cheese." That's a change. It explains why I was served the salty Bulgarian cheese rather than avocado last time. I ask for avocado.

We get through the rest of the order quickly. She asks for my name. I tell her. "Oh! I recognize you now." We had last seen each other before the masks.

On the bus heading back from the mall, the radio segues from Nico's "These Days" to something from the Jackson 5. The DJ yells "Sixties! Sixties! Sixties" – "*Shishim! Shishim! Shishim!*"

We pass murals that say "The City of Culture" and "The City of Freedom." In Hebrew, "Culture" and "Freedom" rhyme.

A man across the aisle from me yells at the driver. The bus has picked up and dropped off a passenger at stops that this line doesn't officially use. The driver ignores him.

I hop off at the Heart of the City and get my usual challah and produce, as well as a salt shaker for spices. It's still early, but I have little else to do. It's too hot to sit around outside. I walk home.

As I walk to the House of a Hundred Grandmothers, I think I see a cat nuzzling a bottle of wine. I get closer. It's a bottle of olive oil and a white plastic bag.

Ahead of me, a young woman walks with four children, dressed in their Sabbath best. The tallest girl wears a white dress made of endless translucent layers. I am surprised when they call the woman "grandmother."

The park on the way is more crowded than last week. Three dogs run around, two on leashes, one without. The freely roaming dog ambles toward me, but darts off to my left when we hear something move in the bushes.

At supper, my family sits as we did last week. I'm in a sturdy folding chair. A step stool takes the place of the chair that broke. I offer to replace it. They decline. Two of the family households are about to move. They will get another kitchen chair from one that has too many.

In the living room, we discuss some tricky language in a Biblical passage that I am translating for a film project. I had tried to use a modern meaning for an ancient word. Wisdom doesn't say that God bought her when he started on his path, but rather than he created her. Oh.

We talk about researching and organizing the books that we're writing. We get tired as it gets late. We have to repeat ourselves when we mumble through our masks. I head home. A Facebook post reminds me to file for my overseas US ballot. So does my mother, over video chat. Done. There's still time for other ongoing tasks before I work again tomorrow.

Sunday, June 14th, 2020

The trash on the rubbish heap looks like modern sculpture. Boxes form a cityscape at the center. Branches rest around them. A set of broken folding chairs is scattered on the pile. One chair has fallen on its back at the left edge, another on the right. A third sticks up from the top, over the boxes. At first, I think it's the handle of a lawn mower. It's just off center, as far off the ground as it is from the chair on the left. The chair to the right is slightly farther away. Without measuring, I imagine that the rubble illustrates the Golden Section.

I think of taking a photo, but any complete image of the pile would also include the six women doing Tai Chi on the plot of grass beyond it. They are already looking at me suspiciously.

Closer to work, on the street where I pick up my packages, three women wearing long off-the-shoulder black dresses drift along the sidewalk. They aren't together and don't seem to notice each other. One is walking a dog. Another heads out of the grocery store with a large cardboard box. The third gets into a silver car and drives away.

Later, I do a web search on "off the shoulder" to be sure that the phrase matches what I saw. It does. An article appears in the search about the loneliness of people who crave physical touch. I assume that it discusses isolation and the quarantine. I click through. It's from February, before the virus was known, eons ago. So much has changed. So much is as it was, only more so.

Monday, June 15th, 2020

A spider dangles from a thread in my bathroom. It's so small that at first I think it's a speck on my glasses or yet another floating wisp in my eye. I whistle a riff from a song I've just heard. My breath gently blows the spider around. It sways in rhythm to the tune.

On my way to work, the street where the bus stop had been is under construction as usual. Workers dig up the asphalt every morning, pulling out piles of dirt and laying pipes. Every evening, they are gone. The street reopens. Cars and buses drive by. I don't know how the workers do it.

The folding chair that had been at the end, next to a vehicle blocking the road, is halfway up the street this morning, on the sidewalk, its back against a wall. One tall worker slumps in it, his legs stretching out to the curb.

I scrape my feet against the pavement as I approach him. He hears me. He pulls his legs inward, his knees touching his chest, until I pass, then slumps back down as he had been.

A few meters beyond him, a blond boy sits on a stone pillar at the end of a fence. His grandmother steadies him. She points to the various trucks and says single words. I think they're in Russian. The boy repeats the words as well as he can.

At the office, a coworker sits in the aisle. His legs stretch across it, like those of the man in the folding chair. We're more familiar. I step over them, carefully cradling my coffee, and continue on to my desk.

Tuesday, June 16th, 2020

I step into the grocery store to pick up my package. The grumpy man greets me by name, in English. That has never happened before. I've been coming here for a year and a half. I didn't know that he could speak English at all. I feel like I've either passed a test or failed one.

The package has arrived more quickly than I expected from the US. It's not a book this time, but a CD. Or, rather, two CDs. I check my order online when I get to work and see that I did, indeed, accidentally order two copies. That explains why it was more expensive than I expected. Oh, well. I know someone here who will appreciate the copy that I don't need.

I eat dinner at a café on the square at the center of town. The seating is outside, though they put glass walls around it in the winter. The tables are reasonably far apart. Most people who are not eating are wearing their masks properly. That's a good sign. I've been seeing people on the street wearing their masks on their elbows or wrists. I suspect that they would only put them on their faces when police approach. But I haven't knowingly seen any police on the streets in a long time. It's a quiet city. There's little crime outdoors.

Wednesday, June 17th, 2020

I'm surprised to see this falafel joint here, one town over. The one just like it in my town is my favorite, though I rarely go there. It's nearby as the crow flies, but I'm too heavy to hitch a ride on a crow, and I don't often walk in that direction. Apparently it's one of a chain. I don't know if more than the two of them exist.

The worker asks me what I want. I say "Falafel." He asks me, in Hebrew, if I want him to speak Hebrew or English. Apparently, saying that one word gave me away. The "F" sound is the same in both languages, I think, but the vowels differ, as does the "L," especially at the end of a word. I ask him to speak Hebrew. I can handle it.

Over a dozen different items can go in the pita along with the falafel balls. He asks me if I want each one. I pause when he says the name of one of them. I don't recognize the word. He says, in English, "it is a garlic and mint sauce with a bit of spiciness." That sounds good.

The shop is called either "Chayim's Falafel" or "The Falafel of Life." Names here are often still active as words. Translations get interesting. Google Translate once told me that someone on the office WhatsApp channel had said, "An angel or tree might know that, but a deer would not." It made sense at the time.

The worker sticks a breaded slice of sweet potato at the top of the pita. I sit down with the falafel and a lemonade at a table far from the others, take off my mask, and eat.

Thursday, June 18ᵗʰ, 2020

The afternoon prayers start a little late. Usually, a guest from downstairs comes in and circles through the office. We call him "the alarm clock." When he drifts past our desks, we know to get together.

He's late today. By the time he comes by, several of us have noticed that it's late and have headed toward the hallway on our own. Just before he shows up, a dispute breaks out. One of our team questions whether we count as a group of ten when some of us are in one branch of the hallway, some are in the other, and the rest are still in the office, just inside the open door. There's a mezuzah posted on the doorway. My coworker questions whether we can be counted as being in a single space if we are on both sides of the mezuzah. He has a point.

I'm surprised that he raises the issue. He's a very precise programmer, but not someone I would imagine being all that interested in the fine points of rabbinic law. The conversation quickly gets beyond me. Some suggest, I think, that we're OK as long as we can all hear whoever happens to be the prayer leader. I don't know if there's any resolution. There often isn't. A lot of Jewish law seems to come down to both sides probably being right, and a consensus that we'll only get a definitive answer at the end of time.

The prayers start up as usual, with the group standing as we usually do. During the silent prayer, a woman emerges from the restroom and looks startled. It's not unknown to see a group of men in a hallway, all facing southeast, most bobbing quietly back and forth, but it doesn't happen everywhere. She stares for a moment, figures out what's happening, nods, and walks quietly down the hall.

Friday, June 19ᵗʰ, 2020

This larger produce market has dinosaur kale. I don't think I've seen that here before. Most leafy greens are harder to find here than where I'd lived in the states. I grab the kale immediately. It will go well in JoeBowls.

When I get to the registers, the cashier asks me if my bags of fruit and vegetables are from the displays outdoors. Those are usually cheaper. The apples and clementines are from outside. The peppers are from inside, as are the kale and a small package of blackberries that I take from a stack on display. They're for the JoeBowls, too.

When he rings up the blackberries, he says in English, "I will give you a special price. Twenty-five shekels for you." That's still steep, but it's my only splurge. He looks at the kale and takes it to another worker. "One moment." They chat. He returns. "Twelve shekels. Good?" That's quite good, less than I expected.

I put them all in my cloth shopping bag. I already have a challah in there. I get my usual hummus at the usual place. The line takes a maddeningly long time. The hummus hasn't been as tasty as it was before the lockdown.

I get an espresso at the cheap coffee chain and some gelato at a good place across the street. I would have gotten them together as an affogato, but the only place that seems to know what those are is at the mall. I got too late a start to get there today. I'll look forward to getting one there next week.

Saturday, June 20th, 2020

As I enter the House of a Hundred Grandmothers, the receptionist waves her thermometer at me. I walk over to her. She's quite short. I have to bend over the counter for her to reach me. I take off my baseball cap. She scans my forehead. She looks at the thermometer when it beeps. She nods. I move on.

At dinner, I sit in the chair that I usually use. Dinner lasts longer than usual. This chair, too, starts to collapse under me. A relative's caregiver grabs me under my arms and lifts me to standing. I'm amazed. She weighs about half what I do and is not muscle-bound, but she lifts me without a problem. She brings me a stool to sit on. She shrugs when she sits down again. "I am thin, but I am strong."

After dinner, the family discusses aspects of Jewish law and other issues. The scholars in the family agree that being on different sides of a mezuzah wouldn't keep a group from praying together. Their precedent: In the face of the pandemic, rabbis have ruled that people can pray together even if each is on his own porch.

They look at the current rash of statues being torn down, in the light of a statement in Deuteronomy about an evil tribe: their memory should be blotted out, but they shouldn't be forgotten. Thus, we shouldn't celebrate and honor the slave traders and other figures, but we can't forget what they did. We can't let it happen again.

Once at home, I get my laundry ready and drag it outside. As I talk on the phone, the largest cockroach I have ever seen wanders up to me. I stamp my foot next to it. It runs off. We'll meet again.

Sunday, June 21st, 2020

A dozen people have gathered for afternoon prayers. The usual leader hasn't shown up. By consensus, a dentist from downstairs takes over. When the usual leader rushes in, he sees that we're already in progress. He takes a spot, properly distanced along the wall, and catches up.

My mind wanders during the silent prayer. I look down into the atrium. I think it's been under construction for as long as I've been here. People seem to work on it for a day or two each month. Last time, laborers dragged gigantic bags of sand into the space. They dumped out several of them. Half of the black plastic sheeting on the ground is now covered with uneven mounds. No one seems to know when they'll be back or what it will be when they're done. The common joke is that they're building a swimming pool. They'll stick a diving board out of our window on the fourth floor.

During the Kaddish, two men come in from the elevator and walk past us through the center of the group. They say "Amen" when we do, and the one line of the liturgy that we say in something like unison. They don't slow down or join us. By the time that the prayer is done, they have disappeared down the hall.

Monday, June 22nd, 2020

The man in front of me in the supermarket line spins around abruptly and drops to the floor. I think at first that he's had some sort of attack. He hasn't. A red pepper has broken loose from a bag on the conveyor belt. He catches it on the first bounce, before it can roll away.

As he stands, I hear a smash and a shout. The woman in front of him freezes. The bottom of the bag she is carrying has torn. A bottle of olive oil has hit the floor and shattered. It's a bad day for bags. The man drops to the ground again. He picks up the rest of her fallen items before the spreading pool of oil reaches them.

The cashier gets on the intercom. "Cleaning worker to lane number nine, please, cleaning worker to lane nine." The woman's left sandal has gotten oily. The cashier hands her a roll of paper towels and places a bottle of hand sanitizer where she can reach it.

I finish putting my groceries on the conveyor belt. The woman looks up at me sheepishly. I tell her that it's OK, that I'm not in a hurry. I say it in English. I heard her speaking on her phone a few minutes earlier, when we were both in the rice aisle. She speaks English with an accent like mine. She may even be from New Jersey.

The cashier first rings up the man with the peppers, then me. The cleaner is gone by the time I'm done. The floor at the end of the line is still slippery. I step carefully, but I still get some oil on my shoes. I skate along the tile floor of the mall, then head out to the bus.

Tuesday, June 23rd, 2020

Freshly printed signs on the doors and elevators of my office building say "Entrance without masks forbidden." I haven't seen this enforced, but people are complying. It helps that the guard at the front desk always looks peeved.

Outdoors, people are less willing. While most people I pass on the way to work are carrying masks, only half are wearing them, and fewer are wearing them effectively. The government has doubled the fine for not wearing masks, though I haven't heard of anyone having to pay it.

The virus is spreading again. They're tightening the rules at the House of a Hundred Grandmothers. No visitors are allowed. The residents may go outside, but some are staying in, just in case.

On the other hand, some shows are starting to happen. At work, I hear from my family that my favorite troupe will perform next week, outdoors at the Dance Center. There's no word of it at the center's website, but the dance company's site has tickets on sale. I grab one immediately for next Wednesday's late show. There's still a chance that the government will shut that down again. I'm gambling the ticket price that the event will happen. I'll understand if it doesn't.

The news shows Orthodox men dancing at a ceremony, holding small hoops together rather than joining hands. Someday, eventually, people will dance as we once did again.

Wednesday, June 24th, 2020

The largest café on the main street has closed. It never came back after the lockdown. I'll miss it, in the way that we miss places that we rarely actually visited.

I only went there once. The salad was good, but too expensive. I was unemployed then. The price might have seemed more reasonable if I had returned once I was working.

Last week, a banner hung from the awning: "café for sale, fully furnished." The sign wasn't there when I passed it today.

The café has a large patio, covered with AstroTurf. It had been filled with tables and chairs and servers' stations. The owners brought them inside when the lockdown started. People now use the patio as an artificial park. They sit on lawn chairs, have picnics, and look out at the traffic.

The other most expensive café on the street, set into the Heart of the City mall, is gone, too, but they closed long before the lockdown. Signs there had said that the bakery across the street would move in. It hasn't yet. The signs are gone, but renovations continue.

Cafés here are nothing like the ones that I miss from the States. Most are full restaurants, with extensive menus. I don't see people hanging out for hours with a cup of coffee while working or reading.

There's nothing like a Third Place. I'm told that that's because life here is based around homes and families. I can easily picture my favorite cafés in most of the cities in which I have lived, though I can't recall many of the names: the diner in Brooklyn where the dishes would rattle when the subway passed overhead, the endless array of all-night spots in Austin, the café in Dallas with the great fruit-laden waffles, the place in Berkeley where I wrote new chapters of The Book of Voices each week, the line of cafés in Cleveland where I performed at open mics, the one in my small New Jersey city where I would read the books that I had gotten on inter-library loan, and all the bookstores in the chain at which I eventually worked.

Many nights, after I leave my office, I just want to sit somewhere for a few hours and write and read. I always end up at home.

A row of signs in the hallway to my office reads, in English, "Fire Handicapped Women." Fortunately, they aren't stating Human Resource policies. They point down another hallway to the left, to an emergency exit and two restrooms. I hadn't noticed them before. They catch my eye today.

Nine of us stand around, ready for afternoon prayers. The prayer leader is late again, caught on a phone call. As he steps into the hallway, someone calls out, "Ten!" Several people start into the first line of the opening psalm.

Someone I don't know stands at the back of the group. He has heard that we gather every afternoon. It's the anniversary of the death of someone close to him. He needs to say the Mourner's Kaddish.

I am distracted during the service. I had a salad niçoise for lunch. I finished it a little too close to prayer time. As I quietly speak the parts of the liturgy that we say aloud, tuna breath bounces back at me from the fabric of my mask. I'm glad that I have another mask in the office. I can wear it on the way home.

Late in the day, I'm hungry again. I don't feel like heading down to the supermarket. Someone has left some small bags of snacks in the kitchen. It takes me some time to figure out the name drawn in Hebrew on each of the bags. They are Cheetos. Under the logo, a bubble of text says "dolphins with the flavor of cheese." They aren't the generic tube shape that I'm used to from the States. They might look like dolphins to someone in a fanciful mood or severely stoned. They taste the same as they always have.

I used to think of Bamba as "Cheetos, but peanut flavored/" I think of these Cheetos now as "Bamba, but vaguely like cheese." Another step in my acclimation. It's a welcome one. I never really liked Cheetos, anyway.

Friday, June 26th, 2020

The supermarket at the mall isn't crowded. I'm surprised. The newspapers say that challah and sliced bread now cost one shekel – about 28 US cents – at that chain, and chicken is one shekel per kilogram. I only see one notice, back in the bread aisle. The single sign says that challah is one shekel. There's a lot of other text on the sign that I don't understand.

I pick up one challah and one loaf of sliced bread, as well as a package of boneless chicken thighs and a bottle of wine. I was planning to get them anyway.

At the register, the cashier works quickly. He grabs the items, scans them, and flings them toward the end of the line. The wine bottle bounces off the edge but doesn't break. It's the least expensive wine in the store, but I only use it for kiddush on the Sabbath. I have never understood the differences among cheap and expensive wines. They taste the same to me. In California, I was happy with Two-Buck Chuck.

The cashier sings as he works. I can't identify the song or even the language. When he rings me up, none of it registers as on sale. I don't know enough colloquial Hebrew to argue about it. As I head toward the exit, he comes running up to me. I had forgotten to pack the bottle of wine. I thank him.

At the café, they've taken down the plexiglass in front of the cashiers, as well as the arch of balloons. At least the workers are wearing their masks. I get my usual Israeli breakfast. This time, I understand the extra question about the added items.

I come home in the middle of the afternoon, put the groceries away, sit down to listen to more of a podcast, and fall asleep.

Saturday, June 27th, 2020

My robot likes chewing on the belt of my bathrobe. When it's working, I make sure to flip the belt out of reach.

Before I head out today, I clean out the robot's dust-catcher and set it to vacuuming. When I get home, I don't see it back in its nook and don't hear it working. I scan the room. The robot is sitting on the floor next to where the bathrobe hangs. Somehow, the belt had flopped back down. The robot had grabbed it and gotten it wrapped up in its works. I pick the robot up, cradle it in my arms, and carefully pull the belt out. I set the robot down and tap its power button. It sets off, continuing on its path.

I turn on the air conditioner, sit down in my TV chair with a book, and doze off. I am awakened by the feeling of something nuzzling at my toes. The robot has wandered over and is trying to vacuum around me. It backs off and comes at me from other directions, gently bumping at the sides of my feet and, once it gets under the chair and comes forward, at my heels. It turns and comes out from under the chair on the other side.

I doze off again without moving. When I get up, I see that it has found its nook again and plugged itself back in. It will hibernate happily for another week.

Sunday, June 28th, 2020

At work, only one email is waiting for me. We'll be interviewing a new candidate for my team. Reading the messages, I learn that we'll either interview her in person or online. I both am and am not invited to the meeting. That's pretty standard.

At just about the right time, the VP sits down in the cube across from mine with someone I don't know. She's the candidate. The VP asks me to join them. They are both wearing masks. I usually don't wear one in the office, since we tend to keep far enough apart. Seeing that they both have them, I put mine on. The VP and I talk with her in English. She's from San Francisco. I like her. I tend to like everybody, though, so that might not count toward whether we should hire her. The VP has me watch the boss's office to see when his current meeting ends. I can see his door from where I'm sitting.

When it's over, the candidate and VP head in. They signal for me to come in, too. That interview is in Hebrew, but I follow most of it. When we come in, the boss isn't wearing his mask. I take mine off. I see that the others have pulled their masks down. A few minutes later, in the middle of a sentence, the boss puts his mask on. The others pull theirs up. I put mine back on.

The interview ends after a while. I head back to my cube. I try to take a sip of the cooled-down coffee in my mug. The mug hits my mask. The coffee doesn't splash or spill. I take my mask off again and continue to stare at my screen.

Monday, June 29th, 2020

It's dark when I head out of the office. It's been a while since that happened, this close to the summer solstice. I'm tired. I'm hungry.

I trudge up the street. It's a slight incline for the four blocks to the pizza place, then a steeper block and a half to the traffic circle at the top of the hill. It's easier most of the rest of the way.

Just past the circle, intriguing music approaches me from behind. A deep melodic bass line booms out under clattering percussion and a keening vocal. The voice and percussion reach me first. A man blasting an unaccompanied song from the phone strapped to his arm darts around me on his skateboard, along the sidewalk's uneven bricks. I turn off the road before the car with the bass line can catch up with me.

I stop at the burger joint for dinner. The same cashier is working as before. She asks my name. I tell her, in Hebrew. Her memory clicks in. "You prefer English, right? And you liked the mushroom burger?" I did. I order it again, along with the sweet potato fries.

I think of getting a milkshake. I had gotten one there when they first opened. It was good, but I get a Coke Zero instead.

After I eat, I dump my trash in the bin, set my tray on the stack on top of it, and put my mask back on.

Most of the rest of the walk back home is easy. The last three blocks, along the pedestrian street, go uphill again. I pause halfway and sit down on a stone pillar where I had once seen a cat balance on a pile of dinner plates.

I tie my left shoe. It won't stay tied for long. It needs new laces. I haven't seen them in drugstores or supermarkets, and haven't gotten the courage to go into a shoe store and ask for them. I know the Hebrew word. I'll just have to do it sometime.

Tuesday, June 30th, 2020

After the afternoon prayers, we all gather in the hallway. One of our programmers is retiring today. He has been with us for almost thirty years.

I don't know if anyone else has worked here for that long. At least one other programmer is older than he is. Both had to work from home during the lockdown.

The boss gives a speech about him, punctuated by comments and jokes from other long-time workers. Someone finds a photo of a company party in 1994 and posts it to the company WhatsApp. I only recognize the boss, though apparently other current workers are there.

The retiring worker spends much of the afternoon with our newest programmer, who joined us on Sunday. They talk together in Russian or something like it. I hear some programming terms, occasional bits of Hebrew, and a few computer-related words in English.

At some point, while I'm in a meeting, he leaves. I don't get to say goodbye. We rarely talked, anyway. He speaks almost no English other than job-specific words, and I have trouble understanding his thickly-accented Hebrew. I suspect I'll see him again. Former workers often drift back in. When you've been with a small company like this for that long, you never completely leave.

July 2020

Wednesday, July 1ˢᵗ, 2020

A scaffolding of metal pipes, in what might be the shape of a geodesic dome, surrounds the stage and seats in the plaza outside the Dance Center. I arrive early, as usual. I wait outside the dome.

Inside it, a worker rakes the red dirt that covers the stage. Three other workers move slowly along the two circles of seats surrounding it. One reads from a clipboard: "47 and 48, a couple. 49, alone. 50 and 51, a couple. 52 through 55, a family of four, together." The other two workers cluster and separate the numbered chairs accordingly.

Two of the dancers step onto the stage. A worker points his phone at them. They record several takes of a plea for funding in well-rehearsed English. Other people standing outside the dome with me call out to them. They also want to take pictures. The dancers strike goofy poses then leave. The man with the rake smooths the dirt where they stood.

When the gates open, workers check the tickets on our printouts and phones and guide us to our seats. The man and woman seated together to my right each carry cameras with huge lenses. The man tries to move his chair closer to the stage. A worker stops him. "I'm sorry. You can't. Corona. Dying is forbidden in the palace of culture." In Hebrew, that rhymes and sounds like a humorous slogan, akin to "Savoir faire is everywhere."

I sit and wait, watching the three-quarter moon rise between the pipes of the scaffolding.

The house lights dim. The choreographer walks along the edge of the stage, mic in hand. She guides us in a seated meditation: feet flat on the ground, backs straight, hands high in the air then down along our faces to our hearts, out toward the center of the space then back and down to a rest position. She thanks us.

The stage lights dim. Five people enter, dressed in red. The dance begins.

I hear loud crying from the boss's office. A coworker emerges. Tears thickening her voice, she tells the people in the hall that one of our programmers has died. I don't hear many details. I don't understand much of what I hear.

He had sat in the cube across from mine. He was quieter than most of the others, except when he coughed, which he did increasingly over the past several months. His English was good. He had lived in Philadelphia for a while. I hear that he was in his mid-fifties, one of the younger programmers on the team. I hear that doctors had told him that the cough wasn't anything serious, until it became impossible to handle.

He had been in the hospital for a week or so. The last person he spoke to was the programmer who had retired the day before. He died suddenly. I haven't heard anything definitive about what happened. I understand that it wasn't the virus. He wasn't Jewish, but I hear that his father was, so he was allowed to emigrate from Russia many years ago.

I hear random bits of information. There is to be a funeral, but I don't hear where or when. In the afternoon, most of my coworkers suddenly disappear. As is usual here, the funeral is right away. He is to be buried immediately. I have a commitment in the evening, so I can't go, even if I had known sooner.

I hear from those who are there that it is a simple, secular burial. Most of the people are from the office. One of them texts to the team: "There is no ceremony. No reading of Psalms. Nothing." The boss gives an impromptu eulogy which is, I hear, quite moving.

Later, someone sets out sweets in the office kitchen. A neatly printed sign above them shows the programmer's name and "May his memory be blessed."

We return to work. The new guy is set up at the now-empty desk. The boss removes the programmer's phone number from the office messaging group.

Friday, July 3rd, 2020

The screen door slams as I leave my apartment for the afternoon. The top of it sweeps through the leaves of the tree above me.

Something falls from a branch onto my shoulder. I feel it skitter up my neck, along my jawline, across my mask, over my closed eye, and into my hair. Simultaneous thoughts: 1: I didn't know cockroaches could climb trees. 2: They climb walls, so why not? 3: Its trajectory across my face is at the same angle as the lines on David Bowie's face on the cover of *Aladdin Sane.*

I brush my hand through my hair. The cockroach falls to the ground. We stare at each other, stunned, for a moment. It runs off across the patio. A cat watches it go past. It doesn't pounce on it.

Last night, I saw a group of roaches gather on my steps. I rarely see more than one at a time. They may have been having a war council to plot their strategy for the summer. It's getting hotter again. I'm told that they need to find water to survive. I don't bear any grudge against them, but I don't feel moved to put a bowl out. They've been here longer than we have. They'll be here after we've gone.

Saturday, July 4th, 2020

The café doesn't put out printed menus anymore. A sticker on each table has QR codes for breakfast, lunch/dinner, and desserts. The only English words on the stickers are "Scan Me!" I'm reminded of Alice in Wonderland.

I scan a code. The lunch/dinner menu appears on my phone. I get through the ritual conversations with the server entirely in Hebrew. I've been there enough times that I know most of what to say. I order a chicken salad and a cold coffee – not an iced coffee, since here that means a sort of granita, but an Americano, cold.

The server puts a small cup of sugar water on the table next to the coffee. I expect the small flies that zoom around me to zero in on it, but they're not interested. I've gotten used to the flies. They seem to follow me every day from a particular tree on the way to the café and to work. Maybe they recognize that I'm less likely to swat them than many other people are.

The meal is close to twice as expensive as at the place where I eat more frequently. This is the only place open on the Sabbath, though, and I had wanted to get out of the house and be among people. I put a fairly large bill on the payment tray. I could get a bit of change back, even after the tip, but I decide not to wait. If the servers are working for tips, they could use a bit of appreciation from the few customers who are there. I leave the whole bill and walk away.

I put on my mask as I step onto the sidewalk. On the way back, I see that the Give-and-Take box is overflowing. I pick up six books in English, by Colson Whitehead, Steven Pinker, Michio Kaku and others, and an intact SodaStream machine and bottle, apparently working. I'll have to clean them thoroughly before I use them. I juggle it all happily as I wander home.

Sunday, July 5th, 2020

I finally get around to cleaning up the soda maker from the Give-and-Take box. Videos online show me how the pieces fit together. It's straightforward, if not what I expect. Pieces flip open that I thought were locked in place. Things that I thought would screw into each other click and hold.

The first thing to do is to sterilize the plastic bottle. That seems simple. I boil water in the electric teakettle and pour it in. Bad move. The bottle starts to melt and droop. The opening that had pointed upward sags and points ahead. It's a real life Pixar moment, as if Luxo Jr. were possessed by Sadness.

I grab a towel, pick up the bottle with it, and pour the water into the sink. I assume that the bottle is ruined. It's not. As it cools, it returns to its original shape, standing tall, its opening pointing once again toward the sky. I didn't think plastic could do that.

I'm reminded of Moses's staff among the snakes. That stands to reason. We've been living through so much of the Book of Exodus this year that we might as well get to the good parts. Of course, when Pharaoh finally let the people go, they were quarantined in the desert for forty years. If we ever get to travel again, I hope we'll be able to do better.

Monday, July 6th, 2020

It's hot in the hallway where we do the afternoon prayers. The air conditioning is on, but light streams in through the tall windows looking out over the atrium. The space heats up.

The man in front of me opens a window. Construction noise blasts in. Workers are finally finishing the flooring in the atrium, securing wood-like slabs over the sand that is over the plastic that is over whatever was there before they started. I think it was cement. It's been so long that I don't remember.

The construction noise drowns out the prayers. The man in front of me quickly closes and latches the window. The prayers continue.

The man who led the prayers for the past few months won't be doing it for the next four weeks. For the past eleven months, he had been saying the Mourners' Kaddish for someone close to him. A myth tells that very wicked people are punished for twelve months after death. Saying Kaddish for them alleviates that. We stop at eleven months. We don't want people to think that the person that we are mourning was wicked. At least that's one of the myths. Twice as many stories have been told about what happens after death as there have been people to tell them.

At most services, whoever leads the prayers says Kaddish, so the usual man isn't doing it. Today, another coworker leads the prayers. No two people lead them in quite the same way. While the other leader's chanting shifts among three pitches like a bugle call, this one rocks back and forth between two pitches a minor third apart. He also tends to pause at the end of phrases rather than barreling straight through. When he says the Kaddish, one of the verses is a lot longer. I have only caught some of the words that he adds.

Afterwards, some of us look out the window. We admire the craftsmanship of the flooring and wonder what the final result will be. In the corner, one of the laborers is doing his own afternoon prayers. He has laid down a rug. He shifts between standing, kneeling, and bowing far forward so that his head touches the ground. Though they flow in different languages and in different directions, the building is suffused with prayers.

Tuesday, July 7ᵗʰ, 2020

We're having a party after work tomorrow. At least, I think we are. It could be next week. I'm keeping tomorrow evening open. I have no plans for next Wednesday either.

I think the party will be outdoors somewhere. Those are still allowed, though I think the rules announced yesterday limit events to twenty people. There are about twenty of us in the office. Maybe that rule is only for indoor events.

As usual, I've seen several different sets of rules. Each is authoritative, ambiguous, and contradictory. I'm reading several of them via automatic translation. That doesn't help.

I think the party will celebrate more officially the programmer who retired a few days ago. He is back in the office today, apparently programming or debugging something. I've heard him talking with the others, discussing the programmer who passed away last week. He may be helping to sort out the projects that that programmer didn't get to finish. Everyone else seems to know what's going on. I feel like the one person on a planet who isn't a telepath.

The retired programmer showed up at the office late in the morning, right when I did. I had been doing some work at home, recording voice-over for a video we're doing. I also wrote some of the script for it, but someone else is making it. He's so much better at what we need than I am that I don't bear a grudge.

I spent much of the rest of the day extracting sections of documents to use in other documents. I like working with modules. I'll be doing more of that tomorrow. Then we may have a party. Or we may not.

Wednesday, July 8th, 2020

The party is scheduled for this evening in the park. During the day, bags of groceries appear in the company kitchen. The meat is in the freezer.

About fifteen minutes before we're supposed to head over, I ask what's happening. No one knows. We can't do it in the park. The city tells us that people can gather there, but they can't use the park's facilities. They specifically tell us that no one can barbecue. They blame the Ministry of Health.

The bosses text the building manager. They ask if we can do it on the roof. We can't. We're not insured for it. We contact the city to ask if we can do it on the beach. We can't. Once again, we specifically can't barbecue. We call the Ministry of Health. After a long wait on hold, we ask if we can do it in a park in another town nearby. They tell us that no one can barbecue in any park anywhere.

One by one, people wander off. We wonder if we can do the party without the meat. We go to look at what we have. It isn't there. Two coworkers have taken the groceries home with them to put in their refrigerators. The refrigerator in the office kitchen is already full of lunches and the like.

We think of trying the party tomorrow. We can't. Tomorrow, many of the workers are fasting. I say goodbye to the retiring programmer and head home.

Later, the bosses send pictures to the staff over WhatsApp. The six people still in the office have scrounged up some hummus, pita, and vegetables. They are together in the conference room. They present the programmer with a collage of photos of the staff. Text printed on it, in a classic Biblical font, thanks him and wishes him well. The bosses let us know that he would be happy to come back if we decide to try the party again.

Thursday, July 9th, 2020

I step into our office building. The guard is carefully placing stanchions around his desk. He isn't using a measuring stick. By now, he knows where to put them so that they are precisely two meters from where he sits. This one is centered on the border between the tiles that runs over from just left of the center of the nearer door, and is a little farther in than the far end of the desk. That one is halfway along the diagonal from the near end of the desk to the Israeli flag.

A woman runs up to him, yelling and waving her blue-gloved hands. "Where are stairs? There are only elevators! Elevators lead to Corona! There is a law. There must be stairs." The guard points to the door marked "Stairs." The woman stomps away.

In the office, I put my JoeBowl in the freezer. I would prefer to order something, but I'm not sure that that will happen, since it's officially a fast day. The coworker who often does the ordering sends us a text message. He's on the phone with a customer. We need to write down our orders and hand them to him, so he can fax the list to the pizza joint.

I decide to get a laflawach. It's not the healthiest, but I get it no more than once a week. I start to write it down in Hebrew. I can think of a few different ways that it might be spelled. I write it phonetically in English. There's a better chance that he'll figure out what I mean.

As I leave for the day, I take the JoeBowl out of the freezer. I immediately put it back in. I'll eat it on Sunday. I hope that I don't forget and bring another one.

At home, I hang out online with friends, posting rock videos to a discussion thread. It's kind of a party. We start with Jefferson Starship and branch out from there, linking, commenting, and giving bits of history. I miss being a DJ.

When I get to the mall, my usual café is closing. On Fridays, they close earlier than I thought. It's later than I thought.

I head up to the food court. It's a gamble. I can't figure out from the new rules whether the eateries or seating will be open. Both are. There are fewer tables than before, but it isn't busy.

I'm not feeling choosy. I go to McDonald's. I enjoy ordering from the kiosks, since I don't face any linguistic challenges. I order, get my receipt, and wait at the pickup point.

A customer is waiting where the line for the cash register should be. The workers don't notice him. He finally bellows "Hello?"

A worker looks over and tells him that all ordering is now done at the kiosks. He's not happy. "That's not normal."

The worker shrugs. "Sir, the world is not normal."

He stomps away to the other burger joint.

The word for "normal" is "*normalli.*" I assume it's a loan-word.

When my meal is ready, they call my number and hand my tray to me. It has a disposable plastic sheath. A few things are jumbled. There's no straw for the soda. They gave me the wrong salad dressing. I decide not to complain, since that would involve words that I don't know.

The food is exactly what I expect, no better, no worse. Short of massive errors or equipment failures, I don't think it's possible for the food to vary much. In a world where the rules seem to change every few hours, that in itself is comforting.

As I walk onto the patio at the Sabbath café, I hear a volley of viscous thuds above me. I look up. The square white umbrellas that cover the space are dotted with stains. They don't only protect us from the sun.

I pull my phone out to scan the icons on the table that bring up menus. Scanning is easy. Finding the scanning app on the phone is hard. I spot it and hold the phone over the table.

The server comes over. "Are you ready to order?" I try to remember how to say "Not yet" in Hebrew. I hear myself say it in English.

She switches languages easily. "Would you like me to bring you a menu in English?" I think of boldly going with the Hebrew menu again.

We're already speaking English, though. I've blown my credibility. I say yes.

She brings one over. I order the Israeli breakfast.

More people are dining on the patio today than last week. Several are smoking. Most of those, but not all, are smoking tobacco. The fumes drift past me in the shifting breezes. Some make me cough. Some don't.

As I eat, I read articles on my phone about the intricacies of identity and community in the works of a Korean pop band and its fans. Intriguing stuff. I'll have to look into it some more.

Later, I follow the live feed from a local news site. Ten thousand people are rallying and marching in a nearby city, protesting what the government is doing about the economy. It's all going precisely on schedule.

Usually, I wish I had heard about these things in time to participate. This time, I don't understand what's going on well enough to want to protest. I suspect that the government, in the time of crisis, is continuing to improvise as well as it can with the information it has. I have to work tomorrow. I'm glad I stayed home.

Sunday, July 12th, 2020

It takes me a moment to figure out which ATM to use. Some handle cash. Others are only for information.

The first time I tried them downtown, I used an information machine from another bank. It simply ate my card. I had only been here for about a week. I showed up at that branch right when it opened the next morning. The teller spoke English. I had my identity card. I got the ATM card back. I now know the words to look for.

There's no line tonight at this row of machines outside the Heart of the City mall. I get the cash and head home.

My landlady had texted me yesterday that my electric bill was due, with the amount. She tends to be friendly but terse: "Electricity:" and a number. I text her back with when I can pay. It's usually a day or so later, since I have to swing by the ATM. She responds with an "OK" emoji, different each time.

I tried once to convince her to let me pay via the local equivalent of CashApp. She had no idea what I was talking about. Texting is as techie as she gets.

The electric company sends her the bills for the house every two months. I don't know if my amount is separated out or if she calculates it somehow. The amount always seems fair. I've never asked.

I get home and ring her doorbell upstairs. She opens the door and says, "Hi." I tell her in Hebrew that I have the money for the electricity. As usual, I hand her the exact amount.

She smiles and says, in English, "Thank you. Bye."

She closes the door. I head downstairs to my own place, and inside.

Monday, July 13th, 2020

They've changed the big sign in the city square. Last week, it had a cartoon of the coronavirus, with text in large letters: "Remember me? I'm still here!" The cartoon is gone. Words in the same colors now say "What to do? Cover up!" In Hebrew, the slogan is catchy. It rhymes.

At a nearby bus stop, the neighborhood graffitist has been scribbling again. What I can read has the usual reference to thirteen commandments. A phrase I can't make out is under it, followed by "corona is because of this."

A couple walks by me as I read the graffiti. The woman says, in a dramatic voice, "Corona corona corona. Corona? Corona. Coroooooooona!" The man laughs.

I take my mask off for a moment so that I can clearly give directions to a woman in a car several meters away. I'm not good at directions in any language, but she's looking for my office building, which is right down the street and easy to describe: It's big and white and has a FreshMarket on the ground floor. It's at the second traffic circle, but I forget how to say "traffic circle." Words that pop into my head randomly when I don't need them disappear when I do.

A breeze blows the mask off my ear. It lands on a box of children's books on a rubbish heap. It's a good collection, including what might be a complete set of "Diary of a Wimpy Kid" in Hebrew. I don't take any, but I hope that someone who can use them finds them.

A large dog wanders by and stops to sniff my hand. I smile at the dog and at the woman walking with it. I think she smiles back. Behind the masks, we can't be sure.

A hundred or so teenagers are standing in the square downtown. One boy with a megaphone leads them in chants. He reads the texts from his cellphone's screen. Many of the teens wave green and black flags or hold long banners. More banners are carefully laid on the ground.

I know that something's happening, but I don't know what it is. I can't make out what they are shouting. From their outfits, I'm guessing that they are scouts or something like it. I only know a few of the words on their flags and banners. This seems to be about something closing, but I don't know if they're for or against it. The word for "education" comes up a lot. Many of the chants start with repeated syllables, much like the "hey, hey, ho, ho" that grew so wearisome in the States.

A little girl, no more than eight, marches back and forth in front, out of rhythm with the chants. A dark green streak is painted in her long black hair.

Small groups of teens freeze in impromptu tableaux with their signs. Grown-ups take pictures of them. The sounds of the chants shift as another group marches toward them, stopping at the opposite corner of the intersection. Cars honk, more or less in rhythm with them.

The two groups chant, slightly off each other's beat. I walk between them. The way that the phrases bounce around to my right and left is marvelous. I wonder if they meant to do that.

I see strips of yellow tape on the ground, placed to keep the people on this side properly distanced. They cluster anyway. At least most of them have masks on.

I walk through the square, away from them. Outside my favorite hummus joint, a woman solemnly places an open container of cottage cheese at the center of a circle of cats.

Wednesday, July 15th, 2020

At 4:30, I go down to the supermarket, as usual, to get a yogurt and an apple. I pause in front of the guard. His thermometer dangles by his side as he focuses on something on his phone. He waves me through.

I know where everything is at this point. I grab a green apple without slowing down. I've settled on them. I haven't had a satisfying red apple since I moved here. I'm told they need a climate with an autumn like we had in the States to grow well.

I walk halfway up the aisle, turn left, and go to the end. The yogurt that I like is about a meter to the right. I have to look at them to see what to get. The ones that I like, with nuts in the lid, are usually at the near edge of that part of the refrigerated section. Sometimes, though, they get shuffled. I'm not interested in the ones packed with candy.

The first open checkout aisle doesn't have any customers. I put my two items down. The cashier doesn't react. I say, "Hi." Nothing. I dig a ten-shekel coin out of my wallet. The cashier is staring either at something on the screen or at the blank space beyond it. Finally, a manager comes over. She stands behind the cashier, says something to me that I don't understand, and points to the next aisle.

I pick up my things and move over there. No other customers appear to be waiting. The cashier looks up at me, says "Sorry," and gestures toward the end of the counter. Someone else's purchase is piled up there. That customer has run off to find another item. It will probably be awhile.

I pick up my things again and head to the next open aisle, two lanes down. I start to put my items on the counter. The cashier gestures for me to stop. "I'm waiting for change." I sigh. I'm annoyed, but I can't complain. Literally. I don't have the vocabulary.

The last aisle is open and free. I walk over with my purchases. "Possible?" I ask. The cashier nods. He rings up the items. The yogurt is always five shekels. The apple varies between three and four, depending on the price that day and its weight. They're expensive now, since they're out of season, but it's not that much of a difference.

I hand him the ten-shekel coin. He hands me my change. He puts my receipt on top of the yogurt container and the apple on top of that. I take the stack and wander back up to work.

Thursday, July 16th, 2020

I walk in to the burger joint, meaning to get a mushroom burger. I change my mind when I see the workers near the front of the shop putting beef burgers together. They look too good to pass up.

The man at the counter looks up at me, ready to take my order. The phone rings. He signals for me to wait, then picks up the phone and takes the order. Whoever is calling is getting six very different burgers. They're being finicky about it. He rings up the order, takes a photo of the receipt with his cell phone, and turns back to me.

The phone rings again. He gestures again and takes the order. This one is simple. He turns back to me.

I ask for a burger in Hebrew. He responds in English. I realize that, while I had the words right, I used the American "b'rg'r" rather than the Israeli "*boorgehr*," and I failed to swallow my "r"s.

I finish ordering, get my soda immediately, and sit outside to wait. About half of the tables are taken. At the table next to mine, two young girls alternate taking selfies. Each clowns in the other's background. They argue about the meanings of the English words "crunchy" and "clicky." Or maybe it's "cliquey." Those are the only words I can identify. They emit a rapid stream of chirps, glottal sounds, extended vowels, and giggles. I imagine that this is how a language written entirely in emoji might sound.

I take a writing guide that I'm reading out of my bag. I rest my arms on the table. My right arm doesn't feel right. I look down. Someone had spilled a chocolate shake and hadn't cleaned all of it up. Some of it got on my sleeve. So be it.

I hear a worker call my name from within the shop. I go inside. My burger is on the tray, but my sweet potato fries aren't. The worker who took my order trots up to the counter with them. "We didn't have enough sweet potato fries, so I put an added serving of regular fries in with it. *Bon appétit.*"

I take the tray to my table. I carefully set it down on the spilled shake, so I won't dredge the muck with my sleeve again. I unwrap the burger and take a bite. I'm disappointed. It looked far better than it tastes. I now know to stick to the mushrooms.

Friday, July 17th, 2020

The shopkeeper steps into the back room where customers pick up packages. I've been waiting for him. I say "Good morning." He doesn't look up. "You said that already." I had. It had taken a while for him to get back here. I had forgotten.

He slaps my packages down on the table. "Your identity number, Mr. Zitt." He knows me by now. I tell him. When he enters it, it doesn't work.

"Your correct identity number." I tell it to him again, identically. It works this time.

"Why didn't you pick up your packages yesterday?" I usually get them on the way to work. I was already at work when I got the text messages. I tell him.

"So you work. Do you do hard work?" I shrug. He pushes the packages forward on the desk. "Good day. Go home." I head off to the mall.

At the café, I order the usual breakfast from the usual person. "What type of bread would you like? Right now we just have white." That choice is easy.

I get almost all the way through ordering in Hebrew. I don't quite understand one question – not because of language, but because of the background hums and chatter. She switches to English. This time I hear her.

When she has all the details, she asks. "What is your name? It's Yosef, right?"

Right. I take my receipt and sit down to wait.

Saturday, July 18th, 2020

I head out for the afternoon. I'm not sure where I'm going. I've heard that restaurants may or may not be closed except for takeout and delivery.

I head to the one café that is usually open on the Sabbath. It is. I check the news. There's been a last minute change. Restaurants have another three days before they shut down, so the food that they have in stock won't go to waste.

About half of the tables on the patio are occupied. About half of the people at them aren't eating. They're just smoking. I think of moving inside, but I can breathe well enough.

I get through everything in Hebrew, ordering a salad that I already know. I discover that I forgot to bring along the book that I've been reading. I look at Twitter instead.

The salad, when it is delivered, is quite different from what I got when I ordered it before. This is better. I'm pleased.

On the way home, I see that the bench with the Give-and-Take box is buried in clothing. So is the ground around it. It looks like someone just dumped three or four garbage bags full of clothes there. Some children's books are sitting, spine up, in the box itself. A fruit juicer sits next to them. I'm tempted to take it, but I don't drink much juice, and I'm running out of room on my kitchen counter.

I stop at the ATM and at the ice cream shop. I get a small cup of gelato, mostly to break the large bill that I got from the cash machine. I procrastinate as long as I can there before heading out to complete the tasks waiting for me at home.

Sunday, July 19ᵗʰ, 2020

I hear a burst of singing behind me. It's the boss's birthday. Much of the team is standing just outside his office. Inside it, a half dozen balloons bounce around. A platter on his desk holds a mound of ice cream sandwiches and cones, each individually wrapped.

Someone's phone plays a lugubrious cover of "When I'm 64." Someone else takes pictures. Someone sneezes. A woman's voice calls out in response, "Corona corona corona!"

A support person wanders down the aisle between the cubes, singing "*Symantec v'Mazel-Tech v'Mazel-Tech v'Symantec.*" I laugh, but I realize that you'd probably have to be a Jewish computer geek to get the layers of the joke: there's another software company called Symantec, and there's a song sung at celebrations that goes "*Siman tov v'mazel tov v'mazel tov v'siman tov,*" and it would help to remember what "*siman*" means, which, at the moment, I don't, and all that probably doesn't help much unless you actually hear it.

Later, as workmen run some sort of cables through the ceiling, I stand outside the kitchen with our company's guitarist, talking about Kansas and Keith Jarrett.

When I get back to my cube, I see that two balloons, one yellow and one pink, have wandered into it and huddled under my chair. I gently kick them out into the aisle and sit down to get back to work.

Monday, July 20ᵗʰ, 2020

I get a text message from my landlady asking me to come outside. Fortunately, I am up and dressed. I put my sandals on and head out.

Her husband is at the top of the stairs up from my basement apartment. A manhole that I hadn't noticed before is open. A pipe stretches out from it. Tools lie on the ground. That explains the strange sounds that I had heard earlier outside my bathroom window.

The landlord speaks almost no English. I understand from what he says that the pump is broken. He says "pump" in English, though maybe the word is the same. I don't understand the rest. He gestures, but I don't know what he means. He hollers for his wife.

The landlady comes out. Her English is better. "The pump is kaput." She actually says "kaput." "Someone will fix it tomorrow. These things will be on the ground until then. We want you to know, so you don't fall."

The landlord picks up a large chair and puts it at the top of the stairs. I can't miss it on the way up. I will have to walk around it.

I ask if the water is working. She says yes. He says no. They confer. She tells me: "The water is OK, but please when you take a shower: chick-chock!" She waves her hands. I get that she means for me to do it quickly. OK. I head back in.

Tuesday, July 21ˢᵗ, 2020

Someone's phone is ringing, here in the men's room. He's not answering. I can't see anyone else in here from within this stall, but I'm pretty sure of the person's pronoun. On second thought, it could be the cleaner, but she tends to answer her phone quickly, speaking in a language that I can't identify.

The repeating ringtone is great. I know the riff from somewhere, but can't recall what it's from. I'm tempted to ask, but people tend not to talk to each other in restrooms, and I don't know how to say "ringtone" in Hebrew. Most of my vocabulary is biblical, and that word didn't come up much.

Neither of the apps on my phone helps, what with the roaring ventilation and the mix of watery sounds surrounding me. The tune gets stuck in my head for a while. I go through my collection and try to narrow it down. It's a guitar riff from a piece of progressive rock or some genre close to it. A keyboard is going in a different time signature with spastic accents from the drums. I can't quite spot it.

When I try again later, I realize that one of the riffs I was checking it against has overwritten it in my ear's memory. I have forgotten what it was. I may never know, unless I'm in the men's room again when the same person decides not to answer his phone.

Wednesday, July 22ⁿᵈ, 2020

I order the root vegetable and grilled salmon salad at the café on the square. As I go to sit down, I'm called back to the counter. They're out of salmon. I'm not surprised. All the restaurants were supposed to shut down after the weekend. They were working through their stock, so they wouldn't have leftover food going to waste.

At the last minute, they were told that they could stay open, with restrictions. No more than thirty customers may sit in their outside area. I don't think it seats that many anyway.

They ask what I would like instead of the salmon. Halloumi? Bulgarian cheese? Tuna? I choose the halloumi. And what type of bread? Multigrain.

I sit down and take a book out of my bag to read. They call my name a few minutes later. I go to the counter and retrieve my salad. The cheese is good.

The weather on the patio, now that it has cooled down after sunset, is perfect. A light breeze drifts past me. I'm not sure if it's natural or from the large humming machine near the wall. I'm not complaining.

Once I'm done with the salad, I sit back with my book and my coffee granita. If this were an American café with its comfortable seating, I would stay for hours. Here, the metal chair eventually starts to dig into my back and legs. I find a good stopping point in the book, put my mask back on, and wander home.

Thursday, July 23rd, 2020

It takes me a couple of days to be certain that the bench with the Give-and-Take box is gone. I keep walking by where it had been, not realizing that it's missing until I get a few blocks past it.

I'm not entirely sure where it was. It was on one of a set of three almost-identical blocks. Now, I look carefully as I pass. I recall that it had been on a stretch of pavement that wasn't curved. That narrows it down.

I find the spot. There's no sign that it was ever there. I'm pretty sure that the bench had been bolted into the bricks. None of the bricks there appear to have been repaired or replaced. I don't know how they did that.

I think some people last week ruined the spot for everyone else. First, several bags-full of clothing appeared at once, piled up on the bench and covering the sidewalk around it. A few days later, it was covered with sheer junk, mostly cardboard boxes, either flattened or just tossed there intact, and torn-up magazines.

I don't know who was responsible for the bench. It may have been the city or the people in the neighborhood. Perhaps the person that the residents of the nearest apartment building had elected to be in charge of its grounds had had enough.

Now the bench is gone. I'll miss it. So, I suspect, will the thin man that I would often see on the bench, smoking and reading, when I would pass it in the evening. Perhaps he'll sit on the low, uneven wall behind where it had been. If he falls, maybe the city, the neighbors' representative, or all the king's horses and all the king's men will show up again to change things.

Friday, July 24th, 2020

I'm not used to the bus to the mall being this crowded. I have stopped by the House of a Hundred Grandmothers to bring some things to family members who are quarantined inside. I could take my usual bus from near there, but I'm not certain where it stops today. On Fridays and some evenings it has been taking an alternate route. I'm not clear when it does that.

This time, I go to a different bus stop, two blocks away. More buses to the mall stop there. On the bus that I catch, given the current rules for distancing, a single seat is available. I take it.

It's very loud in the bus. I hear conversations in what I guess are Tagalog, Hindi, and Chinese. The radio is blasting songs in English, with DJs shouting between the tracks in Hebrew. The person in front of me is scrolling through news on her phone in Spanish. The person across the aisle is texting in some language using the Latin alphabet. She enters words so quickly that her thumbs are a blur.

At the mall, the guard takes a cursory glance in my shopping bag, points his thermometer at my forehead, and waves me in. I realize that I've never seen a guard stop anyone. His presence is enough. It reminds people to put on their masks before they enter and to be careful about what they bring in. When looking in bags, guards used to ask, jokingly, "Any weapons?" I haven't heard that since they started checking temperatures, too.

A different person than usual takes my order at the café. I get through it all in Hebrew. I notice that she does some hand gestures. She acts out the difference between leafy and chopped salad.

The usual cashier is behind her, shining the front of a metal cabinet. When I'm done ordering, she asks the current cashier, in Hebrew, "Is everything good?" The cashier says yes. She looks over at me and says, in English, "Very good." I take my receipt and walk to the counter to wait.

Saturday, July 25th, 2020

The robot is confused. Usually, if it hits something, it either turns a few degrees and tries again, pushes it out of the way, or runs over it. It doesn't know what to do with this chair. Due to the friction of the chair's legs against the floor, the robot can push it forward a few centimeters, but then it grinds to a stop. Continuing to push it doesn't help. The robot has to back up and bang into it again.

I watch it slowly bump the chair across the floor, recalculating after each push. Finally, since I have a vestigial tinge of mercy for some inanimate objects and I don't have infinite time, I walk over, lift the chair, and put it where it was, behind where the robot is now.

I've been thinking of going out to the usual Sabbath café while the robot does its work. I decide not to. It's too hot outside.

I won't spend the day completely isolated. The cleaner will be here in a few hours. She comes to my place about once a month. Cleaning is not my strongest skill, so I leave it to an expert when I can. At the moment, I can afford it.

Today, I'm not absolutely sure she'll make it, since the government keeps playing Mother-May-I with lockdowns. We've decided to go for it, knowing that a last minute ruling might prevent her from getting here.

She arrives as planned, after the robot is done. As usual, she's about twenty minutes earlier than the set time. I know that she does this. I'm OK with that. She deals with the kitchen and bathroom areas. After a month, they need professional help.

I handle the bedroom and living room areas myself. I stay out of her way while she works, dealing with things at my desk. She asks very few questions, mostly about my apartment's inscrutable array of light switches.

I look around my room looking for ways to improve the jumble of boxes. Back in the States, I had put risers under the legs of my bed, lifting it high enough that I could slide the boxes under it. Time to try to figure out how to get them here.

The robot handles the vacuuming. I wish it could sort through the jumble and put it all away. Someday, I suppose, I'll have to do that myself.

Sunday, July 26th, 2020

The balloons from last week's party bob around the office. Over the weekend, one yellow balloon wanders back into my cube. When I come in to work, I find it snuggled tight against the wastebasket. I try not to disturb it as I set up for the day.

Much of today's work is mundane but worthwhile. I'm updating older documentation that was put together well. I'm mostly adding information and graphics to show connections between things. They seemed more obvious before, but now that I've moved the text around into a new medium, I have to make them clear.

Before the afternoon prayers, a coworker tries to get me to speak more Hebrew in the office. Speaking Hebrew feels more stressful as I go on, rather than less. I really should have taken an introduction to conversational Hebrew when I got here. I was told to leapfrog ahead because I tested well on reading and grammar. That hasn't played out well.

On the way home, I see more cats than usual. Several of them lie sunning themselves in the twilight on a patch of pavement on the street with the store where I pick up my packages.

Further down the street, the shopkeeper leans on a car outside the store, smoking. I pass behind him. I don't say hello. People greet each other less here than we did in the States, and a lot less than we did in Texas.

More cats lie around in my yard when I get home. Most of them scatter when they see me coming. One cat, larger than the rest with tortoiseshell fur, glances up at me but doesn't move. I step carefully around where he lies. I don't want to disturb him, either.

Monday, July 27th, 2020

Alarms sound during the afternoon prayers. I don't know what they mean. They go off every few days. No one ever reacts to them.

Each of them puts out a set of continual high-pitched squeals. They may or may not be pulsing. Beat frequencies between the close pitches might be making it seem as if they are. I hear several separate alarms, distributed around our floor of the building. They aren't perfectly in tune with each other. As I move between them, the sound clusters change. The effect is like La Monte Young's music in the Dream House, though not as controlled.

Even standing in place, I hear different combinations. During the prayers, I shift between standing still, stepping back and forth, swiveling left and right, bending my knees, bowing, and, at one point, rapidly rising onto my tiptoes three times in a row. I listen to the changing sound as I move between positions.

The alarms stop abruptly right at the end of prayers. I laugh at the coincidence. A coworker asks me why I laughed at that moment. I explain it to him. He hadn't noticed.

As I sit back down at my desk, I notice that, if I listen carefully, the hums from my twin monitors cause similar effects. I'll try not to find that distracting.

Tuesday, July 28th, 2020

The air outside is hot and soggy, even after dark. I feel like I'm sitting in a vat of chicken soup. That may be appropriate. I'm at a small party, just outside the House of a Hundred Grandmothers. I'm surrounded by a crowd of yiddische mamas, all chattering in Tagalog.

It's the birthday of my family's caregiver at the House. The other caregivers there have cooked a vast and varied meal of Filipino food. It's all laid out in disposable containers on plastic tables on the house's sidewalk. They keep insisting that I eat and drink more, even as I insist that I'm full.

I mostly stay toward the edge of the group. I'm a natural wallflower. I'm also quite aware that I'm the sole medical wildcard in the group. Everyone else at the party lives inside the house and is now tested for the virus once a week. I keep my mask on when I'm not eating, though they keep encouraging me to eat more.

Most speak good English and Hebrew, though I hear one quiet voice come up to me from behind when my plate is almost empty and say what sounds like "Don't shy. More eats."

There's ice cream and a cake, with candles showing our family's care-giver's age. I had thought that she was younger, though when I do the math it makes sense. Besides having worked, if I recall, in childcare for a while back home, as well as for close to a decade in a factory in Taiwan, she has been here for a couple of years. She was supposed to have married her boyfriend, who lives in Canada, a few months ago. That's been delayed until international travel starts up again.

I'm pleased that she insisted that I come to the party. It's been an enjoyable evening, spent with warm and welcoming people out in the hot night air.

Wednesday, July 29th, 2020

The boss brings in a bag of fresh carob pods. He picked them himself in his yard this morning. Some still have leaves attached. In the company kitchen, he offers some to me. "Here, take. Take more. But wash them first. They're right from the tree. You don't know which birds, you know. And be careful of the seeds."

These carobs are the best I've had, sweeter and more tender than what was exported to the States. I was surprised when I first saw carob pods growing on a tree here. I was touring a nature preserve with my Hebrew class two years ago. I had expected that the pods would be larger, perhaps green, and with another, softer layer outside. They aren't. They come off the trees just as we see them: brown, dry, and chewy.

At the nature preserve, they took pictures of us planting small trees, dedicating them to people in our lives. Mine was for my father. I think he would have wanted to move here sometime too. I sent the photo to his branch of the family back in the States. They liked it.

I wash off a couple of pods in the kitchen and return to my desk with them and a cup of strong coffee. It takes me a while to eat them. When they're done, I go back for more.

Thursday, July 30th, 2020

It's a fast day today, for those who observe it. Tradition says that today, a few thousand years ago, a few hundred years apart, both the First and Second Temples were destroyed. This fits with the basic story for fast days: they fought us; we lost; let's not eat.

Some, but not all, of the more religious people in the office are off today. We're not doing afternoon prayers. We probably don't have enough people, and the services today would be longer and more complex than usual.

The people who aren't fasting are being quiet about their eating, respecting those who are. Some carry their lunches from the kitchen to their desks via different routes, so the people who are fasting see them with their food less than they otherwise might. I see one person cover his lunch with a piece of paper when someone who is fasting enters his cube.

Many restaurants that I pass, though not all of them, are closed. Some other businesses are, too. This year, most people are praying alone. Services with more than ten people are not allowed indoors. It's too hot to gather for long outside.

I see online that the Chief Rabbi has told people with symptoms of the virus not to fast. They aren't held to some other rules, either. As usual, those who choose to observe, observe. Those who do not, do not. Everyone figures out a personal path and follows it. For the most part, we get along.

Friday, July 31st, 2020

The mall café looks only a little more crowded than usual, but the line to order is long. The workers are making mistakes. I hear other customers complaining to them about getting the wrong items and about how things were cooked.

When I get to the front, the cashier takes my order in Hebrew. It's my usual Israeli breakfast. When he has to repeat himself over the noise, he says the most critical words in English.

He stumbles once: he asks me which kind of bread I want, but, once again, they only have white bread. He asks the question automatically. He's thrown when he can't actually offer the choice. I understand. In my own time as a bookseller, some things that we would say at the registers got hardwired into our routines. Overriding them when they changed was a challenge. When we were shutting down, the store discontinued the rewards card. I kept asking people for it. I even ended up with a pre-fab way to back out of the question as I was asking it.

At the café, they finally call my name for my order. I carry my tray to a far table. I start to eat. There's no knife. The handle of the fork is slightly greasy. I think of going back to the counter to get replacements, but I see that one aspect of the café is working well: the people who clear the tables are pouncing quickly to take trays away and disinfect the surfaces when customers leave. If I'd go to the counter and back, my lunch might disappear. I decide not to gamble. I stick with what I have. Things may be back to normal next week, unless the government decides to shut down the malls again.

August 2020

Saturday, August 1ˢᵗ, 2020

Approaching the Sabbath café, I pass a man outside its patio. He has a white beard and wears a battered fedora and faded red t-shirt. I automatically think of him as old. He may be my own age or younger. He waves his arms, mumbles in what may be a language that I don't recognize, and spits into the planters that line the patio's edge. No one is sitting near them. No one pays him much attention.

I sit down at a table near the center and scan the icons with my phone for an online menu.

A server approaches me. "Hello! Are you ready to order?" She speaks English to me. She must recognize me. I guess I've become a regular. I order the Israeli breakfast. When she asks me how I want my eggs, I automatically answer "*Ayin,*" in Hebrew. I'm surprised to realize that I don't recall what they're called in English. I tell her so. "They're sunny side up, I believe." OK, thanks. We both laugh.

She brings me my mint lemonade immediately. As I wait for the rest of my order, the man with the fedora walks onto the patio. He is mumbling something about fire. I think he just wants someone to light his cigarette.

A young, thin man who has been hanging out with some customers gets up and stands between the older man and the entrance. The older man tries to dart around him, but he continually shifts his position, blocking the door. The older man gives up and leaves. On his way out, he throws an ashtray from one of the tables out onto the street.

Right as the rest of my meal appears, a police car pulls up silently, its siren lights pulsing. One of the policemen and then the other approach the older man. This may be the first time that I have seen the police actually do anything in this peaceful town. They corner the man on the far side of a translucent bus stop. I can't see or hear what's happening. The man eventually crosses the street and disappears into the town square.

One of the policemen gets back into the car. The other reaches in
and retrieves something. He walks over to a much older woman who is
sitting on a park bench near the taxi stand next door. She isn't wearing
a mask. He hands her one and waits for her to put it on properly. She
only puts it on over her mouth. He pulls his mask down, exposing his
nose, and shakes his head. He puts it back over his nose and nods. She
does the same and nods back. They wave at each other. He gets back in
the car and drives away.

Sunday, August 2nd, 2020

I walk carefully between the shadows of two power lines. The foot-
wide path goes most of the way down this city block. The shadows
and the path should be shifting their location, I think, as the days grow
shorter. The movement is so subtle that I can't tell in which direction
they are shifting. I could probably calculate the motion, but the streets
curve enough that I can't recall whether this block goes north or west.

When I look at maps of the neighborhood, I'm continually surprised
at the directions in which I walk. I have never had much faith in Eu-
clidean geometry. It failed me for good in Greenwich Village, where
West 4th and West 10th Streets meet.

At the end of this block with the power lines, the Street of the Beautiful Heart turns into Kings of Israel Street and crosses Kings of Judah
Street. Or maybe it crosses Kings of Israel and turns into Kings of Judah. I don't notice the names of the streets anymore. I just know to
cross at the corner, turn left, and go up to the pedestrian path, which
takes me past two kindergartens and a vacant lot to the street of the
Sons of Benjamin, where the bus stop used to be.

I work on the Street of the Philanthropist, in a building named the
House of the Philanthropist. But no one sits anymore at the far end
of the street, where AstroTurf and benches once welcomed us. In the
wake of the virus, the café named for the philanthropist has closed.

Monday, August 3rd, 2020

I step outside the power line shadows to duck around furniture
dumped on the ground. Large trash is collected on Mondays. Outside
my house, it all goes on a specific concrete slab at the corner of the
pedestrian street. Elsewhere, people put it on the sidewalk.

Usually, it is quite tidy. Today, it looks like somebody has gone along this street, flipping furniture over and routing through the additional trash that had been placed in bags beside it. On this block, a large sofa turned upside down takes up much of the width of the pavement. I have to step into the street to get around the couch.

Further down, an upholstered recliner rests, face down, on the cement. I could use one of these. I don't know why it was discarded, though. There might be something awful on its front. And I don't know how I could get it home or whether it would fit through my front door.

Along the pedestrian street, a household has renewed its kitchen. Well-used pots and pans lie in a pile around the packaging from new ones. Elsewhere, I pass more upholstered furniture, build-it-yourself shelving that has been torn apart and trashed, and a carefully piled collection of women's clothing and Russian children's books.

I don't pick up anything, but what I see does remind of things that I plan, someday, to buy. First, I have to free up space in my apartment. New stuff will have to wait.

Tuesday, August 4th, 2020

I look in vain on my shelf for a clean shirt that fits. Some of the shirts that fit me when I left the States no longer do. I blame my job at the hotel when I first came here, with the wonderful food from its chefs in the employees' dining room.

I almost give up and decide to wear a t-shirt, when I spot a white bag at the foot of my bed. Oh, right. My laundry had been returned last night. I brought it in, but was too tired to unpack it.

I lift the bag onto the bed and open it. A small rectangle of white, framing a field of black, catches my eye inside. I pick it up and look at it more closely. It's a booklet of some sort. The design strikes me as grim. The strict, sharp-lined black and white evocatively says nothing, as if Mark Rothko, in his late period, had gone into advertising.

I flip it over. The other side is plain blank white. The afterimage of the other side makes it look like it is white-on-white, until the inner rectangle drifts and fades, leaving only the floaters that are always in my eyes to contrast with the paper.

I open the booklet. The design makes sense now. It's a calendar. I hold it so the fold is vertical. Each of the lower pages has a grid of days on one side. The small squares are crammed with the Western date, the

Jewish date, and, where relevant, the name of the day's Torah reading and the starting and ending times of the Sabbath and holidays. Each upper page is lined for writing. Each has words at the beginning of alternate lines, the same for each page. They are written in pale blue on the glossy white. In this lighting, I can't make out the letters.

Holding the booklet open, I flip it over again. The black rectangle is stiff, with a different texture than the paper. I walk over to the refrigerator and touch it to the door. It stays there. It's a magnet. Oh.

The current calendar from the laundry hangs next to it on the door. I had forgotten that that was there. They'll stay on the door next to each other for the rest of August. At the start of September, the old one will be ceremoniously retired and recycled. Assuming that I remember to do so. And assuming that I can recycle a magnet.

Wednesday, August 5th, 2020

I spend the day entangled with my health system. Their Kafkaesque circuitry may be what's brought out this unusual number of cockroaches. I escort the big bugs outside, then go back to crawling through briers of phone systems, websites, and texts.

In the morning, my phone beeps. It's a message from my family. They've read the local Hebrew papers. There's an official announcement: two people with the virus were at the mall supermarket on Friday afternoon. So was I. Anyone who was there has to go into isolation for two weeks. I'm not clear on the details of how this works. I imagine that I'll have to get tested, but I don't know where or when.

I send a text to my team at work: I'm now in isolation. I'll be working from home.

Fortunately, that seems easier today. My internet connection is steady. My landlord, who had been digging in his garden and messing with the cables under it, has gotten into woodworking instead. He's taking a long time to build something in the backyard.

I try to find virus information online. What I can understand is vague, at best.

I call the health system hotline. The phone tree should lead to an English speaker. It doesn't.

I call the Ministry of Health. They almost get me to an English speaker, but then drop the call.

The health system website looks promising, with the help of online translation, but each path that I try leads me to a page that translates to "Due to a glitch in data communications, we are unable to complete your request."

I get through to an English speaker on the nurses' line. He tells me that I have to speak to a doctor. The doctors' line doesn't open until 4 PM. I continue to work until then, getting things done no less efficiently than I do at the office.

I call the doctors' line just after four. An automated system takes my information. A text tells me that they will call me back within two hours. Or perhaps later. Probably tonight.

After three hours, a doctor calls me. He speaks just enough English that we can communicate. Yes, I have to isolate through next Friday. No, I can't get tested unless I show symptoms. If I do, I should call them back. Oh, well.

I'm prepared for this. I've kept my quarantine stash of necessities stocked. I'm almost out of coffee, but I've arranged with a relative to get me some. He can drop it off on my doorstep, so we don't have actual contact. I'm precise about the amount I need, the type, the grind, and the store. It beats guessing.

I let the family know what's happening, then get back to Facebook. The government is livestreaming a wedding with a small, well-distanced party on the roof of City Hall. Today is officially Love Day. At least I don't have a romantic dinner to cancel.

Thursday, August 6th, 2020

My landlady calls me late in the day. She can hear my air conditioning running. She's worried that I might have left it on when I went to work.

I tell her that I'm in isolation and working from home. She doesn't quite understand. We had been speaking in English, but her English is even weaker than my Hebrew. We switch. I tell her what's happening. I emphasize that I don't have any symptoms. We're just being cautious, as instructed by the government.

She's relieved. She asks if I need anything from the supermarket. I tell her that I'm OK, and that I had plenty of things saved up.

Looking around later, I see that I'm out of fruit. Digging into my quarantine stash, I find that I actually have plenty of dried fruit, as well as a fresh pack of frozen grapes in the freezer. They're one of my favorite snacks, like bite-sized all-fruit popsicles without the stick.

I work through the day, sending email and WhatsApp messages to coworkers, and working remotely on my office desktop. My boss tells me that he can see things moving on my screens. It's like there's a ghost in my cube. I think, but don't say, that if there were to be a ghost in a cube, he would probably be across the aisle.

Someone I know who also went into isolation yesterday sends me an eerie picture. He is in his living room. A person in a hazmat suit is testing him for the virus. He doesn't have symptoms either, but apparently his doctor thought getting tested was a good idea anyway. His test has come back negative, after only one day.

When work ends, I shut down the remote desktop for the weekend and put my sandals on. Isolation or not, the trash still has to go out.

Friday, August 7th, 2020

I start to shiver as I work at my computer in the late afternoon. I reach for my hoodie. When it's halfway on, I remember that this is August, and I'm in Israel. I shouldn't be having chills. Is this the virus?

I swivel around in my chair. The air conditioner is running. I clearly don't need it. I walk over to it and see the problem. I usually set the temperature to 25 degrees, about 77 Fahrenheit. That's the setting that my frugal bosses use at the office. It's a reasonable choice. The machine itself, however, wanted more of a workout. It has set itself to 16 degrees, about 60 Fahrenheit. That explains it. The ghost in the machine likes it cold. I set it back to 25, then shut it off entirely.

Now that I'm away from my desk, I start to put together a Shabbat dinner. I moved some chicken from the freezer to the refrigerator last night. Most of it has thawed. I put it in the toaster oven along with a sweet potato. I set it to cook for an hour at whatever temperature the oven uses by default. I've never changed it.

I microwave frozen brussels sprouts. I have another bottle of wine that I got before I got stuck in isolation. I reach into the freezer for a challah that I had kept frozen. It isn't there. I must have used it some time ago. I look at last week's challah. It's only a little stale and isn't moldy. Good enough.

My landlady called me again this morning and asked if I wanted anything. Had I known, I would have asked her to pick one up. Oh, well.

With frozen grapes for dessert, this will all work out.

I get back to my computer and continue uploading one of my early albums. I've been planning to do this for a long time. I'm finally getting around to it.

I can smell dinner cooking as I finish posting the album. The scent of the sweet potato drifts over that of the chicken. It's good. I'll finish getting things done soon. I may even shower before I eat.

Saturday, August 8th, 2020

I wake up without an alarm clock, right on time to go to work. This isn't a workday. Usually, on Saturdays, I sleep until the crack of noon. Now, I'm up.

I decide not to fight wakefulness. I immediately shower. I didn't yesterday. In this humidity, that was a bad idea. When I emerge, I stare at my closet and try to figure out what to put on. I choose a plain white t-shirt. I rarely wear it, since it has a few stains that I can't get out. No one will see me today, though, so it's OK.

I make my usual breakfast and sit down at the computer. I have things to do, but I wander around social media. At about 11 AM, I doze off in my chair. When I wake up, I drag myself to my bed, where I sleep for another few hours.

In the early afternoon, I make lunch. I have had some eggs in the refrigerator for so long that I don't recall getting them. I crack them open. They're still good. I started a new loaf of bread yesterday, but I still have the heel of the previous one. Loaves with odd numbers of slices annoy me. I eat a lot of sandwiches, so I use the slices in pairs.

After lunch, I finally get back to writing a program for a personal project. I'm not all that good at programming. I have trouble remembering commands and the order of arguments, even though I've been using the same language for some 25 years. I look everything up. I move slowly, debugging small things before I fit them into larger ones.

I made my living as a programmer in the 90s. It helped that I had found a useful niche. I was glad to stop programming for a living and to work in a bookstore. Now I work at a desk again. It pays.

In the evening, I have my usual Saturday video chat. I hold my phone so that it doesn't show the stains on my t-shirt.

Afterwards, I try to wrap things up and get to sleep. Even though I'll spend tomorrow in the same room at the same desk where I'm sitting today, it's a work day. If I have any video chats for work, I'll have to look awake and wear a clean shirt.

Sunday, August 9th, 2020

In the late afternoon, I hear glass crash to my right. I walk carefully into the kitchen. Nothing is wrong there.

I see my landlord walk down the stairs to my apartment. He picks up some shards. I don't open the door. I don't ask him what happened. I'm not supposed to be in contact with other people in person, and he doesn't speak English at all.

At some point, I'll look outside. A draining grate lies at the bottom of the steps outside my door. Stepping on it hurts. I always put something on my feet when I go out. My landlord is always very precise about cleaning up after his projects. If any glass is left when I can go outside, it probably won't be a problem. But that won't be for several days.

Otherwise, the day is quiet. I continue to work from home. I listen to music that I've been accumulating for years but have never heard. I eat my usual breakfast. I make eggs again for lunch. For dinner, I cook sweet potato gnocchi, brussels sprouts, and leftover chicken.

As I boil the water for the gnocchi, I only hear the pot sizzle from one side. I wonder if there's something wrong with my other ear. I turn around and stand with my back to the pot. The sound continues to come from the same side of the burner. It isn't my ears. It's the pot, or the burner, or some other freak aspect of the acoustics of my kitchen. I stop worrying.

I take a while to decide whether to eat the chicken cold. I hear myself singing, "Will the Chicken Be Reheated?" Given enough silence, everything is a song cue.

Monday, August 10th, 2020

A drone outside the window howls like a mechanized throat singer. I think the neighbors across the fence are trimming their trees again. A deep tone jumps up and down by about a whole step. Overtones cut in and out. The machine is probably in motion, with different obstructions between the source and my ears. At first, the sound is grating. Eventually, as I sit far from the window, it becomes warm and interesting. When it ends, I miss it.

I turn the air conditioner on, then off again. It's humid but cool. It rains later in the day, or so I'm told. I don't hear it happen. I see an article online that says that it has. I send a text to my family here. "Just traces," they say. "Like snow flurries, it didn't stick."

I open the door to see if the ground got wet. It's too dark for me to tell, but the air smells fresh, like it does after a sunshower. This happens in the summer, but rarely, when there's low air pressure over the nearby sea.

It may happen again tomorrow. One forecast says that we'll have lower temperatures. Another says we won't. Unless I stick my head outside, I may not be able to tell.

Tuesday, August 11th, 2020

I get a text from my landlady in the morning. She asks, once again, if she can get me any groceries. I'll only be isolated for another couple of days. I could probably make it with what I have. I worry, though, that I might violate some social norm if I turn her down a third time.

I give in. I could use some eggs as well as fruit and vegetables. Which fruit and vegetables? I'm tempted to ask her to pick out what looks good, but that would put the burden of choice on her. I'll go with peaches and green peppers. I'm not a big fan of peaches, but I know they're in season.

I thank her. She sends me an emoji of some sort of plant. I think that means she's happy.

I spend most of the day staring at my screens, working. At dinnertime, I decide to settle down with a book, but I can't get my eyes to read clearly, no matter which glasses I wear. I wonder if the usual walk from work, when I'm not trying to read anything, helps my eyes relax. I sit down, put on my headphones, and listen to a podcast, eyes closed.

Wednesday, August 12th, 2020

Another day. Another burger. I don't eat them often at home, but I had stashed away a package of eight in the freezer. They're good, and filling enough that one of them in a small pita, plus a green pepper and a peach, is enough for dinner.

My landlady brings my groceries in the early afternoon. A relative brings the bag of coffee in the evening. I have to give walking directions on how to get here. We both pick up our packages from the same shop. I'm not far from there. The biggest problem: I'm hopeless on right and left. Describing the turns on the phone, I have to wave the appropriate hand in the air and figure out, each time, which word applies. It's no easier in English than in Hebrew.

When he's almost here, I realize that I haven't put the outside light on. I sprint across the apartment and hit the switch. I see him through the small open window at the top of my steps. We talk for a moment.

He leaves the coffee outside. I pick it up when he's gone. I wait a bit longer to turn the light back off. Time to make the coffee. I set it up. It'll steep overnight in the cold brewer and be ready for morning. At least, on my last day in isolation, I'll have an incentive to wake up.

Thursday, August 13th, 2020

My phone rings just as I'm about to get into the shower. It's a delivery from the post office. They're right outside, with a package from the US. That's a surprise. A text from them a couple of days ago said it wouldn't get here until a week from Sunday.

I quickly put some jeans on and head out. After a couple of steps, I realize that I'm barefoot. So be it. I run carefully toward the street. Along the way, I remember that I'm in isolation, and I should get them to leave the package by my door. Explaining how to get to my door would be difficult.

I get to the gate and call out "Hello?" A man appears from behind a truck with a small package. He walks toward me. I reach out over the gate. He stretches his arm out and hands it to me. It's a DVD player. It's smaller than I expected.

I take the package from him. Our hands don't touch. I think for a moment of the Sistine Chapel, where God is shown reaching out to Adam. I imagine, though, that if Adam had been given a DVD player in Eden, he and Eve might not have been tempted by fruit. The snake would have brought them popcorn.

Saturday, August 15th, 2020

A man sits at the first table inside the patio at the Sabbath café. He greets everyone who comes in. "Good Sabbath! Good Sabbath! Welcome to the days of the Messiah!" He smokes a cigarette and sips at a glass of water. He occasionally launches into a further monologue about the Messiah. He has a deeply guttural accent. I can't understand anything more.

As I enter, my usual server calls out to me in English. "Hello! How are you doing? Sit anywhere." I sit and scan the icons for the menu. I decide to get the shakshuka rather than my usual Israeli breakfast.

Another server, who I've never seen before, approaches my table, brandishing his tablet. He speaks to me in English. Maybe he heard the other server talking to me. Maybe she told him. Maybe I just look like an English speaker.

A third server brings my meal soon after I order. She says something to me that I can't make out, but I understand her gestures: The skillet is hot. Don't touch it.

The shakshuka – eggs covered with sautéed onions and tomatoes, cooked with dark, savory herbs – is excellent.

As I pay, I hear the man by the entrance talking to a server. I can't see which one. The server speaks quietly. The man jingles some coins and asks what he can get for seven shekels. The server goes back inside to check. When I get up to leave, the man is gone.

Sunday, August 16th, 2020

I pass two collages hung on a fence outside a kindergarten. The upper left corner of the background on each is a bright fluorescent green. I hadn't noticed that before. Scrapbook photos are pasted on top of the green patches. Those haven't changed. I don't think anyone would have removed them, repainted the backgrounds, and pasted them on again. It doesn't look like moss or any other natural growth.

A few blocks down, three children's sneakers, two left and one right, rest on a low brick wall. The outsides are a vague gray that may once have been white. The insides are the same fluorescent green. I wonder if seeing these identical splashes of color might be some kind of omen. I don't know what they would represent. I don't think we've had any nuclear accidents yet this year.

Across the street, someone has gutted a whole apartment and dumped the contents outside. Appliances, tables, shelving, sinks, and toilets block the sidewalk.

On the way home, I see a fine breakfront cabinet made of elegant carved wood blocking a fire hydrant. I imagine that someone cared enough about it to place it there gently. It's the kind of heirloom that elderly relatives hope to pass on to their descendants. Maybe someone will take it. More likely, it will end up in a massive heap somewhere, where forgotten furniture waits out its days.

Monday, August 17th, 2020

As I zone back in from an unexpected nap at work, I see an enormous pair of eyeglasses on the empty floor in front of me. I wonder if I've fallen into some sort of Claes Oldenburg wonderland.

Looking around, I see a giant computer keyboard lying in front of it, with English and Hebrew letters on each key. An equally large pair of hands rests on it. I wiggle some of my own fingers. The massive hands respond. They are mine.

I shift the hands forward, pick up the glasses, and put them on. Context and proportion return to normal. My glasses had been on my desk. I rarely see that much clear space on it. I hadn't recognized where I was.

Despite the nap, or perhaps because of it, this has been a more productive day than most. I've been working on a single project with few interruptions.

Late in the day, my boss puts an ice cream cone on my desk in front of me. It might be to celebrate something. It might be someone's birthday. I haven't overheard anything.

As I unwrap the cone, I notice that it's 6:18 PM. I think of the Golden Ratio. It's a coincidence. The time doesn't represent a proportion of anything to anything else. The "18" is for sixtieths of an hour, rather than any sort of decimal value. Some numbers stand out for me like that: 618, 613, 316, 433 and others seem to shine brighter than values that are near them. They aren't all that useful, but noticing that I'm noticing them is fun.

Tuesday, August 18th, 2020

The supermarket at the Heart of the City has gone slightly upscale. A bit of pale wood at the edge of bins goes a long way. The store's name has changed to that of the wine merchants who bought the chain a while ago. It's still a bit scruffy, but stark black and white and splashes of bright colors shine out where dull walls had been plastered with shaggy ads.

The bakery at the entrance is far smaller than it had been. A few racks of baked goods have replaced it. Displays of fresh produce greet customers as we make our way past the sleepy guard with his thermometer.

The cheese counter, my favorite in town, is unchanged. Freezer cases had lined many of the walls beyond it. They have been replaced by shelving. Freestanding freezers now run down several aisles. Otherwise, much of the store is the same.

When I go to check out, I see that only two cashiers' aisles are open. Other registers have been replaced by self-scanning stations. Customers poke at machines and look frustrated until workers come over and help each of them.

The queue for the cashiers is chaotic. People fall into a sort of order without conversation. The motor for the cashier's conveyor belt on my aisle isn't working. We have to push our items along. I'm only buying a few items: sliced cheese, white cheese, pomegranate nectar, golden dates, surgical masks, and super-glue.

Once I get to the front of the line, the cashier is friendly and efficient. That makes a big difference. I don't have plans to return soon, but I won't stay away as avidly as I had.

Wednesday, August 19th, 2020

The sign above the counter says "mushrooms burger." I see that kind of mistake a lot. Apparently, that thing we do in English, where a noun modifying another noun is in the singular rather than plural, is weird. In Hebrew, "book store" is "store books." It also drops the "of" that English speakers would expect when the words go in that order. People rarely believe me about the singular noun when I edit their documents. I often wish that I could snap my fingers and have Grammar Girl appear.

When I get to the counter, the cashier greets me in Hebrew and asks what I want. I forget how to say "mushroom" in Hebrew. I say it in English. He looks confused. Another worker comes up behind him. She says the equivalent of "I've got this." I've ordered from her before.

As I sit outside and eat, four young girls play tag on the patio of the pizza joint next door. When any of them falls down, another takes her hands and pulls her back up. They hug and jump up and down like Teletubbies.

The girls run back and forth onto the patio of the burger place. One crashes into my table and bounces off, laughing. One of the men with whom they came in looks over at me apologetically. I shrug and smile.

After I eat, I stop at the café across the street. They just started serving affogatos. I order one. It's OK. The espresso is good, but the ice cream is a generic soft-serve.

I vaguely recall that I may have had another affogato since I moved here. I can't remember where or when. I check my archive. It was last September. I was at an ice cream shop in the city south of here. The affogato was excellent, with cinnamon gelato.

I think back on the many wonderful affogatos I had in Cleveland. I'm told that the place where I got them there has closed, as have other restaurants in the same square. I believe the all-night diner that I went to, wedged between the train platforms, is still in business. I think fondly of their liver and onions. The taste in my memory clashes with the affogato I'm eating. I step out of the past, apologize to the memory, and focus on what I'm eating here and now.

Thursday, August 20th, 2020

The sound of the shofar blasts down the hallway and around the corners of our floor. The leader of the afternoon prayers holds the door to the smoking porch open as the boss sounds the traditional calls: one long blast, three shorter ones, nine staccato bleats, then one even longer tone, lasting until his breath gives out.

The calls don't echo in the atrium, but they do reverberate, hanging in the air for a short while after he's done. Two boys playing on the ground level, one with a mask and one without, don't seem to notice. A woman with a phone on another interior porch, across the space from us and two floors down, looks up and nods.

I was surprised when the boss took the shofar out of its velvet bag a few moments before. I thought the new moon would be tomorrow, not today. Rosh Hashanah is one month from now, so he'll be blowing the shofar every afternoon as we pray in the hallway together.

Last year, we were in the smaller conference room. The shofar seemed louder but reverberated less. Now, we stand out in the hall, masked, several meters apart, as we worship together. More of the workers throughout the building will get to hear the shofar this year, whether they plan to or not.

Friday, August 21st, 2020

The direct bus to the mall no longer runs from my neighborhood. The nearest stop is about a ten-minute walk away. By then, I'm already at the Heart of the City. I can get most of what I need from smaller stores there.

I have to stop at the downtown pharmacy anyway. Even though the pharmacy at the mall is from the same chain, it doesn't take prescriptions from my health plan. This one does.

The café here, where I got the affogato, has the same brand as the mall café, but it's not as good, and the workers are grumpier. I stop into my favorite shawarma joint instead. Then I hit a litany of shops: the produce store for apples, yams, peppers, and pineapple; the cheap coffee chain for an espresso; the pharmacy for my prescriptions and some medical gear for quarantined relatives; the bakery for pita and challah.

They've changed the challah that they make. I had been getting their small sweet challah. What they bake now is larger, with sesame seeds or slivered almonds on top. I don't recognize it at first. They look like pastries. I have to ask. The worker rattles off the possibilities. I don't understand him. He sees that I look confused. "English?" he asks. That helps.

He and another worker somehow ring up several customers at once at a single register. People shove their purchases and money at them. They bag them up and return the right change.

I stop off at the House of a Hundred Grandmothers to bring the medical gear to my family there, then head home. The park on the way to my place is still open. I cut through there. Several dogs run toward me, sniff, then wander away. I think they smelled the challah, which is still warm.

Once at my apartment, I drop my bags on the kitchen table, pour myself some seltzer, switch on the air conditioner, sit down at my desk, and close my eyes.

Saturday, August 22nd, 2020

The dog wanders up to me at the Sabbath café, sniffs my hands, and licks my face. I laugh. I'm still wearing my mask. It hops up and puts a paw on my lap. The dog is big, about the size of a German Shepherd. It may still be a puppy. Its paws are too big for its head.

When the server comes over, it turns to stare at her and growls. I tell the dog in English that it's ok, that she's a friend. It stops growling. I pat it on the back. It steps back down onto the ground. The voice at the other end of its leash says, in English, "You're good at this." It runs in the family.

He sits down at the table behind me and says something to the dog in Hebrew. It lies down under his chair.

I have already scanned and read the menu. I order the shakshuka again. When it arrives, the server warns me again that the skillet is hot. She puts the tray down, though, the same way that she had last week. The skillet handle juts out toward me. I carefully spin the wooden tray around so that the handle faces away. The shakshuka is good. This time, it's more spicy than savory.

Conversations in English surround me. The man with the dog talks about something regarding law and about how dirty Manhattan is. Two men at the next table complain that people don't appreciate how much exposure they give them in getting them to do things for free. Teenage girls ahead of me mostly chatter in Hebrew, but drop in English slang phrases and song lyrics. Two of them smoke thin cigarettes, manufactured with filter tips and translucent papers.

Two men about my age sit at tables alone. One wears a stained white t-shirt. He reads a newspaper and drinks iced coffee. The other quietly eats a sandwich. Eventually a woman joins him, walking slowly with a cane. When I'm done, I get up and look over at the dog. I hope it will notice me. It doesn't. I put my mask back on and walk away.

Sunday, August 23rd, 2020

I see that the Cinematheque is showing *Frozen* outdoors, at a municipal parking facility two blocks from my house. The most surprising part of this is that there's a municipal parking facility two blocks from my house. I've never seen it.

I wouldn't be able to get to the movie tonight, anyway. I'll still be at work when it starts. If I were to go, I don't know that I'd have a way to get into it. They've made the place into a drive-in. Tickets are twenty shekels per car. There's no walk-up price. Without a car radio, I might not have a way to hear the audio anyway. And it will still be hot.

Maybe when I get off work, I'll just head home and put on "Frozen," the air conditioner, and some more comfortable clothes.

Monday, August 24th, 2020

The path from work to the mall is blocked. It was chained off during the lockdown, but that isn't the problem now. The sports complex is open. I walk past people skating, playing soccer and basketball, and running through it as before.

Close to the far edge of the park, a narrow stretch of pavement lies between some cryptic, humorous sculptures and the last unused bit of land. A white metal wall, taller than I am, now blocks the sidewalk, the sculptures, and that field. Through joints in the wall, I can see that construction has begun. I don't know what they're building.

I follow the wall, straying far off my usual course. The metal wall ends at the edge of an ornate skate park that I hadn't seen before. Artfully shaped concrete guides people in knee pads and helmets along intricate dips, swerves, and jumps. It looks as if a block-wide mound of gray whipped cream atop an unseen sundae had melted then frozen again in place.

Across from the skate park, ankle-high walls of cement border six lanes, the size and shape of parking spots, hemming each in on both long sides and one short side. At the open edge of each, men and a few women, my age or older, roll what look like stone balls into the lanes in games of something like bocce.

I finally spot an exit sign. An open gate leads through a fence that runs along that side of the complex. I emerge far up the same street to which I was headed before the detour. I walk back along the road, following the tall white fence, then cross the street when I can and continue my voyage to the mall.

Tuesday, August 25th, 2020

I look down into the atrium as I wait for the afternoon prayers. People are finally using the space. The stain on the gray wood floor is gone. Three round white tables, each with three brightly colored chairs, line one side, a careful distance apart.

It takes a while to pull everyone together. The boss is trying to end a phone meeting. Some people are out today. Others are deep into their work and don't notice either the time or the regular visitor who makes his rounds through our office, welcoming the men to head out to the hallway.

Once enough of us are there, the prayers begin. Just before the end, the boss ducks behind the receptionist's desk and emerges with his shofar. Returning to his spot, he sees a family peeking out of the next office over. A tall man holds a boy in his arms. A woman whispers something in his ear and heads inside. A girl and another boy huddle by his feet. The boss shows them the shofar and gestures for them to come over. They don't.

When it's time, he blows the usual blasts: one, three, nine, and one. The girl runs inside. The boy holds tighter to his father's feet and stares. If he knows what the sound is, he probably hadn't expected to hear it in this context.

One of the regular guests covers his ears. Others admonish him. I'm surprised that a sound could be too loud for him. When he talks, we generally can hear him from the other side of the floor.

When it's over, I head back in. Next to the yarmulkes and prayer books, someone has placed a new bottle of hand sanitizer and a fresh thermometer. The page where we sign in and affirm that we're not sick when we arrive is full. Time to start yet another new one.

Wednesday, August 26th, 2020

A man with a pizza walks up the hallway during afternoon prayers. He comes up to the front just as the boss blows the shofar, less than a meter from his ears. He stumbles and almost falls over. He doesn't drop the pizza. I don't worry whether he might bang his head. He is still wearing his motorcycle helmet.

When I head down to the supermarket a little while later, I see a woman standing nervously by the elevator panel. I press the down button. She asks me if I am going to the ground floor. I am.

I expect that she will choose to stay behind. She might be unwilling to be in an elevator with a strange man. Even though we're both wearing masks, she might be wary of being in an elevator with another person at all. I prepare to offer to let her ride first, since she was there before me. That's not what's happening, though.

I finally figure out that she is terrified of elevators. She doesn't want to ride in one alone. She's been waiting for someone, anyone, to be heading to the lobby. When the elevator arrives, I get in and welcome her to ride along.

We get to the ground floor without any other stops. She thanks me profusely when we get off. I head to the supermarket. She heads to the café.

Thursday, August 27th, 2020

I tear open a new bag of masks as I prepare to leave for work. It's my second bag of fifty. I had thought my first one would last me as long as I could possibly need. I got that one a little over three months ago.

At first, I used each mask for several days. Now, as the high temperatures hover at 90 Fahrenheit or above when I walk to work and back, I use a new one every day. These are generic surgical masks, packaged with a seal of authenticity from China. I keep thinking of getting something that looks better, perhaps a black mask with an appropriate image or pattern. But these are cheaper, all told, and work better. I'm OK with that.

Going through the masks, I could keep count of the days of this never-ending summer. The shofar at the afternoon prayers tells me that autumn is about a month away. Otherwise, I might not know it.

I'm told that the summer is harsher for others, what with hurricanes, the derecho, and wildfires across the US, and violence and the virus seemingly everywhere. Still, I grumble.

Heading out the door on the way to work, I find a piece of unripe fruit on my step. It's some sort of citrus, green and pear-shaped. It may be a very early orange. Whatever it is, I take it as a sign: autumn is coming, should it ever decide to arrive.

Friday, August 28th, 2020

On the main street of the next town over, a colorful troupe of troubadours plays music that I can't hear. The air conditioner on the bus drowns out the sound. Through the window, I see six musicians, playing clarinet, accordion, a bass drum, and other instruments that I can't make out. One wears a gaudy jester's hat. Another has rainbow hair. Each wears exaggerated makeup. Those not blowing into instruments wear multi-colored masks. Children jump up and down around them.

They're playing at the entrance of a supermarket. It isn't a grand opening. There isn't a visible sale. The holidays won't be for another few weeks. The musicians are just there.

The bus is headed into the larger city just south of where we are. It hits a massive detour once downtown. A main street, inbound, is closed for construction. The bus has to navigate narrower roads. Many of them are already clogged with deliveries and double-parking.

Once we get to where I'm going, I try to get something to eat in the double-corkscrew shaped mall. I fail. None of the fast food joints that I think of hitting are visible, either where I remember them or near the glowing signs with their logos. I give up and get an adequate falafel at a corner shop outside.

After eating, I head across the street to the one good record store that I know in the city. It's the prelude afternoon to Record Store Day. The buses don't run on Saturdays, and many people don't shop then, so they've started things a day early. There are discounts on used disks and a few special items.

I end up not getting anything. Most of what I might want and can afford, I already have. After I leave, I think of a few items that I might have gotten. I suspect they'll still be there when I return.

By the time that I get back to my city, almost everything is closed. I'm the last customer at the produce shop. The bakery is out of challah. I forget to hit the ATM. I'll have to go there early tomorrow, so I can pay the cleaning person in the late afternoon.

When I get home, I drink the last of my cold brew coffee and make more for the morning. I still have a lot to do.

Saturday, August 29th, 2020

My table at the Sabbath café doesn't have the icons that we scan for menus. That's OK. I know what I'm getting. The shakshuka is consistently good. There are slight variations each week. Often, the eggs are under the tomatoes. Today they're on top. They're firmer now than before. The sauce is savory, with just a touch of sharp heat.

The server puts the tray down safely this time. The skillet's handle faces away from me. I don't have to spin the whole thing around to avoid getting burned. She also brings out a glass of water in addition to my iced coffee. That's welcome. It's even hotter today than it has been.

A young woman in a black shirt walks across the patio. Several customers try to catch her attention. She doesn't work here. The servers do wear black t-shirts, but the logo is small and only on the front. It's easy to make that mistake. When a real server comes to her table, the woman points to the other customers who had called out to her. The server makes the rounds to them next.

On my way home, I see neat piles of books where the give-and-take bench had been. I look through them. Travel guides in Hebrew for trips to Italy and Paris rest atop an SAT workbook and an annotated paperback of Paradise Lost. Several volumes of an old matched set of hardcovers are stacked next to them. I open the one on top, but the back cover is facing upwards. I can't tell what it is. I don't dig further.

I check the time on my phone. The cleaner is arriving soon. I hurry home.

Sunday, August 30th, 2020

I bounce among media throughout the day. In the morning, I record voice-overs for promotional videos for my job. In the afternoon, I work further on the script, suggesting what will be onscreen. Someone I've never met is doing the visuals. That's OK. He's better at it than I am and has better resources.

In the evening, I collect images for a video project that had gotten stuck. A good dose of Maya Deren and Godfrey Reggio gets me back on track. The logic of dreams frees me to change some ideas.

During the day, in the cracks between work as I wait for documents to compile, I work on a website and mailing list. I'm using obscure software, partly because the developers are helpful. For one project, I have to figure out technology that I've never seen before and two languages I hadn't known existed. The developers give me just enough information to steer me in the right directions and encourage me when I hit successes and challenges.

At home, I try to figure out why things that look good on one screen are illegible on another. I need to bang my head against my monitors a bit more and find the right questions to ask. Eventually, I'll get these things done.

Monday, August 31st, 2020

This frozen candy bar costs ten shekels. That's just about three US dollars. Its unfrozen brothers, sitting on a tray on a stack of boxes in the store, are three for ten. The electricity for the freezer must cost a lot.

When I get off the bus downtown after work, I intend to head home for dinner. It's not too hot, though, and I like the music that I can hear in the city square. A baritone seems to be singing a cappella into a sound system nearby. I can't tell where he is. Sometime later, I hear a group of women singing, also amplified. The sound doesn't seem to be coming from any of the shops.

I get a sandwich and some grapefruit juice and sit down at a table in the shade. The sandwich looks homemade, as do the others that were sitting with it on the display. A handwritten label shows the ingredients: sliced egg, eggplant, mozzarella, chopped vegetables, and a sauce that I can't identify. I sit there for a while, eating, listening, and catching up on Twitter.

After I'm done, I wander through the square. I see that another shop is now empty. The sign above it shows an intriguing name: The Secret of Magic. I have no memory of what it was.

Several shops in a row are gone, including the butcher shop and, I think, the lawyer's office that was where our family's spice merchant had been.

Passing the small grocery store, I decide to indulge in the candy bar. I don't get them often. I sit on a low wall and eat it.

People pass by, singly or in groups, on foot or on wheels. Toddlers chase pigeons past people with walkers and caregivers. A teenager on a bicycle zooms past, doing one of the longest wheelies I've ever seen. Two young girls pass each other, accompanying large dogs. One dog sniffs the other amicably. The other ignores him.

I finish the candy bar, throw the wrapper in the trash can. and head home. When I'm more than a block away, I see a woman with a mask walking toward me. I realize that I'm not wearing mine. I should have put it back on after eating. I do now. The woman and I nod at each other and continue on.

September 2020

Tuesday, September 1st, 2020

I stand behind three teenage girls in the fast lane at the supermarket. Each wears a gauzy white shirt, cut-off denim shorts, and a black mask with a logo that I don't recognize. They lounge against a shopping cart, taking group selfies. The cart only has a couple of items in it.

After a while, a man in a turban comes up to them, takes the items from the cart, and checks out. Two of the girls climb into the cart. The third pushes them down the pasta aisle.

I check out next. The cashier has long, abstractly painted nails. She has trouble gripping change.

Downtown, there's a small dance party at the front of the square. A dozen women in wheelchairs surround several younger women, possibly their caregivers, who sway to the music from someone's phone.

At the café, I only want to get a simple salad. The ones on the menu are too complicated. I decide to get a sandwich. Those come with fairly large salads and are less expensive. I pick the salmon sandwich. It's good. But it's the one sandwich that doesn't come with a salad.

When I get home, I munch on a green pepper and listen to an album that a friend just turned me on to. It's as good as I had hoped. The site has its monthly sale this Friday. The album's on my list.

Wednesday, September 2nd, 2020

My phone falls out of my pocket and clatters to the floor. Nothing's broken. The rhythm of its hitting the ground matches the opening drum riff of a song I'd heard yesterday. The song rattles around in my head for hours.

At the mall, at suppertime, I try a new, supposedly Asian-inspired burger in the food court. The ad for the burger lists exotic toppings. The only one that I can taste is the grilled slice of pineapple just under the bun. That works well. I'm not inspired to get another one soon, but remain curious about the other items in the new line. The downside is that the commercials for them have Asian stereotypes that I doubt would air on American TV.

The food court is still divided by barriers into a maze. It takes me a moment to spot a path from the counter to an available table. Teenagers ignore the barriers and blithely leap over them. The teens with trays who are in groups wait for others to hop over, then hand off the trays before leaping.

After I eat, I get most of the way to the supermarket before I realize that I'm not wearing my mask. We should have signs saying "Thank you for putting your mask back on" at the food court exits.

As I approach the supermarket, I see that the sliding doors are shut. Two young people beyond them are gesturing to me, but I don't know what they mean. When I get there, they open the doors and talk at me simultaneously. I understand neither. I look at them blankly.

The man says, "English?" I nod. The turnstile is broken. People are trying to exit there without paying. "But you are coming in, not going out. So welcome." He waves me in grandly then closes the doors again.

I spend more than usual. I replenish meat, bread, and other items for my quarantine stash, as well as getting some to use right away. Word has it that if the infection rate doesn't ease off in a week or so, there may be new lockdowns. I've been there and done that. I now know how to shop.

Thursday, September 3rd, 2020

The city square is quiet. I'm here later than usual, after shopping at the supermarket downstairs from work. Most of the shops that had been open are closed. I see a woman roll a baby carriage out of a shoe store. A worker locks the glass doors behind her.

I don't stop for dinner. I'm not hungry. But I do sit down and drink a bottle of grapefruit juice from the supermarket. I'm still full after a massive lunch at work.

The bosses often order lunch to celebrate something. Today's celebration seems more ad-hoc than usual. They announce a birthday from a week ago, as well as something or other for one of the other programmers. I think they just feel like ordering out.

Usually, we get falafel or shawarma. Today, they order from a rotisserie chicken place. The boxes are about the same size that I remember from KFC, but are full of food: a quarter chicken, coleslaw, green beans, rice with peas and carrots, and roasted potatoes, sweet potatoes, zucchini, and eggplant. It's delicious.

Somehow we still manage to wobble out to the hall for the afternoon prayers and to get work done afterward. I'm glad that my direct boss has an espresso machine in his office, for just such emergencies. But I only think of eating again after nine PM, long after I get home.

Friday, September 4th, 2020

A boy sits at the table in the back of the store where I pick up the packages. Item 435 arrived yesterday for me. He shuffles through the box with numbers in that range. He doesn't see it.

The shopkeeper comes to the back. "Look again. For this guy, it will be a book." He pauses. "Wait, why are you here? You picked up package 435 yesterday."

I hadn't. I show him that I have the text message saying that it's waiting, and that I don't have the message that I would automatically get when I would pick it up. "No, you were here yesterday and –"

He stops. He bends down and picks up the package from the pile on the floor, where he puts small items for known customers. He hands it to the boy and stomps away.

The boy asks for my ID number and signature. He gives me the package.

As I pass the shopkeeper on the way out of the store, he nudges me with his elbow. I think he smiles.

I stop into the barber shop and make an appointment for a haircut. I need one badly. The elastic straps of my masks are getting tangled with my hair.

The barber welcomes me warmly. As I'm about to leave, he calls over to me. "Joe, take a drink of water before you leave. No, you must. It's very hot outside. The cooler is here. The cups are here. And please say hello to your family for me." I take the water and thank him.

Part way around the plaza, two musicians play live in the shade of a large umbrella. The drummer is very good. The man beside him strums his guitar and sings, "Fly Me to the Moon." They segue into a Hebrew song that I've heard but can't identify. I wander on.

At the nuts-and-seeds shop about a block away, I restock on coffee and other items. When I had been there before, they had had open bins of their nuts, dried fruits, and candies. Most of the other similar stores that I've seen still have the open bins. At this one, however, everything is in bags and clear plastic containers. That may be a good idea.

I get a challah at the bakery, then pick up apples and yams at the produce shop. At the counter, I spot a couple of small wrapped containers of sliced pineapple. I get one of them. The cashier puts the other one with it. "You're getting this, too. It's only ten shekels. I don't want to have to wonder whether anyone will buy it." OK.

He bags it all up and hands it to me. "Wait – did I forget to give you your change?" He had. He nods. He's tired. He opens the register again and fishes out my change. "Here you go. Have a good Sabbath."

He sits back down on his stool behind the counter. Just for a moment, he closes his eyes.

Saturday, September 5th, 2020

The server warns me about the shakshuka, in English, as she puts the tray on my table: "This is boiling. Literally." It is. Bubbles rise and burst at the moon-like tomato-red surface.

She looks over at the package I have set on the table. It still holds the book that I received yesterday. "You order from them? Me, too. All the time."

We talk briefly. She's from New York, but says that she's been here a long time. I tell her that I've only been here for three years. She nods. "You'll catch on."

The Sabbath café is out of the coffee granita that I had ordered. She asks if I'd like an iced latte instead. Sure.

When she leaves, I see that the tray with the sizzling skillet and the rest of my meal is on the other side of the table. I debate whether to just sit on that side. I decide against it. I reach over to the tray and slide it carefully over to where I am, maneuvering around the coffee and the items at the center. It takes a while, but I get it to where I need it. I'm not all that annoyed at the server. I would have been terrified just carrying the tray from the kitchen to the patio.

When I'm done eating, I put my mask back on. She sees me and comes over. "Need the check? You can give me your card now, and I can run it." No problem.

When she returns with the receipt, though, I see that there's a glitch. They charged me for the latte, but didn't cancel the granita. I call her over and show her. She sees what has happened and takes my card again.

After a few minutes, she brings it back. "OK, we canceled the granita from the charge. Sorry." That's OK.

I stand, pick up the book, and reach in my pocket for my mask. It isn't there. I worry for a moment. Looking down toward the table, I see a blur of white and blue at the bridge of my nose. Right. I'm already wearing it. I put my headphones on, fire up my phone, and wander on.

Sunday, September 6th, 2020

I set up my cold brew coffee pot, as usual, with one cup of grounds and four cups of water. I look at the brewing section. There's room for about one more cup. I pour more water in.

In the morning, I decant the coffee into the carafe. Bad move. While the brewer holds more, the carafe doesn't. Coffee overflows onto the counter. Fortunately, I'm only a few inches from the sink.

I let the rest flow into there. It's not much of a loss. The cold brew is so strong that, when I drink it, I cut it by half with even more water.

I clean up what spilled, pour the first cup into my mug more carefully than usual, and remind myself not to do that again.

When I head out for work, my screen door hits an obstruction and gets stuck. One of the fallen fruit has gotten lodged in the grate at the bottom of the stairs, sticking up just enough to stop the door. I give the lower part of the door a sharp kick. It swings open, slicing the fruit in half. There's probably a word for that move in Japanese.

I take a bag of kitchen garbage out with me. Branches of a flowering tree block the door to where we keep the trash can. I duck under the branches and push them aside.

When I get to work and look in the restroom mirror, I see that I'm wearing a randomized garland of small pink flowers in my hair. It's as if I were going to San Francisco, but without the expense or the quarantine.

I think about the flowers as I come in and sit down at my desk. I forget to say "Good morning" to my office mates.

I quickly get up, get coffee in the kitchen, then circle around again. Done with the morning rituals, I settle down and finally start to work.

The nightly dance party in the town square has grown. A dozen wheelchairs and shaded motorized carts sit in a vague circle near its southern edge. An equal number of young people dance among them.

The music plays from a small karaoke system. Some of the young people sing into the mics. They appear to be livestreaming tonight, perhaps to a single person, perhaps to more. A mic stand holds a telephone in a spring-loaded clip. People hand the mic stand around and set it down at spots within the circle. Some speak directly into it.

I stop into a shop and get another cryptically labeled sandwich. The worker behind the counter rings it up and unwraps it. He warms it in a small oven as he meticulously cleans a carrot juicer.

I sit at a table on the square with the sandwich and a bottle of juice. I'm surprised when I drink from the bottle. I thought it was grapefruit juice. It's lemonade.

The innards of the sandwich crumble as I eat it. Bits of dry cheese and diced vegetables fall to the ground. Pigeons will feast on them later.

At the near edge of the party, two of the young people, holding mics, sing a slow song in Tagalog to a woman in a wheelchair. While singing, one of them reaches forward and adjusts the woman's clear face shield.

When the song ends, the beat picks up again. A man with two children dances at a distance. So does another older man with a cane. The people in the circle wave to them. They move closer, but not too close.

I wander off when I finish eating. At the far end of the square, two men at a small table sing as one of them strums a guitar. An older woman at their table digs a pack of cigarettes out of her pocketbook.

A few meters from them, another woman talks to a tall soldier with a gun. She seems to be trying to interest him in calling her daughter. He doesn't look convinced.

Traffic pauses at the circle as several people, including me, cross at the zebra stripes in the street. I think of getting an affogato at the café. I don't.

Tuesday, September 8th, 2020

I get to the barber shop three minutes late. I apologize. The barber is amused. He offers me a cup of water. I drink it in two gulps, lifting my mask for each.

"With the mask," he says, "everything is difficult. It's hard to drink. It's hard to smile. It is hard to recognize each other. And it's hard to know what the rules are each day."

He beckons me to the chair in the back. He removes my glasses and tucks them into my shirt. I tilt far back as he washes my hair. "The water, is it too hot?" It isn't.

We head over to the chair in the front. Rather than the usual black smock, he puts a clear disposable one on me. He knows how I like my hair. I don't want to have to think about it.

He cuts it short, close to a crew cut in the back. "The women like that. They like to touch men's necks with the short hair." Um, OK. "I see you have been out in the sun. Your hair is lighter than before. It looks good."

The haircut costs eighty shekels. I give him four twenties. He is pleased. It makes it easy to give change when other people pay with hundreds.

"You'll be back when, December? January?" I do take a long time between haircuts. Since I've been to his shop enough times, though, and he's punched my customer card for each, we see that the next one will be free. I may not wait as long this time.

Wednesday, September 9th, 2020

I work late into the night, cramming to finish a video for a virtual trade show.

I'm effectively flying blind. Something has gone awry with how the software appears on my screens, so I'm editing entirely by sound. I only see what I've done when I output the result. That takes a while each time.

My boss and I sit in his office and go over changes. We munch on crisp breadsticks. He holds his like a pen. I hold mine like a cigar. I've never smoked, but experiments with celery sticks have shown me that that's the easiest way to hold such things while I work.

When the deadline gets too near, my boss gets on the phone to the person to whom I have to send the files. Through the mystery of boss-to-boss communications and the magic of opposing time zones, we get a day's reprieve.

I close out the project for the evening. The boss offers me a ride home. We head through the main doors together. On the right doorpost, I swipe my time card. On the left, he kisses the mezuzah.

There's little traffic at night. The navigator on his phone guides us along narrow streets. I'm surprised his SUV can squeeze through them.

He drops me off at the end of my road. When I reach into my pocket for my keys, I find my mask and realize that I'm not wearing it. I come into the house, fix myself a cheese sandwich, and sit down to write.

Thursday, September 10th, 2020

The man sings in a high tenor, in English, as he leans against the counter at the café on the square. I think it's a Roy Orbison song.

He hears me order. The cashier knows me by now and speaks to me in English even when I try to speak to her in Hebrew.

The man stops singing as I step away from the register. "So where are you from? New York?" New Jersey, mostly.

"I haven't been to New Jersey much. I used to live in New York. White Plains. Do you know it? I have a brother there. A plastic surgeon. He used to do everything, women's whole bodies, you know. Now he does one thing: the men who lift weights, with the big muscles? Their chest muscles grow, but their nipples fall down. He lifts them back up. Big money.

"I never got big money. I got some, some stocks, but lost most of it. The brokers knew my phone number and wouldn't answer the phone when I wanted to sell high. Do you want to see the market today? Here, on my phone. Green is growing. Red is losing. Everything today is red. Wow.

"I did know one woman from New Jersey. Her car broke down in White Plains. Beautiful car. I fixed cars then. I fixed hers. She said if I come down to New Jersey, she would give me the car. She did. I didn't need another car. I let my workers use it to drive home.

"Most of them were from Puerto Rico, from the islands down there. But one time, one of my men was driving the car to work. He was a Black man. The police pulled him over. They wanted to see his papers. He reached in his pocket, like this. They shot him dead. Bang. Just like you hear so much now from there. I'm glad that I've moved here."

So am I.

Friday, September 11th, 2020

The traveling band moves through the city square, playing in $\frac{7}{8}$ time. They all wear bright colors and white chef's hats. Those whose mouths aren't making music wear flamboyant masks.

The singer, guitarist, and bass guitarist carry small amplifiers on their backs. The tuba player, saxophonist, and drummer move around them. A tall man tosses juggling clubs in the air. A woman in a furry tutu dances with a hula-hoop.

When they get to an open space, the musicians form a circle around the juggler and dancer. The two toss the clubs between them, spinning and jumping as they juggle. A woman with a toddler stands near me, watching. The tall juggler calls out to us, "Come, mother and child! Come, uncle!"

I figure that they're busking for donations, but I don't see anyone collecting them. This doesn't appear to be an official event. The shops haven't turned their overhead music off.

The band sits down in chairs around a table outside the shop with the cryptic sandwiches. They continue to play. After a while, they rise and cross the street.

Outside the Heart of the City, two men from Chabad stand at their usual table, trying to get people to put on tefillin and say some prayers. The band sees them and launches into a Chassidic tune, a cappella. The men join in, singing and clapping on the one and on the three.

The band surrounds them in a half-circle behind the table as they sing together. They gradually switch to their instruments, accompanying the chabadniks.

At the end of the song, they all wish each other a good Sabbath. The band plays another tune and dances into the open space at the center of the mall. The song plays in my head for the rest of the day.

Saturday, September 12th, 2020

The Sabbath café has returned to paper menus. The scannable icons are gone. The tables on the patio are also much closer together.

I'm surprised at these changes. Word has it that another major lockdown will start next week. The indoor seating and patio will shut down again. Maybe they figure that they might as well set things back to how they were.

A server whom I don't know brings me the English-language menu without asking. I decide to be a bit extravagant. I probably won't be here again for a few weeks.

I try to order the Israeli breakfast. I can't. They now only make it before noon. So be it. I order the shakshuka again. I want to order an American-style iced coffee, without all that milk. After some negotiation, I get a large cold Americano over ice. It's just right.

A couple with a young child comes in after me. The server brings out a high chair. The couple cleans it themselves, using wipes from a container in the back of their stroller.

Another woman talks to people at the next table. She stands so close to me that all I can see of her is her round bare midriff. A bandage covers her navel. A metal stud sticks through it.

Near the patio entrance, two large dogs lie under a table. Men in muscle shirts sit in the chairs. The two dogs play with each other and lap up water from a plastic container between them. When other dogs walk past with their humans, the two dogs bark. The men pat them on their sides and ask them to calm down.

One of the men sees that his dog's leash has gotten tangled around its leg. He squats next to his chair, lifts the dog's foot off the ground, and slides the leash off of it. The dog licks the man's face as he rises. The man and the dog sit back as they were.

Another man dressed in white, with a white yarmulke, dangling tzitzit, and a white-covered prayer book, walks past the café. Neither the dogs nor the men notice him. Our eyes meet. He nods toward me. I nod back. He walks on.

Sunday, September 13th, 2020

These fresh dates are a revelation.

When I first saw them in produce shops, I had no idea what they were: hard tan fruit, an inch or so long, still attached by slender threads to flimsy branches. I had brought some home in the past and eaten them. They were crunchy and somewhat sweet, with a large seed in the center.

I got another bunch of them a week or so ago. They got lost on my kitchen table. Today, they have emerged from behind a forgotten plastic bag. They have turned a deeper brown and gotten wrinkled. Some are further along than others. None are moldy.

I try one that looks roughly like it looked when it was new. It's quite good, a bit softer and sweeter than before. I decide to risk one that is further along. It's now mahogany brown with deep creases.

I pop it in my mouth and gently bite down, wary of the pit. I am amazed. The inside has turned into a soft paste, with a texture rather like apple butter. The flavor is smoother, with a deeper sweetness that lingers on my tongue even after I have swallowed the fruit. This is the missing link, the stage between the fruit that I get fresh here and that which I had known in the States.

Dates apparently don't grow on their trees as sticky, tooth-challenging masses that look like vegan water bugs. They go through stages, and end up in that form, in which they are easily packaged and shipped and are found in stores.

I try another of the darker ones. It's equally good. I'm tempted to eat the whole set of them. Most haven't reached their finest form yet. I can wait.

Monday, September 14th, 2020

I can't turn off the water to my shower. There's one simple faucet. The water runs from it into a heater near the ceiling, then out again.

I had known that the faucet would fail sometime, but didn't know when. While the water turns on easily, part of the faucet has been coming loose. It's been getting harder to push in on it clockwise so that it moves whatever doohickey inside actually controls the water flow. Now it does nothing. I put all of my weight into it. It doesn't help.

I think about telling my landlady. In the year and a half that I've been here, I've never complained to her about anything. I don't want to break that streak, but I can't let it run all day.

I put on some clothes and pick up the phone to text her. I pause and put the phone down. As far as I know, she hasn't been in here since I've moved in. It's a mess. I do a quick clean up in the kitchen, sweeping up the dead bugs in the corners and wiping down the counters. A tiny lizard darts past my broom as I sweep. I let it run free.

I type the text to her into my phone's translator. I have to do one fix: by default, it chooses masculine forms for the words addressing her. I send the text, along with a photo of the faucet.

My phone rings almost immediately. It's her. I go to my kitchen door and open it to get a better phone signal. She's sitting at the top of her steps, which zigzag up from mine. No need for the phone, then.

I describe to her what's happening. I demonstrate the connection within the faucet with hand gestures, trying not to make them look obscene. She understands. She turns off the water leading to the apartment. Her husband will be home in half an hour. He'll fix it. I can go off to work if I'd like. I do.

I get a text from her a couple of hours later. The faucet is repaired. I thank her. When I get home, I see a pair of gleaming new faucets in the shower. The one that I use works beautifully. I've never figured out what the other one is for. Someday, I'll have to ask.

Tuesday, September 15th, 2020

I wake up in the morning, looking forward to easily taking a shower. I'm excited that the faucet worked last night. The water goes on again well. When I try to turn it off, though, it fails, in the same way as it had yesterday morning.

I step out, frustrated. I put some clothes on, then send another text to the landlady. After a few minutes, she hasn't answered. I have to go to work. I text her again to tell her that I'm heading out, but that I'll leave the door unlocked.

I leave. About three blocks from my house, I see someone pass me wearing a mask. I realize that I've forgotten mine. I head back again.

Right when I get in, she calls. She seems to be in traffic. She wants to know if I'm home. I am. She is talking quickly, in a mix of English and Hebrew. I can barely follow her. She tells me to go turn off a faucet outside. I don't understand where it is.

She repeats herself a few times. I gradually figure out the words that I couldn't make out: garbage can, parking spot, water meter.

Her voice guides me to a hidden gate in the outside wall, between the main gate and where we stow the trash can. There's a spigot inside. I also note that there's a cable connection in there that doesn't look all that solid. I turn the spigot all the way off.

I head back to my apartment. The water is still running. I may still be misunderstanding something. Neither she nor I can figure out what. She has to get off the phone. I go to work.

A couple of hours later, she sends me a text: "The faucet is fixed." I thank her.

When I get home, I turn it gingerly. A bit later, I think of testing it and taking a real shower. If it fails again, though, I would have to wake them. They are early risers, getting up at about 5 AM, and I don't know when they go to sleep. I'll see how it goes in the morning.

Wednesday, September 16th, 2020

Lou Reed speak-sings "Walk on the Wild Side" as I wait for my mushroom burger. The music inside the shop was so loud that I had trouble ordering. Outside, it is almost drowned out by the sound of the giant fan blowing onto the patio.

The unintended remix brings out details in the music. The percussion is more varied than I had thought. I don't recall having noticed the way that the women's voices appear for the first time: rather than a fade-in, it sounds like they are walking up to the mic.

The song segues into "Free Fallin'." Most of it is a blur, but Tom Petty's voice rings out when he hops the octave for the chorus.

After that, I'm not sure that anything is playing at all until I hear unmistakable whistling. Even separated from its context, I know that it's "(Sittin' On) The Dock of the Bay."

I'm not sure whether to bus my own tray or leave it when I'm finished. When I let go of things, they start to blow toward the street. I catch them and bring them to the trash bin myself. As I shovel them in, the burger wrapper comes loose, flies into the air, and smacks the guy at the next table in the face. I apologize. Both he and the woman with him laugh.

I return to my table, pick up my bag of groceries, and continue on home.

Thursday, September 17th, 2020

The whiteboard at the ice cream shop shows unexpected combinations: "Figues & Roses," "Peach with Amber" (though I may have read the last word wrong), "Oasis Bananas & Dates." The card for their strawberry sherbet suggests "Try it with pepper on top!"

I'm here for the cinnamon affogato. It's as good as it was when I had it before, two days short of a year ago.

I've taken the day off from work to get some things done before the lockdown. Most of the shopping has been for naught, but it's good to relax.

This cobblestone street has changed since then. More shops are empty. More buildings are being renovated. Fewer tourists go by, though I still hear conversations in English.

Four scooters roar past together, each with a cooler from a different delivery service. Two tiny girls in tights and tutus try to pilot a foot-powered scooter together. They fall off, but they don't fall hard. They get right back on. A large man in a black hat and white beard ambles up behind a party at the coffee shop two doors down and blows a shofar. The people look neither inspired nor amused.

Five young people emerge from behind an ornately carved door across the street. Were it anywhere else, I would assume that the building was a synagogue. A large Star of David is centered at the top of the carving. One panel near the bottom appears to have been kicked out. One of the women is saying to one of the men, in English: "You know her. She's my roommate. You've been in her bedroom."

My phone buzzes with a text from work. They're having a ritual "raising of the glass" in the afternoon, ahead of the New Year. For those of us who aren't in the office, there's a Google Meet link. I think of connecting to it, but forget until afterward.

When I've finished the affogato, I put the paper cup in a metal trash bucket on the table. I put on my mask, and walk around some more, taking photos. Later on, I'll want to double-check my memory.

Friday, September 18th, 2020

The bakery where I get my challah seems radically different, but when I look closely, I see that little has changed. They have finished moving the registers to the front and updated the technology. Customers can swipe their own cards and sign on a screen on a device facing out toward us. I had only seen those before in cafés in the States.

The area in the back, behind where it had been, now holds more dark-wood shelves. The counter is the same shade. The flow of customers is smoother. There still isn't a clear queue, but there's less crowding.

I come up to them with a prewrapped challah from the shelves. "Do you know that that has raisins?" I didn't. I do now, since I now also know the word for raisins. It's just right.

The workers at the registers keep running out of the right change, The technology develops glitches. They shift back and forth between the machines, still able to keep the transactions straight in ways that baffle me.

Outside, the street is swarming with shoppers. The lockdown starts in a few hours, and the New Year starts in the evening, so people are grabbing last minute items. The shinier new bakery around the corner has two large signs: "During lockdown, we will be open as usual." I suppose that they will close off the seating area.

I get lunch at my favorite shawarma joint. The owner and I wish each other a good year. The street corner violinist sits a few meters from where he usually stands. Rather than the usual pop and classical tunes, he is playing languid melodies against a recorded drone. The sliding and wavering pitches and continual double-stops sound more like carnatic music than his usual, very Western playing.

At the phone store across the street, I pick up some video equipment that I'd been wanting. It's inexpensive consumer tech, but it puts together pieces that I've been wanting more affordably than I'd seen them separately. Once home, I work on launching my newsletter, now that I've hit my self-imposed deadline.

I doze off for some of the afternoon, then hunker down for several quiet days of holiday isolation.

Saturday, September 19th, 2020

I only get around to watching Rosh Hashanah services online at about 3 PM. Before that, I watch and read tributes to RBG.

I follow links to the services and flip listlessly among those that I find. Some are dull and droning. Some are too jokey. Some are directed at people who know little about the holidays. Some are stealth recruitment efforts from yarmulke-clad preachers who pretend, for the moment, to be Jewish.

One pair of livestreams kicks in at 5 PM my time. I watch one for a while. It seems to consist of vaguely-related musical performances and stories. I flip to the other, which follows the form, at least, of the liturgy. After the first hour, my attention wavers. I keep the audio playing, but look at other things online. Most of those, too, are about RBG.

I stumble across information on how to get local shows on my TV. I set it up. When the service is done, I heat up pretty much the same dinner that I had last night: roast chicken, frozen Brussels sprouts, and a sweet potato.

My favorite of the neighborhood cats sits outside my window and meows as I eat. Maybe she wants some chicken. I don't open the door for her. I don't know if it's good for the feral cats to come indoors, and I'm not allowed pets.

I don't go outside at all. With the holiday and the lockdown, there's nowhere to go. I don't see anyone all day, though I hear my landlord and landlady walking around upstairs. I sit back down at my TV after I eat. Maybe there will be something fun to watch.

Sunday, September 20th, 2020

I approach today thinking that it's my 63rd birthday. Then I do the math. It's 2020. I was born in 1958. I'm only turning 62. I've been wrong about this for months. It's disorienting. But I do feel younger.

I've never been good at remembering information without double-checking. That's one reason I'm more comfortable with people online than in person. Online, I can fact-check myself.

On Friday, at the phone store, I signed a receipt for some equipment. I had to put down my local phone number. I forgot it. Fortunately, I soon remembered a mnemonic, decoded it, and wrote it down.

The salesman was not amused. He pointed out the window at the people on the square in wheelchairs and, as he put it, "their *filipinim*." He suggested that I might need one soon. It was my turn not to be amused.

Yesterday, I had to fill in my American phone number on a web form. Even with a similar mnemonic, that took several tries.

Today, like yesterday, I am at home, alone. I wake up early after a bad night's sleep with too much dreaming. I get breakfast, get online, and get the first stream of birthday wishes. I fall asleep again and wake up at 2 PM. I get lunch, get online again, and get further wishes. My music library finishes indexing itself after churning for five days. I wrestle with the server. It eventually works well enough. I haven't seen anyone else in person in two days. I haven't spoken to anyone today.

Headlines tell me that the lockdown may become tighter in the morning. At least the government thinks my job is essential. Tomorrow I will go to work.

Monday, September 21st, 2020

The office hallway smells, pleasantly, like burnt toast. I don't know why. We are standing out here, waiting for ten of us to come together so we can start the afternoon prayers. Between the lockdown and the holidays, we think that we might not make it, but most of the regular people appear.

Today's prayer leader starts as usual. Soon, people are calling out corrections. The boss puts his hand on the prayer leader's shoulder and announces "Gentlemen, we are in the Days of Atonement. There will be some differences in the prayers."

We continue. I get lost a few times. For convenience, I use a very small, easily held prayer book. It shows the texts that we should substitute this week, but it doesn't show clearly what we should omit when we say them.

Today is also a minor fast day. I think we should be adding even more texts, but people appear to be skipping them. At least, I think that's what's happening. Most of this is within the silent prayer, but people often mumble sections of them audibly, especially when they aren't what we usually say.

The boss steps forward to stand next to the prayer leader. He leads the *"Avinu Malkeinu"* himself. Most of it is spoken, but the last line is sung.

I'm surprised to hear my own voice ringing out above the others. I know the text well, and it's a familiar melody – the one recorded by Phish and Mogwai, rather the one that Streisand has sung.

The service runs slightly longer than usual, with another psalm and another recitation of the Mourner's Kaddish at the end. I go back to my desk, still humming the melody. I look forward to singing it again.

Tuesday, September 22nd, 2020

The cashier at the supermarket insists on spraying alcohol gel on my hands after I check out. "You must always be clean. Your hands must always be clean. You should also clean that apple before you eat it. But not with alcohol gel."

The café on the other side of the building entrance should only be doing deliveries. It's open for takeout. The tables on its patio are gone. The built-in benches remain. Customers relax on them, drinking coffee from to-go cups.

Downtown is less deserted than I expect. The groceries and produce shops are open. The usual cluster of wheelchairs and caregivers is in its place near the street. Doors are open at a lawyer's office and a butcher shop. I thought they had shut down. The lotto booth has a vague line of customers. It might be a protected business. The burger joint's inside lights are on. Its patio is dark. The end of the square smells like fresh, warm hummus, but the shop is closed. Maybe they, too, were open for deliveries.

Dogs and people walk by. Cats dart in and out of the bushes, keeping their distance.

Much of the square looks as it might if I were walking through at midnight. No one is protesting the lockdown. The people that I see mostly look tired. Everyone is ready for all this to be done. But we'll still be wandering, hidden behind masks, for several more months, maybe for years.

Wednesday, September 23rd, 2020

The boss calls us into his office, one or two at a time. I come in alone so he can speak to me in English.

One of our programmers has tested positive for the virus. He had had a fever over the holiday and was tested immediately. He is in isolation.

According to the Ministry of Health, any of us who had spent longer than fifteen minutes closer than two meters away from him in the past week or so also needs to go into isolation. None of us had. His cube is about four meters from mine. He's quite friendly, but I only speak to him if we're working together on a project or if we pass each other in the kitchen hallway.

He's a regular at the afternoon prayers. He often leads them. He's the cantor of his congregation and has the best male voice in the office. But otherwise, he's quiet and focuses on his work.

Later, the boss comes around with a tape measure and a thermometer. He makes sure that we have a sense of how far two meters is.

He points the thermometer at us and takes our temperatures. We're all OK. Another programmer tries it on himself. He gets varied enough readings that he suggests that the thermometer might really be a random number generator.

The boss leaves it on the receptionist's desk, next to the pens and prayer books. We're supposed to log our temperatures when we sign in. No one has used the more conventional thermometer that has been there. Maybe people will actually give this one a try.

Thursday, September 24th, 2020

The shopkeeper where I pick up my packages whistles and waves at me. It takes me a moment to notice, since I'm listening to a podcast on my headphones. I cross the street to him.

"Why haven't you picked up your package? It's been waiting for two weeks." I hadn't been notified.

"Yes, you have. You received the SMS. Package 1077."

We head to the back of the shop. He pulls it off the shelf and scans it. Nothing happens. He scans it again. He slumps into his chair and runs the scanner very slowly over the sticker. Nothing. That explains why I wasn't notified.

He types in the code. It takes him a few tries. Humans shouldn't have to type arbitrary letters and numbers. Finally, he gets it right.

"ID Code!" I recite the number, then sign the screen with a finger. He shoves the package at me. I thank him. He grunts.

Down the road, a man wearing tallit and tefillin sits, his legs straddling a low wall, as he says his morning prayers.

When I get to work, the woman who fears elevators is standing in the lobby, waiting frantically for someone to help her.

"Sir, are you taking the elevator up?" I am.

"To what floor?" The fourth.

"I am only going to the second." That's OK. We can stop there.

"Thank you, sir!"

The elevator arrives. Another woman is already on it. Normally, I would wait for the next one, since no more than two people should be on an elevator. The woman who is already there waves us aboard. She is going to the fifth floor. I press the buttons for the second and fourth.

When we reach the second floor, I hold the door open for the fearful woman. She blesses us, singularly and together, in the masculine, feminine, and plural forms: "Be well. Be well. Be well."

Friday, September 25th, 2020

The pharmacy is mobbed. A crowd stands behind the line, brandishing the numbers they got from the machine when they came in.

An increased lockdown starts later today. The shop will remain open, but people don't want to count on it. That's not surprising. The rules seem to change every few minutes, as the government's Coronavirus Committee, the Ministry of Health, the Economics czars, and the full Knesset give conflicting signals.

There are four pharmacists on duty, but people want them to move more quickly.

A mechanized voice calls customer 132 to window number 4. Within seconds, a man near the front of the crowd yells, "132? 132 isn't here. 133? 134? Come on, it's Friday! It's Friday!"

A voice on the overhead system finally announces, "Sir, it is Friday for everyone. There is a line. Thank you."

After a while, number 148 is called. He yells "148? 148 is not here. I am 149. I need –"

A much older woman comes up behind him and gently whacks him in the ankle with her cane. She shows him her number. 148. He grumbles, backs off, and hovers near the pharmacists' windows, as if he is one of those people in American football who has to be ready to dart in any direction based on what the other team might do.

149 is called. He jumps to the next window. "One moment," the pharmacist says. He shuffles some papers, consults with a colleague, opens and shuts the register drawer, then slowly turns to the customer. "Yes, sir, how may I assist you?"

I am number 152. When I'm summoned to the window, I hand the pharmacist my number, my health provider ID card, my debit card, and the empty box of the prescription that I need refilled. He scans them as another worker reaches around him and plonks boxes of what I need onto the counter. I take them and start to wish him a good holiday. He is already shouting for the next customer. So be it.

I make my way through the crowd. I have more groceries to get and a newsletter to complete. I can breathe later.

Saturday, September 26th, 2020

Outside my basement window, my landlord is watering plants. Or maybe his son is. The sandals, olive-skinned legs, and khaki shorts could belong to either of them.

As I look up and out, I see a cluster of fresh dates that I had left on the window sill a week or so ago. I had hoped that they would ripen more quickly in the sun. They haven't.

I reach up and take them down. I'm surprised at what I see. While the dates in the direct sun hadn't ripened, the ones in their shadow had. Perhaps, rather than light, the dates need darkness. Some of the dates on my kitchen table had ripened, too, but I hadn't noticed if they'd been in more or less light than those that hadn't.

The ripe dates that haven't fallen off the branch on their own come off easily. The fruit is so soft that it leaves the seeds behind, still attached to the branch by the stem. The ones that I try are as sweet as those from a week ago. I leave the rest in a loose pile on the kitchen table.

I think of stepping outside to check how hot and humid it is out there. I know that it won't rain.

I hear someone sweeping my steps, removing the remnants of other fruit that has splattered down from the trees. I choose to remain invisible.

I won't get outside at all today. In the new lockdown, the Sabbath café is closed. I stay in and handle things at home. Tomorrow I should have half a day's work. I might see and speak to people then.

Sunday, September 27th, 2020

The boss sends a group text overnight. In the automated English translation, the genders of some nouns and people get scrambled. A reference to "coronavirus" becomes "coronary heart disease."

With some work, the meaning comes through. Another programmer on the team probably has the virus. His partner has been ill and has tested positive. The programmer has lost his sense of smell. He shares a cube with the other coworker who has the virus. They sit with their backs to each other, somewhat over a meter apart, but that may not have been enough. He's also friendly, but we don't talk much or work closely together. He sometimes comes to my cube for a moment to ask how to phrase something on an interface in English.

Only two other people are in the office when I come in today. It's a half-day, stuck between the Sabbath and a holiday, so few people show up. I could have taken a vacation day, since we have a lot of them. When I asked the boss last week, he answered in circles. I think I was supposed to pick up on something that was not being said, which was either that I should come in or that I shouldn't. I don't know what he meant.

I work for a few hours, then run into the supermarket downstairs just before it closes. In the cashier's line, I get stuck behind someone buying a lot of bottles of different kinds of beer. A voice overhead wishes for us all to be sealed in the book of life for the new year, and tells us to check out and go home.

As I walk away, the bus that I often ride passes me. Due to the new lockdown, I didn't think that it would be running today. Oh, well. It's not like I'm in a hurry to get home.

Monday, September 28th, 2020

The city sits silently.

It was full of bicycles last year and the year before. On this one day of the year, there are no cars, trucks, or motorcycles. People can walk down the center of the street if they want to. Most keep to the sidewalks. At intersections, even those walking on the asphalt obey the traffic lights. It's hot. Air conditioners drip on me as I walk in the shadows. They're a relief.

All the shops are closed, even the 24/7 market and the small sweets shop where men sit every other day of the year, drinking Turkish coffee and chatting in what sounds like Arabic.

The glass door of a bistro bar has been smashed in. It looks like an accident. The few people who walk past shake their heads and walk on. I don't think anything has been taken. The police or owners may do something after dark, when the holiday ends.

In the city square, a cadre of young girls rolls past me on scooters, wearing pink crash helmets. Other than them, I only see one or two children on each block.

I sit and try to write on my phone. I have to change locations every few minutes. The flies quickly find me and regroup.

At the bus stop at the center of town, moving text on an electric sign announces that buses will start running again at 9 PM. The fan inside the sign is shockingly loud. I'd never heard it before.

A poster hastily pasted on several storefronts shows a picture of the Prime Minister and two large words: "The lockdown is because of me." An asterisk beside the words leads to a smaller word at the bottom: "satire."

The doors to the Grand Synagogue are open. A few men pray inside, in the afternoon gap between services. More may gather toward dusk, indoors or outside. Or they may not. I've lost track of the rules. I'm not going to sit here much longer to find out. There are too many flies.

Tuesday, September 29th, 2020

We don't do the afternoon prayers today. We try to gather for them, but there are too few of us.

A third programmer now has the virus. He's already been off in isolation for a while. His cube is in the same row as the others, across the aisle from mine, but much farther away, behind a glass wall.

The boss is now allowing anyone who wants to work from home to do so, as long as they fill out timesheets. Several more workers are now staying home.

Those who are in the office gather for an informal meeting. Each of us sits or stands in a different cube. The boss tells us what is going on. I understand most of it. We have a meeting online later for everyone to say what they're doing. I understand almost none of it.

The usual guest appears at ten minutes to two and comes around to gather us for the afternoon prayers. Several of us wait at the receptionist's desk. People call the other usual guests. None are available. Of the needed ten men, we only have seven or eight. We disperse. The rhythm of my afternoon is thrown off.

Late in the day, I get a message from the post office that a package for me from Amazon has arrived in this country and will reach me soon. Moments later, I get a message from Amazon that the shipment has failed and that they will reimburse me for it. I don't know if it is or isn't on its way anymore. Both may continue to be true, at least until someone opens the box.

Wednesday, September 30th, 2020

One of the teams at work is having an online meeting. Most of the people are calling in from home. A few are here.

I hear two of the ones in the office twice: first, through the open air as they speak, then, about a half-second later, through their speakers as the sound is carried to others in the chat. One, when interrupting, repeats a word incessantly until he finds a way in. His rate of repetition is about the same as the speakers' delay. When he repeats himself, the word ping-pongs back and forth across the space for several seconds.

The office is about half-empty, with the same workers as yesterday. The usual guest tries to gather us for the afternoon prayers. Even with two additional visitors, the dentist from downstairs and a friend of his, we're still one short. We disperse.

On the way home, I see more cars than I did last night. I don't recall what level of traffic was normal before the lockdown.

On the city square, a worker drags a child's coin-operated ride, shaped like a Minion, away from the front of the café with the mystery sandwiches. He unlocks the gate in front of the toy store two doors down, rolls the ride inside, then locks the gate again and heads back to finish closing down the café.

A few blocks closer to home, I see a handwritten sign from a lemonade stand, taped to the gate of an apartment house: three shekels for one cup, five shekels for two, and ten shekels for five. It's hot enough that I would have been tempted, had I gotten there before dark.

October 2020

Thursday, October 1st, 2020

My cellphone rings while I'm at work. I don't know who it is. The same number called me six times on Tuesday while I was in the shower, as well as once yesterday.

I finally answer. It isn't spam. It's the delivery guy with the package from Amazon. He speaks in rapid Hebrew.

I struggle to respond. Words that I otherwise know disappear under pressure: gate, office, mailbox.

He finally says "Hey, don't panic, man, I can do English." That's a relief.

I talk him through where to leave the package. The house is a custom-built side-by-side duplex with two nearly identical gates. I ask him to drop the package behind the fence, below the mailbox. I know the contents aren't fragile.

"OK, by the green mailbox?" I have no idea if our mailbox is green. I have a terrible memory for colors. He leaves the package.

When I get home, it isn't there. I use the flashlight on my phone to see better in the dark. Nothing. And the mailbox isn't green. I decide not to worry for another day or so.

In the morning, when I head out to work, it's on the steps to my door. My guess is that the delivery guy dropped it at the other gate. The folks there probably saw it and brought it to my landlord (their brother-in-law) who put it there for me.

It all works out. Maybe when I get home I'll be awake enough to open it.

Friday, October 2nd, 2020

The line for the new bakery stretches down the block, past the entrance to the Heart of the City mall. Red stripes mark the pavement every two meters. People should be standing at them, not between them.

In practice, they stand about half as far apart. That's better than the clustering I see elsewhere.

A man with a cane sits on a bench nearby. Every few minutes, he walks up to another man in the line to ensure that he is keeping his spot. Everyone understands this. It's OK.

A woman walks up to the guard. He knows her. She isn't trying to barge in, but wants to know if the bakery has a particular item in stock.

The guard asks how many she wants and says that he'll check. He goes inside. She goes to the end of the line. He returns and waves a plastic bag with baked goods in the air. He has found what she wants and is holding them for her.

A car with a gaudily-decorated trailer moves slowly down the street, blasting music for the holiday that starts tonight. A little boy in line dances to the sound.

The usual chabadniks aren't at the mall entrance. They gather there on Fridays to try to convince men to put on tefillin and to show them how. Getting that close to strangers isn't possible during the lockdown.

I finally get to the front of the line. A mic stand next to the guard holds a scanning thermometer. Each customer has to wave a hand in front of it. I do. I pass. I enter. I already have a challah from the bakery around the corner. I get large and small pitas and a loaf of sandwich bread here, as well as a coffee granita to go.

I sit in the city square on a bench away from other people, take down my mask, and drink the granita slowly. I don't want to get a brain freeze.

Several meters from me, a shabbily dressed man bangs away at a single chord on an acoustic guitar and shouts words that I can't understand. After a while, he pauses, takes a recorder from his pocket and plays a beautiful, complicated melody, full of unexpected turns and melismas. When he reaches the end, he jams the recorder into a different pocket and goes back to banging the guitar and shouting.

The city billboard near us has a new sign. Tonight's holiday usually features people going around to visit one another. The sign acknowledges that, using the classic terminology, but says we're not to do it this year. To fight the virus, to preserve the rules, to preserve life, this year we will just stay home.

Saturday, October 3rd, 2020

A young mother runs in exaggerated slow motion across the grassy plot where women do Tai Chi. A toddler tries to follow her.

Few other people are outside here. I've waited until late afternoon to head out of my apartment. It isn't too hot. I'm OK in my long-sleeved t-shirt.

I head down to the city square to see if my Chromebook can find open Wi-Fi. My connection is OK at home at the moment, but I like to have options. I only see a few people between my house and the square, mostly accompanying dogs. I hear a few families along the way, hidden behind high stone walls.

The square itself is busier. Parents sit and watch their children roam around on bicycles. Older people sit at small stone tables and talk. Three white-haired men around a backgammon board share a thermos, espresso mugs, and a can of Raid.

My phone app claims to find several open Wi-Fi signals here. My Chromebook sees none of them. Apparently, the local cafés shut their signals down when they're closed.

A woman walks past with a large Israeli flag. I don't know why. It's a national holiday, but between the Sabbath and the lockdown, there's no sign of it. Two more people walk by with handmade placards that I can't read. A man carries another flag past me, a blank field of black or dark blue. I follow them. At the front of the square, where the caregivers have their dance parties, a dozen masked people, properly distanced, stand quietly along the curb with flags and signs. Cars honk their horns rhythmically as they pass. The only sign that I can read says "There is a Future." That's the name of a political party. I can't recall which one.

Night falls. The crowd thins. Buses start to roll by. I still have a lot to do before work tomorrow. I wander home.

Sunday, October 4th, 2020

The café at the entrance to our office building has roped off the benches on its patio. People, despite the lockdown, sat and ate there last week. Not anymore.

The café's only supposed to be doing deliveries, but the doors are still open for takeout. No one's staying there to eat. Whoever decides these things must have figured that this compromise works.

In the building's atrium, there's now a sukkah, the thatch-roofed hut used in this week's holiday. People are bringing food down and eating in it. That's apparently OK. It's a small space. The top, at least, is open to the air. And everyone who enters the building must wear a mask, so there's at least some sense that those who go through to the atrium will follow the rules.

I only see two sukkot on the way to work today, one in a yard and one on a balcony. In other years, I've seen far more. We still only have about half the usual workforce in the office. No one even tries to gather a group for the afternoon prayers. I go to the front, open the office doors, and straighten the prayer books, but no one else comes by, either from within the office or outside.

After work, I stop into the supermarket. Some fall fruits are in, right on schedule. But the clementines and pomelos are still green, and the persimmons are small and hard. It's too early to buy them. I get shelled almonds and several kinds of cheese.

When I emerge, I see that the next bus isn't for half an hour. I walk home.

Monday, October 5th, 2020

My family can't get at some things downtown. The House of a Hundred Grandmothers is back under an even stricter lockdown than the rest of the country. They ask me to run some errands for them.

I leave work early. Other people leave early, too, a little before me, so I'm not all that inspired to stick around. The buses stop running now at around 8 PM. I want to be sure to catch those that I need.

The bus from work to downtown winds past the college, as usual, before I get off at the Heart of the City. I run my errands, then hop another bus at the same stop. It's the line that used to run past my house. I'm told that it will do so again, if they ever finish fixing the road. At least I'm not surprised now when it takes the long way around.

I get off at a large intersection about three blocks from where I'm going. I call my family to say that I'm almost there. I think of cutting across a lot on the way, but it's dark. There's no danger from people, but I might trip over something.

The street that I walk down is quiet. Its sidewalk took so long to be renovated last year that, long afterward, I instinctively duck around where the barriers had been.

In the small park just outside the House, a tall woman in black workout clothes jumps rope. I cross the street. By the time that I get to where she was, she is gone.

Pairs of people sit on benches in the park and talk. Streetlights in the distance outline them as silhouettes. Just outside the House, two women in wheelchairs laugh and talk loudly in what might be Romanian.

I stand on the sidewalk near the lobby. Inside, the guard at the desk appears not to see me. An exhausted woman rolls a large basket on wheels up to him. She reaches in, puts a meal in a clear plastic box on his desk, then heads down the hall.

A relative appears on the other side of the window. I hand him what I've picked up for them. He hands me a bag with a book that they had set aside for me. We talk briefly. Neither of us has much going on.

He returns to their apartment. I put my headphones back on, start up a podcast, and walk across the dimly lit park toward my house.

Tuesday, October 6th, 2020

The streetlight on the walkway past the kindergartens is out. On my way to work, that's OK. When I walk home, it's a problem.

The path has two sets of stairs, one with about six steps, one with something like four. The flat part of the walk is safe. It gets enough light from nearby apartments and the moon. The steps, in the dark, spawn illusions. Both sets of steps lead downward on my path toward home. Each uses two different kinds of paving. They look about the same as the shadows and the pale moonlight.

I move carefully as I approach the first set. I tend to anticipate the stairs too early. I step forward, expecting my foot to meet the ground a few inches lower than it does. I'm wrong. My foot hits the paving stone too soon. If I didn't prepare myself for this possibility, I would stumble. I'm ready. I know that I might make this mistake.

When I do reach the first step, my foot finally landing lower than it had, I reach out to my left. There's a metal banister, invisible in the darkness, about as high as my elbow. I find it and hold on. I step down again, then further down. I never remember the exact number of steps.

I make a matching mistake at the bottom. My foot hits the paving stone where I expect a few inches more of air. I wobble slightly, then straighten up.

I head for the second staircase, a few meters ahead. The banister on this one is too low for me to reach while walking. The canopy of trees is thinner here. A little more light splatters onto the stones. I can just about make out the edges of the steps. I walk as carefully as I did before.

As often as not, I also guess the start of the steps wrong here. I stumble, but I know how to recover. Without a banister, I have to rely on memory and what inner balance I retain. I feel as if I'm on a tightrope at the circus, performing for the cats and birds.

Another step, then three or four or five more, and I'm back on solid ground. I stand tall and walk more confidently. Here, of course, where there is no more danger, the streetlights are working just fine.

Wednesday, October 7th, 2020

The boss emerges from his office. He bellows, "We have ten. Let's go!" Most of the men in the office come out of their cubes and head down to the hallway for the afternoon prayers.

We have a couple of more people now. One of the programmers with the virus has officially recovered and returned. The boss's son, who had been away for a couple of weeks, is back.

We meet in the hallway. Before starting, we count again. Only nine of us are there. One worker, who has filled in before, has decided not to today. That's OK. There's no pressure. People get on their phones and try to reach the usual guests elsewhere in the building. The insurance agent, the building manager, and the dentist all are away. A few other people have shown up on occasion, but we don't know who they are.

We stand around for a while. One of us circles through the office to be sure that we haven't missed anyone. We haven't.

Someone remembers that, a couple of weeks ago, a guy with a yarmulke came through. He told us that he worked in a new office down the hall. The worker standing nearest to that office heads over to ask. It works. He emerges with the new person. The boss makes sure to get his name and phone number. He switches his phone to the liturgy app and faces forward.

The prayers begin.

Thursday, October 8th, 2020

The man in front of me at the supermarket has a Whole Foods bag. It's been a while since I've seen one. I think of commenting on it, but he's wearing one of those deadened stares that says "I'm on an important secret mission and if I notice anyone other than myself, the fate of life itself could be at risk." OK, then.

The supermarket is crowded. It usually is, on Thursdays. People shop to prepare for the weekend.

I would have skipped it tonight, but I needed to get chicken. There are other butcher shops closer to me, but I'm more comfortable here.

The fall fruit still isn't quite ready. I hold off on it. I get more peanut butter.

While waiting in line, I check the bus schedule on my phone. The next one isn't for half an hour. I could walk home faster than that, but I'm tired. I appreciate the chance to sit quietly for a while and not have to do anything. We're in the midst of yet another heat wave, but the sun has set, and the air has cooled.

As I wait at the bus stop, a stream of joggers flows past me. So does an array of dogs, mostly with people. One, off leash, wanders over and sniffs my hands. He gets the information that he needs. He wanders on.

I think of counting the dogs that go past. I don't. Just sitting here and watching is enough.

Friday, October 9th, 2020

The tiny pharmacy inside the Heart of the City is quiet and fast. There's no need to take numbers.

The lockdown only allows five customers inside at a time. A short line of people waits outside, where the doorway opens into the center of the mall. Many wear the black and white garb of the ultra-Orthodox. Others stand in flip-flops and jeans cut off so short that their pockets dangle beneath the edge of the denim.

I only need to wait behind one other person. When I reach the counter, I hand my health plan ID and the empty box of what I need refilled to the pharmacist. He opens a drawer and pulls out another box. It costs fifteen shekels, less than five dollars. I pay, drop the box and receipt into my shopping bag, and leave.

I get my challah at the usual bakery. Watching the workers, I figure out some of their rhythms. The two of them use a single register. One worker handles cash transactions. The other handles credit. The cash and cards move between them so quickly that, in other situations, I might expect a scam.

At the produce shop, I look for leafy greens. I'm pleased to find kale. At the counter, the workers stand behind a sheet of clear plastic. That's new. I get the kale and, on a whim, some sliced pineapple and a package of dates with walnuts inside. I know that if I bring snacks home, I eat them too quickly. These, I can justify without too much guilt.

Across the street, the café with the mystery sandwiches is open, though without seating. I see that they have homemade burekas for sale. The worker meets me at the doorway. I order a cheese burekas (the singular and plural are the same) and a large iced coffee.

I step inside as he prepares it. I pay at the counter. "You have to stand outside now. I have to hand this to you there. It is now the law. Your coffee is on the counter. Don't forget it."

I take the coffee and step outside. He comes around and reaches over a display. The burekas is on a plate, with a chopped egg and separately packaged sauces, neatly tied up in a red plastic bag. I will eat it when I get home.

I am hot and thirsty and need the iced coffee right away. I sit on a low wall and take off my mask. I breathe in what I recognize as a thick cloud of pot smoke, though I don't see anyone smoking nearby. That's OK. In its presence, even the flies are calm.

Saturday, October 10th, 2020

I head out for an afternoon walk at 6 PM. It's later than I intended. It's getting dark. I planned to do too many things today. Each has taken too long. I still haven't gotten to some of them.

Outside, the streets are quiet. It's the last day of the holidays, but it's hard to tell. Outside the country, today's a solemn holiday followed by a joyous one tomorrow. Here they happen on the same day. It's also the Sabbath, but that doesn't complicate things much.

Today's morning prayers would normally take much longer than usual. As part of the joyous holiday, congregations dance outside, carrying Torah scrolls from synagogue to synagogue. Not today. With the lockdown, few synagogues are having services. No one can go between places that are more than a kilometer apart.

At dusk, the city square is busy. No shops are open, but families swarm about. I sit silently on a stone wall, observing.

Many of the people go past me on wheels: baby carriages, strollers, tricycles, scooters, bicycles, skateboards, walkers, and wheelchairs. The caregivers and the elderly gather at the front of the square. The dance party hasn't started yet.

I expect to see the usual Saturday evening protest. One woman stands by the curb. She may be waiting for others. Another younger woman walks past with a flag, but she doesn't stop.

When night has fallen, I get up and head back. The Sabbath café is dark. In theory, they're doing deliveries, but the chain may be handling them from a central kitchen.

As I turn the corner onto the pedestrian street, a family passes me with flags, balloons, and protest signs. Democracy proceeds as usual. I could join in, but I have cooking to do.

Sunday, October 11th, 2020

The lampposts on the way to work are out of sequence. I pass three of them. I notice, for the first time, that the numbers stenciled on them are 2472, 2473, and then 2471. That bothers me more than it should.

The one a little past them is 18172. It and the rest appear to be numbered arbitrarily. That's OK. But these three look like they had been planned and set down as a group. I would think that they would be sequential.

I wonder about it for a while, but there's nothing I can do. I go back to my usual pastime of sorting the digits on the license plates of the cars that I see so that, in my head at least, the numbers are more symmetrical.

I usually walk up this side of the street on the way to work and down the other side on the way home. This evening, I walk down the morning side, so I can double-check the number on that last lamppost. I make a note of it and continue walking.

Despite all the streetlights, this side of the street is darker than the one on which I usually walk at night. The sidewalks are narrower here. I avoid several collisions with people going the other way. I have to silently negotiate who is to step aside and who is to keep going when I encounter other people who, like me, are wider than most.

The streetlamp on the walkway past the kindergartens is still out. When I think that I have reached the first set of steps, I remember to pull out my phone and light the way. I see that the staircase isn't for another few meters. Where I had paused, the stones dip a little, but not as much as at the stairs.

I walk both sets of steps easily, then go on to where the streetlamps work again. I juggle my groceries and the phone to get it back into my pocket, then continue on.

Monday, October 12th, 2020

The line of people waiting for takeout at the city's most popular shawarma joint is gone. It had formed there every weekday evening throughout the lockdown. Tonight, the doors are closed almost all the way.

A worker sits at a makeshift booth several meters to the right. A sign on the booth reads, "Orders for delivery people only." A cluster of scooters and electric bikes surrounds it. Another worker shuttles back and forth between the shop and the booth, darting inside the half-open door and retrieving the orders.

The large bakery is open, as usual, but without seating. I go inside and get what I think is a cheese sandwich and a bottle of soda. I take it to the city square.

The last few caregivers and elders are dispersing for the evening. At the toy store, someone is yelling at someone else in English to shut the lights off and leave, already.

I sit down at a stone table with a built-in chess board. I bite into the sandwich. It isn't what I expected. I remember that the word that I had thought was "cheese" actually means "omelette." It's good. A whole wheat bun and the usual vegetables surround a flat layer of chilled scrambled eggs, with a sauce that I can't identify.

As I eat, I see a woman quietly going around to the trash cans and digging out plastic bottles. People can return them to stores for about a dime apiece. She's halfway across the square when I finish my supper. A coterie of cats surrounds her. She bends down and places some sort of food on the ground for them. I leave my soda bottle next to a trash can, in her line of sight.

I walk over to a small grocery store to get a frozen candy bar. The owner sees me, nods, and taps the side of his face. I have forgotten to put my mask back on. I do. I buy the dessert and sit down on a stone wall to eat it. It's a cool night. There aren't any flies.

The grocer is talkative tonight. He's eating a sandwich as I come in. He calls out from the back of the shop, still chewing. "Hello! Peace and blessings! Welcome!"

I consider getting some of the small green apples from the tables outside the store. I don't. Those that are left don't look good. There aren't any apples left inside. I get plums instead. I look for peppers. There aren't any on the shelves. I see them in the refrigerated case. I get a few and try to shut the case's door. It doesn't close completely. I try again. "Don't worry. You have to do it exactly right. And it doesn't really matter."

He keeps talking as I come toward the front. I understand little of what he says. He talks with his hands. It helps. I try to open a plastic bag for grapes. I can't get the right grip on it. I'm wearing a mask, so I slide my finger along my forehead, hoping to pick up some sweat. There isn't much there.

The grocer steps behind the counter. He hands me an open bag. "I know how hard those are to open. I cheat. You see this glass of water here? I'm not drinking it. It's for the fingers and the bags."

I get a small package of blueberries and put everything on the counter. He combines most of what I've gotten into a single bag. He puts the grapes in another, even though they're already in one. "You need another bag for the grapes. They would spill from a bag this small."

He rings me up. The register calculates the bill from the weight of the items. He rounds it down to an even number. "Here you go. Thank you. We'll see each other again. Peace and the best of health." I head out. He goes back to his sandwich.

In bright light, this shirt is army green. In shadows, it looks like it's navy blue. If I were to jump up high, it might turn some other shade. I don't know for sure. I'm not good at jumping. And I don't know what color represents the air force.

My current set of masks is purple. I was planning to stick with the usual pale sky blue, but the supermarket downstairs from work is out of them. I got what they had. It's a good shade of purple, lighter than grapes but brighter than lavender. In a world of uniform blue masks, they stand out a little, but not too much. The only other people I've seen wearing them are the supermarket workers. Since I don't wear a yellow vest, no one has mistaken me yet for one of them.

I see fewer distinctive masks now than I did when people started wearing them. Maybe they've stopped thinking of them as fashion statements. The newest person at work wears a lovely floral mask. The purple streak in her blonde hair almost matches my mask, though she's so tall that I only noticed it when I was standing, and she was sitting down.

Most of the masks that I see at the supermarket today are either the usual surgical blue or black. Many of the black ones have a small Adidas logo in the lower left corner. Some children have fancier and more whimsical masks. A small boy in the cereal aisle has a mask that looks like Spider-Ham.

They seem to call most cereal here "kornfleks." I've never seen anyone eat them. A lot of people eat salads at breakfast. I don't think I would have the energy in the morning to prepare one. I miss the cafés' Israeli breakfasts. I look forward to having them again, if the lockdown ever ends.

I've gotten making breakfasts here down to a pattern. It does involve vegetables, but that's usually just a pepper, washed, torn apart, and munched as I sit at my computer. When I buy them, I try to get peppers of a uniform color, different from the last time. It helps me know which I should finish first. It works.

In the morning, I have just enough energy to grab a shirt from the stack and put it on. I find out what color I've chosen after the coffee kicks in.

Thursday, October 15th, 2020

The power goes out while I'm in the shower. It's just a blip. The light and the water heater go off, then, almost immediately, back on.

When I emerge from the bathroom, I see that the digital clock is still correct. The room is too quiet, though. My computer is off. That isn't good. I have been doing a full backup of a very large hard drive. It was supposed to take a week. I was four days into it.

I sit down at the computer and boot it up again. It starts without a problem, as do all the apps that had been running, except for the backup. I start to set that up again.

I remember one thing that I had forgotten to do before starting the last one. I was going to move some files from a drive that doesn't regularly get backed up to the one that does. I set that process up. It will take three hours. OK.

Moments after it gets rolling, the power goes out again. This time it doesn't come back on. I have to get to work.

I pull my stuff together and head out. My landlady is at the top of the stairs. I tell her, in Hebrew, that there is no electricity. She answers in English. "Yes, the electric company is working." That tends to take all day. I leave everything as it is.

I see more people and hear more voices than usual. The weather is relatively cool. The temperature hasn't gone above 90 degrees Fahrenheit for a couple of days. People are walking their dogs and sitting in their yards. A city worker is sweeping up fallen purple petals from a jacaranda along the pedestrian street. More grapefruit and oranges have dropped from the trees.

A toddler struggles to walk past me, holding on to his stroller as he stumbles along. When he lets go, he falls in front of me. He looks up at his mother. He didn't expect that to happen. His mother lifts him off the ground, stands him up, and puts his hand on the bar of the stroller. They continue on. So do I.

I hear several air conditioners come back to life. A light in a yard comes on. I wonder how long that will last.

Friday, October 16th, 2020

I see a man with a black mask on my way to the nearest supermarket. I suddenly realize that I've forgotten mine. The supermarket is only a block away by then. I continue walking toward it.

When I get there, a guard scans my temperature. I apologize for not having a mask and ask if they have them. She holds up her hand in a crossing guard's "stop" gesture. "Wait here."

She walks to a bin a few meters away. The overhead speakers blast an announcement. "Attention. The lady with the blue mask in the wine aisle. Your mask must cover your nose. Yes, you. I know you heard me. Your mask must cover your nose."

The guard returns with a small package of masks. She opens it. I pull one mask out and put it on. She hands the package to me. "You will have to buy these, of course." Of course.

Online ads have suggested that the supermarket has been spruced up and renovated. I can't see any difference. It's still cramped and scruffy.

I manage to find what I need: white cheese, persimmons, frozen fruit, chicken thighs, Sabbath wine, and paper towels. The overhead system announces that credit card purchases should go to aisle 4. I do. I start to unload my shopping bag.

The cashier stops me and points to my left. "He's next." A man with a white beard and black coat is slowly going through the pomegranates, holding each one up to his right eye as if he were examining a diamond. This will take some time.

I move to the next aisle. When that cashier's done ringing me up, she tries to upsell me a half dozen items arrayed at the end of the counter. She's good at it, but I don't need any of the things that I can recognize.

I put my purchases back in my shopping bag and head out. At the door, I thank the guard. She grunts and continues to stare at her phone.

Saturday, October 17th, 2020

A rocking chair sits alone on the concrete slab where the neighborhood dumps its trash. It's pale gray and small, not one of the formidable dark wood chairs that might dominate a sitting room, but an unimposing object that people might place next to a crib. It still looks usable.

I go over to the slab and sit down. The chair doesn't collapse under me, which is a good sign. I fit into it well, although its back doesn't come up very far. The padding is comfortable. At one spot, the cloth has torn and pulled back, revealing foam rubber. I think I could fix that. I continue on my walk, wondering how I would use it.

Three kitchen chairs sit, abandoned, in the city square. Green cloth covers the seats and backs. At some spots it has turned white. Bent metal tubing forms their frames. They could do well there, at least until the rains come, but I can see how someone might want to replace them.

I head past the square to the ice cream shop on the main street. Its door is open, though blocked by the shop's own chairs. It should only be doing deliveries, but I see people standing nearby with cones.

I ask in Hebrew if it's possible to get a cup of ice cream, but I hear myself saying "ice cream" in English. The worker replies in English. "Yes, but I'm busy, so you will have to wait for five or six minutes." OK.

After a while, she returns to the door. I get a cup of gelato, flavored with hazelnut and cheesecake. It's in a to-go container, much larger than the usual cup. I take it back to the square.

Up near the main street, I think I see the usual caregivers and wheelchairs. Looking more closely, I see that I'm wrong. Teenagers have gathered with bicycles. Their wheels line up closely enough that they look like they are connected. Nearby, a tiny girl chases after pigeons. I have never seen a child that young run that fast.

On the way home, I pass a hybrid vehicle that I have never seen before. The back half of a bicycle, with a more comfortable seat, is connected to a stroller. The handlebars form the stroller's top bar. It works well.

Close to home, I sit on the rocking chair again. It's comfortable, though the arms are a bit low. I try to picture it in my apartment. I can't see where it would be useful. Someone else could probably use it. I leave it behind.

Sunday, October 18th, 2020

Workers swarm behind the counter at the burger joint. It's the first night of the lighter lockdown, so they can do takeout.

Over a dozen buns are arrayed on a countertop, with burgers in various states of completion. Most have lettuce and tomato, but they offer a lot of other elements. Many have hummus and tahini. Some get fried eggs, but only as the very last thing put on them before the bun is closed.

The boss is taking rapid fire orders on the phone at the register. My usual cashier, who is slicing buns, sees me come in. "Hi! How are you?" I'm doing OK. They're going crazy.

The boss looks over to me. "You want takeaway?" I do.

"We have a lot of orders. It might be maybe twenty-five minutes. Is that OK?"

I'm in no hurry. I order my usual mushroom burger, sweet potato fries, and diet soda.

"Give me your phone number. I call you when it is ready."

I pay and take the customer receipt. There's a bench outside the medical center across the walkway. I sit down, put my headphones back on, and continue listening to a symposium on radical Jewish poetry.

People and animals wander by. Many of the men carry bags from the burger joint and pizzas from the place next door. They drop the bags into containers on powered bikes and scooters and zoom off. Teenage girls in cut-off shorts walk in pairs, each staring at her phone. A dog, off leash, trots by. Every so often, it stops and waits for a man walking with a cane to get nearer, though he never catches up. Cats dash across the street. Many double back abruptly when traffic comes around the bend.

About half an hour later, I wander back to the burger joint and wait outside. After a few minutes, the boss sees me and calls my name.

"We're sorry. Your order is not yet ready. This has been the busiest night that we have seen. Can you wait another ten minutes? Can I give you something to drink, a soda or ice tea, for free while you wait?" Thanks.

I stand outside with a soda. Just as I finish it, he calls my name again and holds up a bag. "Here you are. Thank you very very much for your patience." No problem.

I take the bag and head home. Along the way, I pick up a foot rest from the trash heap. It's dusty, but otherwise it'll be perfect for in front of my TV.

Monday, October 19th, 2020

Our newest worker comes around the corner from the elevator. A crowd of us are standing in the hallway outside the office.

"Has something happened?" It's the afternoon prayers. We get together every day just before 2 PM.

"But we have a conference call at 2 PM!" It'll work out.

"Only for the men, right?" I nod. She heads into the office. Her back is to me, but I can feel her rolling her eyes.

A dozen of us gather more quickly than usual. All three of the programmers who had had the virus have returned. Several others who have been working from home are in today.

As we wait, one of the workers and one of the guests talk loudly in the back. The boss drowns them out by bellowing the first line of the opening psalm.

During the silent prayer, a little girl emerges from the restroom. She runs up the hall, barefoot, then sees us each standing still quietly or bobbing back and forth. She wanders up to several of us and stares, as if she were in a sculpture garden or a grove of murmuring trees. Few others notice her. Our eyes meet. I smile at her through my mask. She smiles back, then runs to the office next to ours.

The prayers end quickly. The guests head to the elevators. Most of the rest of us head back into the office for the 2 PM conference call.

Tuesday, October 20th, 2020

A man nearly collides with me on a narrow sidewalk. He's looking down – not at a phone, but at a small painting that he has picked up from a trash heap. He moves and tilts it to catch the light from streetlamps as he walks.

As I wait for a traffic light down the road, I look back to where he was. He is gone. The painting rests on a bench, facing out.

A few blocks further on, I get another omelette sandwich at the new bakery. They are priced at twenty shekels, but a worker, without prompting, sells it to me for ten. The bakery is about to close for the night, so I guess he figures that selling it to me cheap is better than throwing it out.

I flash back to when I would travel from Delaware to Philadelphia every other weekend, some twenty-five years ago. I would hang out in the bakery at the railroad station until the last train arrived. When they closed, they would give the remaining unsold goods away to whoever was around.

Across from the new bakery, the much smaller storefront where it had been has been gutted. Piles of trash lean against stripped drywall and punctuate the cement floor. I wonder what will go in there. I don't expect anything new to show up until after the lockdowns end.

I sit in the city square and eat the sandwich. The usual crowd of caregivers and elders gradually leaves.

A young man at the next table plays show tunes from the speaker on his phone. He finishes his falafel, attaches his phone to his bicycle, and heads off. The voice of Barbra Streisand echoes and fades as he rides away.

Wednesday, October 21st, 2020

Another day made of words: in the morning, a worker asks for a better word for "accompany," as in "Our staff will accompany you in installing the product." Assist? "Yes. Assist. That is the word. Assist."

In the afternoon, someone wants to know if the screen should say that a line can have "many" or "several" asterisks in it. Multiple? "OK."

Someone else asks if "subset" means "substitute." I hold my hands in the air, facing each other. Here's a set of things. I bring my right hand closer to my left. I chop the air, swipe imagined objects away with the back of my right hand, then move the hand back to where I had chopped. I move my hands, and the objects that would be between them, closer to him. These are a subset. "OK, got it."

At the end of the day, the boss and I talk about the American election. I tell him what I've heard about the odds of each candidate winning. He doesn't know the English word "odds." I tell him that it's the ratio of the probability of one outcome over another. He understands that.

We talk about gambling and the stock market. I tell him how I used to walk down an alley off Wall Street at lunchtime when I worked there, through a throng of men in suits, all getting stoned. He asks if they were just smoking marijuana. Well, that's all that I could smell there. That and aftershave.

He hollers for another worker to stop what he's doing and come to his office. He announces, officially, that he will now tell a joke. It's a long, intricate story about a Yiddish speaking parrot, with a punchline referring to probability. It's quite funny.

We laugh. "And now I know that I will remember the word 'odds.' "

Thursday, October 22nd, 2020

The butcher sits outside the supermarket with his thermos and cigarette. His break is between 4:30 and 5. I see him when I go downstairs for a yogurt and an apple. A couple of plastic containers rest beside him on the stone planter. A plastic bag from the supermarket is at his feet. I can't see what is in any of them.

A teenager with ostentatious headphones rolls past us on a scooter. He sings Springsteen's "I'm on Fire" off-key. He may have cranked the headphones so loud that he can't hear his own voice.

Inside the supermarket, I translate for the customer ahead of me. She only speaks English. Fortunately, I know the Hebrew phrases she needs. "Another bag, please?" And I can translate what the cashier is saying. "This is a half-shekel piece, not five shekels. Do you have another five shekels?" She does. She takes a while to get organized and head out after she's paid.

As the cashier rings me up, I shift to the head of the line, past the plastic barrier. The cashier scrubs her hands with alcohol gel as I stand there. My purchases are out of reach. She sees this and slides them over to me. She only touches the yogurt with a fingernail. She picks the apple up by its stem.

As I head out, the butcher finishes his break and stands. His apron is faintly stained. That's why he wears it. The rest of his clothes are pristine.

Friday, October 23rd, 2020

I haven't walked through this park, north of my apartment and south of the House of a Hundred Grandmothers, in several months. The few times that I have gone to the House, I have either come from different directions or have been walking after dark, when the park is closed.

It's quiet this afternoon. I would expect to see families, but none are around. On the grass near the entrance, two young women are sitting and reading. They may be having a picnic. There are no dogs. The garden is barren, but it often is when the caretakers are changing the flowers for a new season. The fruit of the giraffe tree, as large as my head, hangs in clusters from its branches. None has fallen yet.

I don't continue to the House when I leave the park. It's Friday afternoon. I'm going to the small supermarket to the left before it closes for the Sabbath.

The shop is crowded with people doing last-minute shopping. I find everything that I need there: white cheese, sliced cheese, hummus, eggs, apples, peppers, pecans, and the first pomelo of the season.

My aisle moves quickly. The other one is slower. The cashier there is babbling a monologue in English that I can't follow. I get the sense that her customers are used to her doing this. They nod on occasion. No one seems rushed. Everyone has allocated enough time to do what they need.

After I head out, I realize that I forgot to get challah. I still have much of last week's. It's slightly stale, but sufficient to eat with tonight's supper.

The park is still open when I get there. I walk back through it. It is still quiet. I see one cat, but it darts under the bushes when I get near it. The women are still on the grass. They are playing a board game. From a distance, I can't tell which one.

Saturday, October 24th, 2020

I don't get outdoors today. I wake up in the mid-morning, check messages, eat breakfast, and doze off at my desk. Somehow I end up back in bed.

I wake up again at a little before three in the afternoon. I can't gauge how long I've slept by my dreams. I tend to have what feels like a full night's dreams in the first hour that I'm asleep, and then nothing else that I recall until just before I awaken.

I check more messages and finish backing up my network drive. I try to play some music on my TV, but the app locks up. When I try to stop it, nothing works short of shutting the TV off. I look for another app that would work better. I don't find anything. The new audio interface for my computer should arrive in a few days. I look forward to listening to and making music on it again.

At about 5 PM, I get lunch: hummus left over from yesterday and a microwaved pita. By the time that I shower and get dressed, it's after six. There's little point in going out. I continue with what I'm doing.

I make supper at about eight: the last piece of last week's chicken, gnocchi, and a green pepper. I pack my bag of laundry to put out on the porch.

The clocks change tonight. I hope I can get to sleep at a reasonable hour.

Sunday, October 25th, 2020

I should know not to shop for groceries when I'm tired and hungry. I stand, uncertain, at the entrance to the supermarket at the Heart of the City. I think of skipping it, but I need some things for breakfast tomorrow.

I tell myself to stick to my usual shopping list, just getting things that I had planned. I do make one impulse purchase, a package of yellowfin tuna steaks that are surprisingly cheap.

I still haven't gotten used to how this place has reorganized itself, but I find what I need. The bread aisle slows me down. I know I have to get sliced bread, but hadn't thought much about what kind. Multigrain, definitely, but there are too many choices. I close my eyes, open them, and get the first appropriate loaf that I see.

Otherwise, it's my usual haul: boneless chicken thighs, peppers, persimmons, small and large pitas, and rice desserts. I forget to get butter.

Once out of the supermarket, I realize that I need to eat something. All the falafel joints are closed except the big, popular one, and that place confuses me when I'm at my best.

I carry my groceries into the city square, find a remote bench, and take a persimmon from the bag. Two benches down, the woman who collects the bottles sits with an array of cats. A man with very little Hebrew tries to ask or tell her something. They communicate through gestures. She corrects his grammar. I never figure out what he wants.

I finish the persimmon, put my headphones on, and wander the rest of the way home. I unpack and stare at my groceries. Rather than choosing, I make myself a cheese sandwich.

Monday, October 26th, 2020

The landlord's woodworking projects cluster together in the back-yard. I can't tell how many there are. A dismantled coffee table rests on the ground, with additional boards underneath the top. The body of a skateboard sits on a metal table, its wheels removed. What looks like a bird feeder camps in a corner where cats sleep in the winter. Its pointed roof, about a foot above the base, covers a flat tray with low walls. Any of these objects could turn into something else. I hadn't expected the elements of the bird feeder to take the form that they have now.

In the front yard, as I pass, the landlord is buffing a fresh coat of bright orange paint on a child's bicycle frame.

On the way to work, I stop at the shop to pick up a package. I find that there are two. Both are books, from the same vendor. The smaller package is in a plastic wrapper. In Hebrew and English, the postal service apologizes profusely for having damaged it. I open it carefully. The book is fine. The bookstore knows how to pack them to survive shipping. I'm tempted to sit on a bench and read the books, but that would mean deciding which to read first. I really should get to work.

Another package comes for me at the office: the new audio interface for my computer at home. It's supposed to be new. The box is open, with a label torn off of it. The contents appear to be intact. I blame it on customs inspectors, or whoever guards the country against hazardous hardware. I keep glancing at all of the packages while at work and eagerly carry them home.

In the backyard, when I get there, the birdhouse is on the metal table, next to the skateboard. A cat is sleeping in it. I juggle my packages as I dig for my keys. Once inside, I'll figure out what to do next.

Tuesday, October 27th, 2020

The cashier at the supermarket downstairs asks me if I want a bag. This time, I do. I'm picking up a few other things while I'm here to get my yogurt and apple.

Rather than the usual shopping bag, she picks up a much thinner one, usually used for produce. She stuffs my items into it as she scans them. That's never happened before. We've always had to pack our own bags.

She asks me if I want a spoon for my yogurt. I don't. I have a spare one from when I made coffee earlier. The plastic spoons we have in the kitchen are thin enough that I often pick up two when I only mean to get one.

My debit card doesn't work when she scans it. Some machines have trouble with it. No problem. I use a different one. She insists on spraying alcohol gel onto my hands. OK.

The bag of groceries doesn't have handles. It starts to slide out of my hand while I'm in the elevator. I reach down with the other hand and cradle it from underneath. I have to do some juggling to enter the code to get back into the office. The bag tears just as I get to my desk. Nothing breaks. I have a cloth shopping bag in a drawer. I'll use that when I go home.

Wednesday, October 28th, 2020

All the tables are taken in the city square. People sit at each of them, eating, watching each other, or looking at their phones. The caregivers and elders have clustered near the main street.

The butcher shop may be open. I see someone moving around behind the counter. I don't see any customers. The rest of the shops are closed.

I sit down on a bench near the edge with another omelette sandwich and a soda. Cats rest on the bench next to me. Fewer people move through the square than usual. It's cool outside, but not chilly.

In the morning, my laundry doesn't appear until after I'm dressed. I dip into my shelf of less-used clothing and put on my vintage Electronic Frontier Foundation t-shirt. It looks pretty much like it did thirty years ago. No one that I see today notices it. Few here would know what it represents. It's just right for the temperature today.

In the square, when I'm done eating, I toss my trash in the bin and leave the bottle beside it. When I get home, I see a bicycle frame hanging from a tree in the front yard. I guess the paint is still drying.

A gray cat runs up to me as I open the gate. It hops onto the fence, stares at me, then jumps back down. I take care not to trip over it as I walk to the back and down the stairs.

Thursday, Octover 29th, 2020

A cluster of children in costumes, carrying plastic pumpkins half-full of candy, passes me after work. That's a surprise. I've never seen anyone trick-or-treating here. I wonder where they are headed. Most people would be puzzled and unprepared if these kids rang their doorbells.

I'm on my way to the usual burger joint. It's fairly quiet when I get there. Their boss is at the register. He says something to me in Hebrew that I don't understand. I tell him that I'd like to get an order to go. That's redundant, since they're only doing takeout, but it's a start.

He switches to English. "One moment." He answers the phone and takes an order from the caller. He looks back at me when he's done. "You would like to order?" I ask for a mushroom burger. He takes my name. "And you would like the sweet potato fries and a diet cola? See, I remember you!" I do. "It will only be a few minutes. Stay close."

I step outside and lean on a high table as I flip through the news on my phone. I've only read two articles when he calls my name. "You see? This time we are fast. Last time, I know that we were very slow, but you were patient. I remember." He puts my items in a bag. We thank each other.

Two blocks from home, I see images of witches and pumpkins on the stone fence of the newest house on the pedestrian street. A plastic chair blocks the gate open. A large bowl on it holds even more candy. I hope the kids find this place. When I saw them, they were headed the other way.

Friday, October 30th, 2020

A small crowd surrounds a table in the city square. Young women stand behind it. Jars of something I can't identify from where I stand sit in a row on top. A neatly printed sign hanging from the front has several lines of information. I can sound out the words, but don't know what it means.

A man, turning away from the table, sees me standing a couple of meters back from it. "Are you OK? Can I help you?" He has a gentle voice. He looks sort of like our mayor, from what I can see behind his black mask.

I try to form a question, but end up just sounding like the Third Son: What is this? He reaches into a cloth bag and hands me one of the jars. "Take this, It's for you. Courtesy of the city." I thank him and wander off. Even close up, I can't tell what's in it. But it's a lovely jar.

Further in on the square, I get a burekas to take home for lunch. The man there asks me something. I can barely hear him over the hip-hop playing in the store. I don't answer.

He sees my American t-shirt and asks "English?" Yes. He asks again, in English. I don't need to hear as many phonemes to figure out what he's saying. Yes, I would like him to add an egg and tomato sauce. And an espresso. He prepares it all and puts the plate with the burekas in a bag.

I sit on my usual spot on the stone wall and drink the espresso. He comes by with some food that he's taking to a table farther back. It isn't one of the tables from his shop. I guess that counts as being to-go or delivery and is thus allowed.

"There's a chair next to you, you know. You are allowed to sit in it." I hadn't noticed. I'm quite comfortable on the wall. But I move to the chair, since he had offered.

I pass him again when I go to throw out my espresso cup. He is bringing a beer and a tall shot glass with what might be arak to an old woman at another table near the center of the square.

At home, at dinner, I open the jar and have some of what's in it on challah for dessert. The image on the jar is of a strawberry, but this is something like an orange marmalade. It's delicious. I try to read the label. I recognize words about the virus and donations. I should have given someone some money, had I known. If it happens again, I will.

When I'm done, I go to my computer, type in a name, and look for images. I was right. That was indeed the mayor.

Saturday, October 31st, 2020

The billboard in the city square no longer speaks about the virus. It bears a pink poster with a message about breast cancer. I don't know if that's an improvement, but at least it's a slight return to things we saw before.

A floodlight shines on it in the dark. I like walking at night. I usually come home from work around now, so I've seen these paths in the dark, but things look different when I'm walking away from my house rather than toward it.

The middle of one block on the pedestrian street has no light. I hadn't noticed that before. Looking around, I don't see any streetlights that would illuminate it. Heading home, I must have just walked straight through the shadows.

The Sabbath is over now. Downtown, a few small groceries and take-out eateries are open.

As I walk past the open counter at one shop, a car pulls up and stops in the middle of the road. If there were any other traffic, it would be blocking it. Men yell from the car window, "Falafel? Falafel?" A woman inside yells back, "Pizza! Pizza! Pizza!" The men yell again, "Falafel? Falafel?" Again, the woman calls back, "Pizza! Pizza! Pizza!" And again, the men yell twice, the woman three times. I wonder if I've just witnessed some sort of ritual or coded message. The men drive off.

Several of the pizza places are open. The only open falafel joint is the popular one downtown.

I hear loud music from the square outside the Great Synagogue. A man's voice wails and slithers. I don't know if he's singing words, or, if so, in which language. The instruments roar along, playing something like "White Rabbit," but in $\frac{7}{8}$ time. It sounds like a celebration.

When I get there, though, I see just one man, sitting, reading a newspaper, with a Bluetooth speaker the size of a large thermos beside him blasting the sound.

I take a different route than usual home, down the main street then up the one near mine where buses used to run. When I get in, I figure that I've been out for close to two hours. It's only been 45 minutes. I have time to relax. I have fulfilled my mission. I have enough to write.

November 2020

Sunday, November 1st, 2020

Four or five pigeons gather around a single crust of bread. There may be more. They come and go quickly enough and look so similar that I can't keep an accurate count.

Only one bites at the bread at a time. Whichever one has the crust pecks at it until it can lift the bit of bread from the ground, then shakes it until it falls. No one else tries to get at it while one is in control. If one is trying to get it but doesn't yet have it in its beak, another might approach, but the one working on it often coos menacingly and pecks at the air toward the other bird. The other one usually backs off, though, rarely, the one working on it gives up and walks away. It looks like a sports match or a ritual, with well-defined rules.

When a human comes through on foot or on a scooter, the pigeons scatter. They return when the intruder has passed.

I'm sitting on a bench about a meter away with a falafel and coffee, but I'm relatively motionless. My feet aren't moving. I doubt that they see anything higher. They continue to work on it until they have nibbled most of the softer bread away from the hard crust.

When they are almost done, a human in a yellow vest comes by with a broom. He sweeps up the crust and disrupts the scene. When he's gone, some of the pigeons return, but there's nothing left to interest them. They move on.

Monday, November 2nd, 2020

The US branch embassy is surprisingly scruffy. I don't know if it was like this before. The governments recently switched some signs around and declared the branch in another city to be the main site. There might be a grander facade hidden behind the construction barriers.

Everyone here is friendly. Getting in is trickier than I expect. Before I can get through the standard airport-style screening gate, I have to rent a locker at a café down the street and stash all electronics, down to my earbuds, in it.

Once inside, I go to window six. I tell the young man in the booth who I am and where I'm from. He has a brother a few towns over.

He goes through documentation. It turns out that I can't vote here. I can, however, fax my ballot to New Jersey. As he guesses correctly, I don't have a fax machine. No problem.

He gives me an email address provided by the Department of Defense. If I scan and email my ballot to them by tomorrow, they will automatically fax it to the right place. I head out, get my stuff out of the locker, and wander through the city, looking for someplace to eat.

Tuesday, November 3rd, 2020

I wake up early with a plan. I will take the fast train to Jerusalem. I don't have a particular destination there. I just want to take the new electric train out and back.

I get on the railway's website, and then on my phone, to get a ticket. First, I have to get confirmation that I can take it, since the trains can't be too crowded. Fair enough. I select my departing station and destination. I set the time that I want to travel, then choose a particular train near that time. I enter my name, email, national ID number, telephone number, and travel card number. I get an authentication code on my phone and enter that. The national railway confirms that I am cleared for the trip.

I then have to book the trip itself. They need my credit card information, even though it is already associated with my travel card. I haven't yet had a chance to indicate that it's a round trip and when I will return. I imagine that I will have to clear that, too. I worry about having to pay for the trip out before I have selected a trip back. The bureaucracy drains my enthusiasm. I give up.

Later, I decide to take the bus to the mall. The supermarket there should be open. I need a few things that I've only seen there. I tear myself away from the computer and get my phone, wallet, travel card, and shopping bag. I start to open the outside door. I realize that I've forgotten my mask. I double back to my desk and get one. I tie up the garbage bag to take out to the trash.

I put on my mask and open my front door. For the first time since early spring, it starts to rain.

Wednesday, November 4th, 2020

Finding the one open entrance to the mall takes me a while. Inside, it is dark and grim. Few shops are open: the pharmacy, the supermarket, and a store with supposedly natural stuff that has just enough edible things to qualify. People are standing around in a sushi kiosk in the middle of the mall. Maybe they're doing delivery or takeout.

The supermarket is less crowded than usual. The produce is inexpensive. I suspect that they are under pressure to sell it to the few shoppers before it goes bad. The butcher's bins of featured meat are full. Those of prepackaged meat are not. I get fruit, vegetables, some spices, bread, rice desserts, and a zero-calorie cola syrup for my seltzer maker.

The aisle for buying less than ten items appears to be closed. Three young boys are sitting on the floor at the entrance to it with bags from another store. Apparently, their mother has dumped them there while she shops.

The cashier waves at me as I approach. The aisle is indeed open. I step over the boys to get there. When he takes my store credit card, he asks me to enter my secret code. I've never needed that before. I have no idea what it might be. He says that he can enter my national ID number instead. OK. He inserts my card into the machine. Nothing happens. He flips it over and tries again. Nothing. I point to the smart chip in the card, which is outside the scanner. He spins the card around and inserts it. Now it works.

I exit the same way that I came in, walking around the outside of the mall to get to the bus stop. The bus's heat is on. This may be the first time they have used it this season. It blows so hot from under my seat that I worry that it might cook my food.

The rain resumes before we get to my stop. I have my baseball cap and my rain jacket. I get off the bus along with a young man in a Cleveland basketball shirt. He shivers. I am prepared.

Thursday, November 5th, 2020

Another day when I don't get outside. I'm on vacation. There's nowhere to go. I have already gotten all the groceries that I need, other than picking up a challah tomorrow.

It's raining intermittently. Most places are closed. There have been rumors that the shops on the street may open again on Sunday. People in charge say that they might not. The virus transmission rate is rising again.

Online, I compulsively reload the pages about the US elections. The news is generally favorable, but not certain. Everyone I voted for won in my district. The national vote is still up in the air. Friends are interested in organizing back in the states. I do what I can to connect them to people who are putting groups together.

I record a 75-minute piano track for a film score. I have to record three more layers to go with it. I go back and edit out wrong notes. Some may remain. I'll only worry about them if I can hear them.

Partway through the evening, my internet connection goes out. I'm upset. Then I'm not. I put on a sweater and queue up some Kate Bush videos. If the power goes out, I'll go to bed.

Friday, November 6th, 2020

I finally get to see my family for a little while at the House of a Hundred Grandmothers.

Their lockdown has lightened up a bit. The workers have set up tables outside. Residents can schedule to get together with their families. I get there right when my family is coming out the door, headed to a table. I meet them there. I haven't seen some of them in months.

We talk about what's been happening, the US election, my disappointing vacation, and the cascade of problems caused when their ceiling leaked. Depending on how quickly that can be repaired, they may have to move to another apartment in the House.

They had just rearranged their small space, fitting things in with millimeters to spare. Moving all that will be difficult.

The roar of small planes from the nearby airfield halts conversation every few minutes. After half an hour, they have to head back inside.

I walk home through the usual park. A few dogs and their people wander about. Someone whom I don't recognize, with a mask and a child's bicycle, says hello to me. I say hello back. I see him a few minutes later, heading into my yard. It's my landlord. I rarely see him with his mask on.

I head inside and get to work on my newsletter. I pause to mark my calendar. I'll see my family again at the same place and time next week, assuming that nothing further goes awry.

Saturday, November 7th, 2020

I'm awake at 7 AM. I don't know why. Today I should sleep late.

I have a list of things that I want to get done. I check the news and my mail. I make breakfast.

I set up my computer so I can record another track of my 75-minute piece. Just as I'm about to start, the power goes out. I check if it's just my computer. Nope. It's the entire neighborhood. I go back to bed.

When I wake up later, I have lost the momentum that I had. I catch up on some tasks and make my lunches for the week. I've been watching US election news compulsively. I put on some music instead while I cook.

When I check my computer again, I see that I have missed the moment when the race has been called. I don't feel exuberant so much as relieved. Of course, a lot of wrenches can be thrown in the path of history in the next two months. I flip between networks online. They all are saying the same things.

Eventually, I pull myself away. The mundane returns. I still have to get ready for work tomorrow and pull my clothes together. After the elections, the laundry.

Sunday, November 8th, 2020

When I get to work, people greet me with "Mazal Tov" and pepper me with questions about the election. The big question, of course, is whether the new guy will be good for this country. I think so, but people mean different things by that.

I haven't missed much in my week off. I talk with my direct boss and show him how to use some software he needs. I get back to work, doing what I, apparently, do best: going through a lot of text on screens, following a careful path to reach all of them, and fixing the English.

On my way home, I find the dance party in the city square in full swing. Someone has hooked up speakers to a phone. They boom out a bass-heavy cover of "Stand By Me" in mixed Hebrew and English. Purple and green lights flash with the rhythm.

The street-facing shops are open again. A long line of modestly-dressed women stretches into the square from a shoe store. Under the new rules, no more than four customers can be in a shop at one time.

Four boys in black and white, with their tzitzit flapping, use the chairs and tables on the square as a jungle gym.

I stop into the burger joint to get my usual order. Three older boys in green soccer uniforms talk to the workers, showing them something on their phones. I think they may be intentionally trying to confuse the grownups.

Neither the boss nor the cashier that I've gotten to know are there. I start to try to order in Hebrew. I forget how to say "mushroom." The worker from whom I'm ordering calls over another one with better English. "We'll have to put it in a bag to go, but you are welcome to sit here while you wait." I do.

They fill my order quickly. I head out, passing the three boys, who are rough-housing on the AstroTurf outside the pizza joint next door. I pause, put on yet another election postmortem podcast, and wander home.

Monday, November 9th, 2020

When I get home, I see that there has been another power failure. It hasn't even rained today. My computer has rebooted, but the programs that had been running have stopped. My file server is up and OK, though it had been down for a little while. Flashing digits on my electric clock tell me that the power came back on six hours and eleven minutes ago.

That corresponds to when I couldn't get at the files on the home server from work. I poked at it while waiting for processes to run, during another day of fixing the English on screens. Some of it needs more than a proofreading. I have to make a plan for it. That will involve some other people.

It looks like what I'm editing had a stone soup evolution. It started small. People, without consistent planning, added content and features as they created them. As usual, I may be the first person to go through everything, page by page, in order. What I'm finding would work better as soup than as screens. I think I know what I'll be doing for quite a while.

At home, I reset my clock and restart my computer. The TV has to reboot, too. Everything is working, but this is definitely the week to get that uninterruptible power supply.

Tuesday, November 10th, 2020

Several trees on the way to work are missing limbs. Last week's storms didn't do it, at least directly. Each was cleanly amputated. The city's trimmers must have been at work while I was gone.

Some trees had doubled trunks. Which trunk was removed looks arbitrary now, The choice might be clearer if I were to see both together again.

Branches are piled on the sidewalk. Most are gathered neatly, though some are scattered.

On the street where I get my packages, the claw of a trash truck tries to pick up piles of branches and other debris. It has trouble getting a grip on them. It lifts what it can grab. Much of what it gets falls out. A workman with a broom sweeps what has landed into a neater stack. It tries again.

I cross the street to avoid walking under it, then cross back a half-block farther down. I can only cross the next street from this side. A temporary fence has blocked the sidewalk on the other side beyond the intersection for as long as I have been walking to my office.

Halfway to work, rain starts to fall. At first, it's just a few drops at a time. The sound when they hit the sidewalk blends with the noise of distant construction. About a block from work, it begins to fall much faster. I hold my shoulder bag over my head. I'm wearing a dark shirt and jeans. They won't show how drenched I am.

Wednesday, November 11th, 2020

A young woman rushes up to me as I enter the supermarket. She waves a six-pack of paper towels in the air and asks me a question in rapid-fire Hebrew. I have no idea what she is saying. I tell her I didn't understand.

She repeats the question, almost identically. This time I catch the words for "telephone number." I think she might be saying that if I give the store my phone number, I'll get a free pack of paper towels. I did the rewards card spiel often enough in my retail days that I recognize the cadence.

I tell her again that I didn't understand. She glares at me, says "I have to say this a third time?" and repeats it verbatim, at the same speed. I finally wave my hands and squeeze past her.

I'm only getting a few things. I look at the clementines, but they're still green, quite late in the season. Maybe it's because the rain took so long to get started.

I get persimmons instead. When I get home, I put them down on the kitchen table, right next to another bagful of persimmons that I had picked up yesterday. Oh, well.

I sit down at my computer and immediately make a purchase online. I had researched it for hours last night, but delayed getting it until now. I tend to do that with expensive things.

Yesterday and today are a sort of unofficial shopping holiday here, where the online shops gang up and offer discounts. I understand that in years past, it was an inducement to get people to shop online. This year, everyone already does.

I look for some more bargains, but don't find anything. I'm told that the selection and deals aren't nearly as good as before.

I add a note to the order form for my purchase asking them to deliver it to my office, if they're delivering it during the work week. I try putting my message through the online translator, but it keeps timing out. I end up pasting it into the form in English. Someone there should understand.

I sit back with a burger, a persimmon, and my TV. Time to wind down.

Thursday, November 12th, 2020

I've passed this pizza place on the city square hundreds of times. Tonight, I want a calzone.

I walk in and order one. The man behind the counter answers me in English. "Just pizza. I make you any kind, or you can get from the slices here." The loudspeaker to my left is blasting aggressive rap. It isn't too loud. I can understand him.

I get prefab slices, one of tomato and onion and one of pineapple and cheese. "This will be few minutes." He scoops each slice up on a large spatula, opens one of the four ovens, and puts it in. I step back.

The next customer wants a pineapple slice with no added cheese. The worker picks the little blocks of cheese off of a slice with his gloved hands. He tosses it into the oven next to mine.

A woman comes in with a small blonde girl in a pink tracksuit. The mother picks up a full pizza that she had ordered. She turns and sees the girl dancing to the music. She starts to say something to her, and then doesn't.

I stand and wait. The scents take me back to the best pizza I ever had. It was thirty-four years ago. The pizza place had a large stone oven outdoors, near an old bus station. It was just a slice of cheese pizza with spices, but it was magnificent. I recall being told that the pizza place had been bombed some years later. The old bus station itself is gone now.

After a few minutes, I hear the pizza oven clank open. The worker scoops out my slices and puts them in a box, with thin cardboard between them and a bag with packets of spices.

I pay him and head home. The mother and girl walk several meters in front of me, hand in hand. The girl continues to dance as she walks, well after the music has faded away. They turn the corner at the hummus joint and disappear.

Friday, November 13th, 2020

It's donut season. They always appear around now, about a month before Hanukkah. Since our national body clock is off, what with the lockdowns, late rains, and unripe clementines, I'm surprised to see them. I get one at the bakery where I buy my challah.

I do my usual Friday rounds. I get groceries at the supermarket in the Heart of the City. They're out of chicken breasts, so I get a turkey breast. I see that they have liver on sale. I pick out a package of it.

I stand in the cashier's line behind a man with only two items. The cashier takes a long time with the customer before him. As she does, a woman repeatedly appears next to him. She hands him more and more items. He has to put some down on a display to avoid dropping them. It takes much longer to ring him up than it would have for just the original two items.

Heading out of the store, I realize that I have nothing on which to cook the liver. I go into the cookware store and ask for an inexpensive grilling pan.

The worker asks me a litany of questions. Price range? Size? What kind of stove? What will you be cooking? I get a pan for only a little more than I had expected, since it's forty percent off today. The cookware here is good. It's worth the money.

I get a shawarma from my favorite shop. I sit down in the square to eat it. The shops there are all open and busy. There's still a long line at the shoe store. My boss comes past and sees me. He's on his way to the shoe store. I warn him about the lines.

Somehow, when he gets there, no one else is waiting. He sails right in. A few minutes later, the line reappears. I wonder how he does that.

The table with the jars of jam is at the front of the square again. The sign is now clearer. They cost twenty shekels apiece.

I go up to get one. The teenager behind the table says that they have grape and carambola. I pick up the second one and ask again what it is. Carambola. I have no idea. I get one. It's in a flimsier jar than what I had gotten before.

By the time I get home, the lid has popped open. Carambola has oozed all over the bottom of my shopping bag. I look it up later. I know it as starfruit. It tastes much better than I remember starfruit tasting.

I spend the rest of the afternoon finishing the newsletter. As I'm about to send it out, the server goes down.

I make dinner: liver, spinach, and, as a dessert, challah with the starfruit jam.

I upload the newsletter and put on the TV. Later, I eat the donut with some cola-flavored seltzer. The season has begun. It is good.

Saturday, November 14th, 2020

Close to twilight on a Sabbath afternoon, the city square at first seems deserted. I look and listen more closely.

Across from the shoe store, two women stand talking. Each has a hand on a wheelchair. The man in the chair doesn't appear to be listening to them.

Further down, another man sits at a stone table. He sips something from a coffee cup with a plastic lid and eats something from a clear container. His phone softly plays music that I can't identify.

Two young men on a bench talk in what I think is Arabic.

Two children zoom down the path in front of the stores. The girl, dressed completely in white, rides a bicycle. The boy, wearing bright colors and patterns, rides a scooter. They come to a stop at the front of the square. A pair of grownups eventually catches up with them. They all sit down in a group of chairs there. The girl gets up several times to circle the square on her bike. Each time, she goes around once, then returns and sits with the others for a few more minutes.

Near the street, an older woman twists and bends, waving her hands in the air. It looks like she is doing some kind of exercises. Another woman walks through the square toward her. When they meet, they walk together, arm in arm down the street, away from the square.

Children's voices echo from outside the Great Synagogue at the far corner. Their screeching merges with that of the invisible birds in a tree outside the Heart of the City mall.

As the sun sets, more people appear. After dark, the sidewalk fills with people. Some shops open. Traffic gets busier. Buses line up at the stops. The week begins.

Sunday, November 15th, 2020

Someone else is ordering when I walk into the burger joint. That's good. I have time to grab a Hebrew menu and remind myself how to say "mushroom burger."

When the customer before me is done, I tell them what I want, in Hebrew this time. I've preloaded everything that I would have to say into my memory. I have to ask the cashier to repeat himself on a couple of things. He's drowned out by Hall and Oates blasting overhead.

I stand outside while I wait. After a few moments, a worker calls to me and asks if I'd like the regular bun or the vegan bun. He asks it in English. Either he knows me from before, or my accent is that obvious.

I step back outside. Apparently, the rules against eating outside at restaurants are honored loosely. There are no chairs on the patio, but a few tall tables remain, rooted into the ground. They aren't moving anywhere. While stuff had been stacked on them before, they're clear now. Three men are standing at them, talking and eating. Their take-out orders have only traveled a couple of meters from the counter.

A family sits cross-legged with their dog on the AstroTurf at the pizza shop next door, eating their own burgers and fries.

My order is ready quickly. I head out of the shop. I'm wearing a baseball cap and a rain jacket. I had heard a thunderstorm when I woke up this morning, though the rain stopped by the time I got outside. It's too warm now with this jacket, and the cap gets in the way of my glasses when I try to wear them along with my earbuds and mask. I regret wearing them.

I wander home, listening to podcasts. Right when I get inside and close the door, the rain starts up again.

Our office runs on coffee and cookies.

Right after I sit down this morning, my direct boss puts two cookies on my desk. As I head out, the big boss is also handing out cookies. I decline, but he insists. When I take one, he says that I should take more, "to eat on the road." I eat one right away, and put the other in my pocket. I think of eating it as I walk home, but my mask would get in the way.

I meet with both bosses earlier in the day. That usually involves more obligatory cookies, but this time, they have put what they call American peanuts in a bowl on the desk. Apparently, "American" means that they are dry roasted. The usual peanuts available in the nut and grain stores here aren't. My bosses grab them from the bowl by the handful. I take one at a time.

We each have cups of simple coffee. To make it, we just put a spoonful of Turkish-ground coffee in our cups and pour hot water right in. The direct boss has a good espresso machine in his office. We're welcome to use it, but it's more of a complex ritual than what we usually do.

Others in the office drink the simple coffee with a lot of milk. One worker, now gone, insisted on a complex process, filling the cup with boiling water, dumping it, filling it part way again, adding the grounds, filling it the rest of the way with milk, then putting the whole thing in the microwave. At least, I think that's how it worked. I would get lost trying to follow the pattern.

At home, I drink cold brew. I only have to make it up once a week or so. I don't have cookies in my apartment. If I did, they wouldn't last long.

Tuesday, November 17th, 2020

I feel something squishy as I put my hand down on the kitchen counter in the dark. I can't identify it by touch. I cross the room and turn on the light. Looking back, I see what I felt. A large slug has come in overnight and climbed up onto the counter. It curls up as I watch. They don't like being touched.

I wonder what to do about it. If it were to stay on the counter, it would probably be injured as I make breakfast. I don't have much room to maneuver. I detach a paper towel from the roll and pick the slug up with it, as gently as I can, rolling it off the counter's edge until it drops into a pocket I've made in the towel. I carry it outside and place it on the step.

From its color, I wonder if I might be mistaken. It could be a segment of a plum. But I haven't had any plums in the kitchen in months. And it's moving, very slowly.

As usual, it takes me awhile to make breakfast and get dressed. When I head back outside, the slug is gone. I worry that a cat or something might have gotten it. Looking closely, I see a slim shimmer of slime leading from where I had put the slug down into the grass at the steps' edge. I am relieved. As far as I can tell, the slug is free.

Wednesday, November 18th, 2020

Early in the day, a coworker and I try to decode some cryptic hand-written notes for a PowerPoint presentation.

We eventually have to ask the person who wrote them. We can tell from the alphabet that they're probably in English. What we read as "INGRID" means that the image below it should be in red. "FB LATKE" means "isolate."

We cram to get the project done by the 4 PM deadline. By midday, we learn that the matter is moot. Due to a constellation of issues, the invitations for the online event never went out. We'll try it again for tomorrow.

I spend much of the day trying to integrate images from screenshots and videos made on several different quirky systems. I try to work through things methodically. Others bounce around within the project, going off on new tangents before reaching the end of anything. By the end of the day, I'm exhausted.

I get a falafel and a donut at the Heart of the City and eat them at a table in the square. The weather is perfect.

Three little boys run after one another not far from me. One trips and keels over. His palms hit the pavement. He flips upside down, walks on his hands for a few steps, then kicks his legs into the air and lands back on his feet.

A large white dog blocks my exit from the square. It's friendly, as is the human with it. I drop my hands. It sniffs them. I pass the test. It lets me go home.

The doctor has more energy than I do, this early in the morning.

"So you haven't been here since, when, January?" That was when I had what we thought was a heart thing. "Or maybe it wasn't your heart. We don't know for sure. You didn't do your stress test. I'll authorize you for one again."

I have been staying away from medical things since the virus landed. I have some issues and questions to catch up on.

A virus test? "Are you having symptoms? We're only doing them for people who need them."

A flu shot? "You can schedule – wait, I have them right here. I'll just do it now."

My ears? I'd had an earache last week in my right ear, and some hearing loss in it since then. She looks into them. "Weird. You say your hearing loss is on the right? It looks fine. Your left eardrum looks odd, though. You should see an E.N.T." I already have an appointment for next Wednesday with one.

"Anything else?" Well, the joint of my left big toe sometimes hurts when I walk. Some of my family has gout. Should I worry about that? "Does it hurt when you touch it lightly? No? Then it isn't gout. Though you would be an excellent candidate for it."

That's all the questions. She renews my prescriptions and writes me up for some other tests. "OK, bye. Oh – hang around in the waiting area for about fifteen minutes. See if where you got the flu shot starts to hurt. If not, you can go. Set up a phone appointment after you get the tests. Bye."

I sit in the waiting room for a while. Nothing happens. I continue on to work.

Friday, November 20th, 2020

A thunderclap awakens me at five minutes to 5 AM. Torrential rain quickly follows. Through my windows, it sounds like a wall of white noise, joined by other plonks and hisses.

At five after five, just as abruptly, it stops. I go back to sleep.

I wake up again a few hours later. It's earlier than I'd like, but we've managed to work out a half hour slot when the meeting place outside the House of a Hundred Grandmothers is available. I can get together

with my family. The weather remains uncertain. If rain starts, there's a
backup meeting place in their auditorium.

We sit and talk. Some technology I've set up for them is working.
That's good.

After the half hour, I take a bus to the mall. Inside, one take-away
coffee shop is open. I haven't had much of a breakfast. I get a muffin and
coffee to eat on a bench outdoors. The muffin is messy. I get chocolate
on my mask. When I go back inside, I pick up another package of masks
at the pharmacy. I should keep some spares with me.

Almost everything on the ground floor is closed. The top floor is
dark. The escalators up to it are off, but the ones to the basement are
working. Nothing that I can think of should be open there, other than
the parking exit.

I'm surprised to see that the computer store, appliance store, and
home center are functioning. I don't know why they're allowed to be
open. I go into each of them. I think of getting a UPS, but I wouldn't be
able to carry home both the unit and the groceries that I need.

I head up to the supermarket. I look for ingredients for a beef stew.
The recipe calls for tomato paste. There are signs on the shelves for it,
but the containers all say tomato sauce. I finally find two packages of
tomato paste. I get them.

Later, my family tells me that laws have changed. Since much of
what had been labeled as tomato paste has added sugar, it now has to
be labeled as tomato sauce. I get what ingredients I can find. I drag
them home.

Once in the house, I sit down at my desk. I doze off, listening to
thunder. It doesn't rain again until after night falls.

Saturday, November 21st, 2020

The cleaner is coming this afternoon. She hasn't been here since
August. I really need help about once each month, but we've been delayed by the lockdowns and all that. I texted her a few days ago. I'm
tempted to warn her that she might need a hazmat suit, but she might
not know the word.

This morning, I sleep later than I expect, get up, get breakfast, then
sleep some more at my desk. I don't get outdoors at all.

Rain falls for much of the day. The sounds of rain and thunder lull
me into inaction. I do a bit of cleaning on my own after I eat lunch,

putting away stuff that needs a clear place to go.

I run the vacuum robot, but it doesn't work as well as it usually has. It drops some things after picking them up and acts as if it's bumping up against things that I can't see. Before I run it next time, I'll have to flip it over and see if I find what's making it do this. I have some ideas.

I set up my keyboard to record another 75-minute solo, but don't have time before the cleaner arrives. The music has to wait until later, along with my laundry and other obligations.

A busy evening awaits, then on into the week.

Sunday, November 22nd, 2020

The burger joint is empty when I come in. No customers are waiting. No burgers are in progress. One worker stands at the register. Another is in the back, prepping things. A third is hanging out on the patio.

I step up to the counter. I haven't seen this cashier before. He starts to take my name. He stops. "You know what? Have you earned a free meal from us yet?" I haven't.

"Ok, this one's on us. Congratulations." Thanks.

"Let's see, you're ordering the cheeseburger, with no sauce and fries without salt?" No, I want the usual mushroom burger and sweet potato fries.

His face falls. I'm guessing he had thought I was someone else.

He recovers quickly. "OK!" It's too late for him to rescind the free offer. He finishes typing in the order and wanders over to the grill. He pulls a breaded mushroom burger from a plastic container and slaps it down to cook.

"Vegan bun?" OK. He takes a bun from another container and puts it on the moving grate of the toaster. He pours some fresh fries into a basket and lowers it into the cooker.

Looking back, he sees that the bun is ready. He takes it out of the toaster, looks at it, and shakes his head. Something's wrong. He tosses it in the trash and puts another bun on the grate.

A few minutes later, everything's ready. He puts it all together, piling the burger, sauce, and vegetables on the bun and deftly juggling the fries into a box.

"Something to drink?" I had been thinking of getting a milkshake, but that might take too much advantage of the free offer. I get a diet cola. He puts it all in a bag and hands it to me over the counter.

"Here you are. Congratulations. *Bon appétit.*"

I go back outside and put on my headphones. On the pedestrian street, I see my first two snails of the season. They only come out after the rain. I say the blessing for occasional events. Their presence is an official announcement: Winter is here.

Monday, November 23rd, 2020

The afternoon prayers get rolling half an hour late.

It's the birthday of one of the programmers. He's turning sixty. He tends to work late, so he shows up close to noon. He walks among the cubes, handing out candy.

To celebrate, the bosses order lunch for us, not from the usual shawarma joint but from someplace else. They specialize in roast chicken and schnitzel.

Lunch shows up much later than we expect, almost at the time that the prayers usually start. The insurance agent from downstairs who tends to round us up appears on time. The boss asks him to come back in a little while.

The lunch is excellent. I get the roast quarter chicken with a plateful of vegetables. Two workers stand in the small kitchen and pass the meals out to us.

The birthday lunch isn't as festive as it had been in the past. Due to the virus, we eat alone in our cubes, not together in the conference room.

The agent shows up again after half an hour. He gathers us for the prayers.

One former worker who has come back for a brief project joins us. He always wears the standard back and white of the ultra-orthodox. He puts on a wide-brimmed black hat. When he gets out to the hallway, he pulls a long black rope from his pocket, wraps it twice around his waist, and knots it loosely in front.

We're still short by one person. The guest sees the building manager in the atrium, three floors below us. He hollers down. The manager hollers back and heads to the elevator to join us. A soldier in the atrium dozes in a plastic chair. A toddler runs back and forth between her and another child.

The boss invites the programmer with the birthday to lead the prayers. He declines. Someone else takes charge.

When we're done, people give the programmer the traditional wish to live until 120. The boss says not to rush him. He's already halfway there.

Tuesday, November 24th, 2020

The shop window at the international store in the Heart of the City is only as wide as the folding table in front of it. A doorway takes up the rest of the storefront. A wire rack at the far side of the doorway juts over to the front of the shop to its right. No one seems to mind.

I need two more ingredients for my stew. I haven't seen them elsewhere. I duck around the table and go in.

The shop is much deeper than it is wide. Wooden shelves line the walls. A lower table running down the center holds bins of seeds, spices, and other things that I can't identify. I have just enough room to squeeze down the aisles.

The store is enormously popular with foreign workers and gourmets. The shelves are roughly organized by region. One set has a daunting array of types of coconut milk. Another has boxes and packets of soup mixes, labeled in various languages that I can't read. A small freezer case sits in a corner in the back.

I go completely around the inside of the shop without seeing what I want. When I get to the front, the owner asks if he can help me. I'm looking for Worcestershire sauce. He points to the end of the wall to the right and says something that I don't catch. A small woman turns around. I had thought she was a customer.

"I show you." She goes right to it. It's exactly what I want. "I can help you find anything else?"

I ask for beef broth. She doesn't understand. I see cubes of chicken bouillon. I pick one up. Like these, but for beef?

"No, no beef. Just chicken. Sorry." That's not as crucial.

I bring the Worcestershire sauce up to the register. She starts to ring me up, then stops. The owner comes back and completes the sale.

I head out to do more shopping at the supermarket at the end of the mall. I can get my mundane groceries there.

Wednesday, November 25th, 2020

I get to the ear doctor fifteen minutes early. I wait for an hour and a half.

In the lobby, half the chairs are marked with signs to keep them vacant for social distancing. Families sit together anyway. Single people sit alone. I have to wait a few minutes for a seat.

Some people read. Some people watch videos on their phones. Few of them use earbuds. A young boy sprawls across his parents' laps.

A girl whose family sits across from them runs up and down the hall. Her tiny sneakers are surprisingly loud. She spots an empty chair, apart from the others, and darts over to it. She tries to jump up and sit on the chair. She succeeds after a half dozen tries. She sits upright for a moment, her feet dangling halfway to the floor, then swivels around and hangs off of it upside down. She slides off, her hands hitting the tiles, lowers herself into a clump on the ground, and laughs.

An electronic voice finally calls my number. The doctor checks my ears, prescribes an ointment for when they itch, and tells me to go to the nearby hospital for a hearing test. He wants me to go tomorrow, since it's already been close to two weeks since my initial earaches. I can't do it. I have to do some emergency video edits before an online presentation in the afternoon. He grudgingly lets me wait until Sunday.

Downstairs, a pharmacist looks at my prescription. He rattles off a long string of high-speed Hebrew. I only recognize the words "health plan."

I tell him that I don't understand. He speaks more slowly. "All you have to understand is that it's forty shekels." OK.

I try to swipe my debit card on the device on the counter. I get it wrong six different ways before I succeed.

Heading out, I think of getting dinner at one of the many eateries nearby. I don't. None are serving indoors, and it's starting to rain. I pull my sweatshirt's hood up and catch a bus home.

Thursday, November 26th, 2020

Someone whistles a Sousa march as we wait for the afternoon prayers. I don't know which one it is. I can't remember their names. I know that the Monty Python theme is the Liberty Bell March, since I heard a band play it when I saw Yitzhak Rabin across from Independence Hall. My father used to sing the one I'm hearing now as "Be Kind to Your Web-Footed Friends." I think my mother's orchestra has played it.

My socks are slipping on the hallway's tile floor. I have to walk carefully. I have left my shoes at my desk. They are still soggy after the morning's rain. So are my jeans. I wore my rain jacket today, but it only keeps me dry down to my waist. The street where I pick up my packages had flooded, higher than the curbs. The only way ahead was to walk through it.

It's been a morning of frantic video editing. The boss looks at what I've done and makes some requests. Some I'm able to do easily. Some I have already done, but a little later in the video. When he gives the presentation in the afternoon, it all works out. Afterward, he tells me, "Your work today gets not just a ten, but a ten of tens." I'm pleased.

More people come together in the hallway. A woman walks through with a lace facemask. It's lovely, but utterly useless.

A dozen men finally show up for the prayers. We seem louder than usual. The hard surfaces amplify the sound. We often open some of the windows over the atrium for ventilation, but we don't want it to rain in. The floor is slippery enough already.

We snare my direct boss as he tries to leave early. He ends up leading the prayers, then, picking his umbrella and briefcase up off the floor, heads home.

Friday, November 27th, 2020

I finish sautéeing the onions and garlic, cube the beef, put it all in the refrigerator, and head out.

It's after noon. The stew is never going to be ready for even a late dinner tonight. I need to do my Friday shopping, finish my newsletter, and then get back to it. I'll put it in the slow cooker overnight for tomorrow's lunch.

Everything is wet outside, but it has stopped raining for now. As I understand it, an entire year's worth of rain fell yesterday. We're told that climate change will be giving us longer dry spells between more of these intense storms.

I don't see any snails on the pedestrian street. They were out last night, but must have headed back under the shrubs. There are few cats where they usually gather. They may still be hiding out in case it rains again.

The city square is crowded. Long lines stretch back outside the hummus joint and the shoe store. Across the main intersection, the street corner violinist plays a slow blues over an orchestral recording.

I quickly do my shopping. As I enter the supermarket in the Heart of the City, the loudspeaker is already telling customers, once a minute, to finish up and to have a good Sabbath. I buy some fruit and vegetables, a loaf of bread, and chicken breasts to cook for dinner. I get a challah and a donut at the usual bakery, an espresso at the cheap coffee stop, and a shawarma at my favorite place, and head home.

I go directly to my desk and get back to work. I'll have to finish cooking later on.

Saturday, November 28th, 2020

I take the bones out of the stew first. A lot of the meat was still attached to them when I cubed the beef. They're larger than what I had cut away.

I figure I'll have what's on them in this first meal, so I don't have to deal with storing them. I don't need to. After seventeen hours, stewing overnight in the slow cooker, the meat has come right off of them on its own.

Everything has cooked down just as I'd hoped. With the flour coating the meat before I browned it, the added tomato sauce, and the other ingredients, the texture of the gravy is just what I wanted.

The recipe was vague on spices. I should have put more in. I had guessed on how much sumac and baharat to add. I also didn't have beef broth. Following other recipes, I just used water and a splash of wine.

I eat two servings for lunch. It's too much. I feel heavy for the rest of the day. I pack up and freeze eight more servings.

There is still a lot of the gravy left. I freeze that separately. I may add it back in when I make the next stew, in lieu of prepackaged beef broth. And next time, I may add beans and barley back in. I could adapt it into an excellent cholent.

Sunday, November 29th, 2020

The municipal billboard has changed again. At first, I think that it's about being safe in traffic, but it's not. The city wants our help in keeping its "green light" status in the face of the virus.

At the front of the square, several people sit in intense conversation. Hand-drawn signs say "We're here to listen" and "Let's talk about the situation."

Further back, running along the center walkway, barricades bear printed posters about the Day to Eliminate Violence against Women. Against a common background, each has a black and white death notice, four times the usual size, giving the name of a woman and how she died.

Heading in to work late after an appointment, I get a falafel at a nearby shop and sit down on a bench to eat it. I make a phone call and head up to the office.

A couple of meters in front of me, a white-haired man falls off his bicycle into the street. The cars stop in time. I think of helping him, but I wouldn't know what to say. Three other people rush over and rescue him and the bicycle. He seems OK.

Down the street, a soccer ball flies out of a schoolyard and lands near me. Another man about my age trots over and expertly kicks the ball over the tall fence back to them.

I pause closer to the office as a car parked in front of the supermarket plays chicken with an SUV who wants the space. I wait until I'm sure they're stalemated, then walk around them and in.

Monday, November 30th, 2020

I finally get to play back my long piano score.

I'd recorded its four lines, one line a week, performing each without listening to the lines that preceded it, over a month of Saturdays. Each follows the same structure, beginning and ending at the same place at the same time, but wandering in between through a field of possibilities.

I'd recorded each in the same octave, then arbitrarily assigned them to different ones, low to high, in the order that I recorded them. It sounds like a single piano, though I would never be able to play the result. Unexpected melodies occur. A phrase starts in one octave and continues in the next. Chords appear, and moments of harmony. Silence has its place. Stretches of four or five seconds at a time, though rarely more than that, pass without new notes being played. I may add a pedal to everything, so a haze of tones drifts in the background. I may not.

I planned it to be played by others, and eventually it will be, but this is what it has become for now. It's one layer of several. I have already recorded four tracks of my voice reciting a text, similarly connected and separate. There will be sounds from the environment and elsewhere. Birds, seascapes, and children will appear, as well as clusters of massed violins that I played some twenty years ago. All this goes along with visuals: pillars of text, images of my city, and other layers not yet known.

I like what I hear in the piano score. I know that I made mistakes, but I can't hear where they are. I leave them in.

It's time to start combining things. The whole thing is soon, though I don't know how soon, to be a minor motion picture. I want to watch it as I fall asleep. If only I can understand and enjoy what it becomes, it will be enough.

December 2020

Tuesday, December 1st, 2020

A bicycle darts past me as I wait for a traffic light across from the city square. It zooms ahead, not paying attention to much. A dog crosses into its path. The bicycle rolls over the dog's leash, inches from it. The dog flops onto its side. The bicycle just keeps going. The dog gets up. It doesn't look pleased.

I cross the street and step into the pizza shop. The worker asks me what I would like. I point to the one remaining slice of Sicilian pizza.

She tries to scoop it up on the large pizza peel. That's the English name for the tool they use, somewhere between a spatula and a shovel. I don't know the word at the time, but look it up later to write this. The pizza keeps sliding off the peel. The other worker turns and takes the peel's handle. He gives it a quick flip. The slice slides forward, seated securely.

The woman with the dog comes in. A little girl is with her. The girl disappears almost immediately. She emerges near the ovens on the other side, having walked under the piled-up tables that keep customers out of that area. The woman yells at her. The girl grumpily stomps back under the tables to our side.

The woman wants four slices. The other worker tells her they add up to the same price as a large pizza. He uses the English word "large." She doesn't like that. "But they're slices!" Yes, but they add up to a full large pizza. He spins the slices around on the metal counter and forms them into a perfect circle. The woman doesn't like the price, but she gets them.

The worker who took my order tries to scoop my slice out of the oven. She fails. The other worker shows her, again, how to flip it onto the peel. She rings up my pizza and a soda, but gets confused at the register. The other worker shows her how it works.

I take the pizza and soda and try to leave. The girl is leaning up against my leg. The dog has wandered between us and wrapped its leash around my ankles. I gradually extricate myself without dropping anything. I look down at the girl and smile. She smiles back. The woman doesn't notice. I carry everything over to a chess table, take off my mask, and eat.

Wednesday, December 2nd, 2020

I stare at my phone yet again, trying to figure out what has gone wrong with it. Ever since last week's storm, I can't get online via mobile data.

I have gone into the settings screen and checked that mobile data is working. The screen claims that it is. It isn't.

I depend on the phone in all sorts of small ways. I don't notice them until they're gone. Without the mobile data, I can't get at WhatsApp at work, since it depends on my phone having a connection, and the Wi-Fi is flaky there. It's how our team communicates, as well as my family. I can't check when my bus is coming. I also can't use the bus, since my transit pass ran out at the start of the month, and I use the phone to recharge it.

I stare at the phone some more. On the top bar, I spot an icon that I've never noticed before, like an N with two crossbars. I swipe down from the top. There's a whole array of settings for things that I've never seen. The odd N is for NFC, which is how the phone talks to the transit card. It's off. I turn it on. There's a setting for Mobile Data. It's off, even though the other screen said that it's on. I tap it.

The phone immediately begins buzzing and beeping with incoming messages and alerts. Apparently this hidden screen overrides the one that's easy to see. I must have fat-fingered the interface as I tried to hold onto the phone while walking through the flood. Odd are the ways of the Android.

I'm relieved. In the states, I would have taken the phone in to the AT&T store or the equivalent. Here, it seems you buy phones and get them repaired from small shops, many of which look sketchy. I'm glad that I didn't need them.

I press my transit pass to the back of the phone and start the app to recharge it. My email comes in. My podcasts update. The world begins to get back to normal.

Thursday, December 3rd, 2020

I take a 5-shekel piece out of my wallet on the way from the bus to the bakery. The baker sees me coming. He's seen me before.

"One donut?" I nod. He takes the coin and hands me a bag. All they have left are jelly donuts with powdered sugar. They usually have a wider array.

A group of teenage girls wearing identical white t-shirts are carefully picking through what's on the rack. To me, the donuts look identical. I pick up the tongs from the top shelf and take the nearest one. I drop it in the bag. A cloud of sugar poofs into the air. Much of it gets on my shirt. I brush it off.

The street corner violinist plays a klezmer tune along with a recording of an orchestra. A man on a chair near him stomps, claps, and shouts in rhythm, speeding up and slowing down along with the music.

I've heard the tune before, though not in a long time. I think my parents had a record of it. My mother may have played it when I was young. Bartok may have done something with it.

I can still hear it clearly when I cross into the city square. I think of getting a mushroom burger, but I'm too hungry to wait for one. I didn't get to eat anything in the later afternoon as I hurriedly edited video for another webcast.

I stop into the pizza joint and get the nearest slice. It's wonderful, with olives and other toppings that I can't identify. Olive oil dribbles off of it as I eat. I catch the oil on the piece of cardboard with which I carried the slice to the small stone table. I avoid dripping oil on the chessboard embedded in the table-top.

The violinist stops playing right when I sit down. I had looked forward to hearing more from him. I settle into the silence and the sounds of the square.

Friday, December 4th, 2020

This sahlab is the best I've ever tasted. It's dense and smooth, somewhere between foamy and creamy, topped with ground peanuts, spices, and other items that I can't identify.

For lunch, I have a sabich, like a falafel but with grilled eggplant and an egg instead of the chickpea balls. I eat it at a chess table in the square.

When I'm done, I think of getting coffee. I see that the store with the mysterious sandwiches has sahlab. I get a large one. The worker asks me what I'd like in it. I say OK to everything. It's easier than trying to figure out what he's saying. I go back to the chess table with it.

A grizzled man walks over to the next table and unpacks a guitar. He sits down, tunes, and plays a sensitive version of "Knockin' On Heaven's Door." He shouts above it, sounding like a less melodic Captain Beefheart, using random fragments he seems to recall from other rock songs. There are lines from "The Letter," "I Saw Her Standing There," and "Satisfaction," tied together with a repeating "Mama Mama Mama" that might actually be from the song that the guitar is playing.

He finishes the single song, packs up his guitar, and wanders off. Stores around me start to close for the Sabbath. I slowly finish the sahlab, then head back home.

Saturday, December 5th, 2020

I combine the piano and spoken tracks and listen to how they go together. I'm pleased. Both function as music.

I have to slide the voice track ahead by half a second. The first piano chord is accented, while the first syllable isn't. Once positioned and balanced, neither outweighs the other.

Two minutes before the end, where I will insert a song, each comes to an appropriate pause. I put a layer of visuals on it. For most of it, pillars of English, formed from the text, slowly slide past, echoing the image of a Torah scroll. In the last two minutes, a paragraph that the voices repeat zooms in to focus on its unison last sentence.

I didn't intend, when creating the text, that it would repeat at the end. A bug in the program that generated it made it do so. I kept working on the program to fix the bug, but liked that version best. I didn't save the buggy code. I no longer know exactly how I did it.

I expect that the pillars of text will form a backdrop to whatever else happens in the visuals. I start to render out the film, but it will take too long to let me back everything up this evening. Other programs, running at the same time, stumble and glitch. I may be reaching the limits of my sturdy computer. I stop and render out only the audio.

I listen back to what I've made as I continue with the weekend's mundane tasks: making lunches, preparing laundry, sorting out tasks for tomorrow. I miss some of the sound due to the noise of the other things I'm doing. It's OK. The music can roll on without me.

Sunday, December 6th, 2020

I spend the work day drifting, unmotivated. A couple of people ask me brief questions about English. Yes, the proper noun forms are "improvement" and "approval" and not vice versa. No, I don't know why.

I flip through an old manual and find that little of it can be salvaged. The structure is OK, but I'll have to rewrite most of it from scratch.

My mind is taken up with thoughts of the film project. I realize that I can't shoot or generate what I need by myself.

I had planned to do the entire project on my own, but I want to incorporate dance. I'm not interested in seeing my ungainly body wobbling around on screen. I think of what dancers could do that would fit with the project.

I pull up an old idea for four dancers, moving to the soundscape independently, passing through one another like ghosts when their images meet. I sketch out a few lines of instructions in my head. This becomes more complex as I work on it.

Toward the end of the day, it becomes radically simpler. Much as I did the sound with a single speaker and a single player, the visuals should include a single dancer, recorded four times.

My brain is tired when I get home. I prepare something quick to eat, and sit down to watch an hour of television. I'll work on the movement score afterwards.

Monday, December 7th, 2020

I don't feel like going straight home after work. I head to the city square. I think of getting a mushroom burger, but can't get myself to spend that much for dinner, especially to go.

I stop into the pizza place again. I don't recognize the worker who greets me, but he speaks to me in English right away. I get a slice of what's on display and a soda.

While I wait, I realize that, even though he seems to have an Israeli accent, he is speaking with everyone in English. Either he is practicing the language, or he doesn't speak Hebrew well and comes from somewhere else with an accent that sounds the same to me.

I sit down at a chess table with the slice. I figure I'll get some writing done on the dance scenario. I had written some notes down at work. I take them out and fumble around in my pockets looking for a pen. I don't find it. I must have left it at work. So much for writing.

I finish the slice fairly quickly. It's good, as usual, simple cheese with a thin, crisp crust. When I'm done, I realize that I hadn't opened the soda. I put it in the bag with the groceries that I got in mid-afternoon.

The shop with the sahlab appears open. I want another one. I go into it. The teenager smoking outside tells me that they're closed for the night. Oh, well.

I head home. I'm not tired. I should be able to get more writing done tonight.

Tuesday, December 8th, 2020

I do get the mushroom burger tonight. I may not be able to get another one for a while.

A curfew may start tomorrow night. Or it may not. If it does, the word is that it will start at 5 PM. Or maybe 6. Possibly 7. The Coronavirus Cabinet has announced it. Members of the Supreme Court have said that it may be illegal. A contradictory law passed earlier this year.

I take the bus from work down to the city square to get the burger. When I buzz for the next stop, a shabby-looking man across the aisle mumbles something at me that I don't hear. I stop the podcast I'm listening to and take my earbuds off.

He says it again. I tell him I don't understand. He switches to English. "I need to go up the street to get Chanukah presents for my children. Will you come with me?"

I've heard this line before. He'll want money. I tell him that I have to head straight home.

"Please, it will take a short time." Sorry, I can't.

"It will only take ten minutes." No.

"Then can you help me with some money?" There it is. Sorry, no.

I get off the bus and head to the burger joint more quickly than I otherwise might. I pass a lot of people sitting at the chess tables and in the clusters of chairs in the square. They all seem to be enjoying a last warm evening before the curfew starts. Or doesn't.

Wednesday, December 9th, 2020

One of my favorite gelato joints, "Doctor Lick," is now "Aryeh's Ice Cream." As I walk toward it, I see the new sign.

The curfew didn't happen. I'm downtown. The place where I had gotten the great sahlab is closed for the evening. This other shop is across the intersection from the city square, on the edge of a smaller plaza next to the Great Synagogue. It's still open. I haven't had dinner yet, but I'm in the mood for sahlab. I've gotten it here before.

The worker is dishing sherbet out from a large tub into a container that fits in the counter display. There aren't any other customers right now. He asks me what I want, then says to wait a moment.

It takes him a couple of minutes to finish transferring the sherbet. He picks up a metal instrument and guides it along the top of the sherbet to give it a fancier surface, He puts the container where it goes, then scoops out a sample with a small spoon and hands it to me. It's apricot. It's good.

He pours some of the sahlab mix into a paper cup and steams it with a cappuccino steamer. Coming around front, he puts crushed peanuts, coconut, and spices on top and sticks a spoon into it.

I pay. It's fifteen shekels, slightly less expensive than the other place. I hand him a twenty shekel note and put the five shekel piece he hands back as change into the watch pocket in my jeans. I'll use it to get a donut tomorrow.

I take the sahlab to a bench in the square and sit down. Few other people are around. A man reads a newspaper at the other end of the set of benches. A woman paces between me and the gelato shop, speaking on her phone in what may be Russian. At the far side of the square, three young women sit on the ground, against a wall. From where I am, I can't see what they're doing.

This sahlab is good, but not as good as at the other place. Once I get past the top layer, the body of it is liquid, like eggnog, not foamy. I don't have to use a spoon. I can drink it. The flavor is a little less rich. Still, it's a good second choice. I drink it slowly, watching and listening to what's around me.

When I'm done, I drop the empty cup in the trash can a few feet away, put my mask back on, and continue on home.

Thursday, December 10th, 2020

We gather in the office hallway to light the first candle. There isn't quite enough room for us to space properly. We do the best we can. Some of us wear masks. Some don't.

After some negotiation, the youngest worker, the bosses' son, does the actual lighting and prayers. We respond appropriately. Our staff sings rather well.

Someone has ordered donuts, jelly-filled with powdered sugar. They're still warm. They're delicious.

I take the bus downtown after work. I think of getting another donut but don't. I'm limiting myself to one a day.

I get a coffee and sit down in the city square. It's relatively quiet. The three young women that I saw sitting against a wall yesterday come by again. Two of them are carrying skateboards.

A mother cat and two kittens come through a hole in a fence and sit outside the toy store. One kitten jumps on the mother repeatedly. She doesn't react. The other kitten sits and watches them. A large black cat comes over and sits about a meter from them. The mother walks over, swats the black cat in the face, then sits down next to it. The kittens join them. A soldier with a yarmulke and backpack walks by and crouches in front of them. He wants them to play with him. They aren't interested. He walks away.

I head home after a while. When I get in, I put my bag down, take off my mask, and reach for the menorah and candles. They're right where I left them last year. This time, I put a large piece of aluminum foil under the menorah. I had trouble getting the wax off the table last year.

The matches are in the drawer. I haven't used them since then. They're still good. I say the blessings, light the candles, and put dinner together. The holiday begins.

Friday, December 11th, 2020

Six men huddle around a backgammon board on a stone table in the city square. What hair each still has is white. Those who are watching wear masks. The two who are playing are smoking cigars. I can't see the board clearly. It wouldn't matter if I could. I can never remember how the game works.

A block away, several men stand on the steps of the Great Synagogue. They are worshiping individually, holding prayer books from a table at the top of the stairs. The doors to the synagogue are closed, but they are still facing in the proper direction. To their right, someone is moving slowly. either putting up or taking down posters from a board on the wall.

The pharmacy on the far side of the bus station has the prescriptions that they couldn't fill when I was there last. No one else is in line when

I go to the window.

As I approach, a woman barges up and asks if they have a particular item. She is desperate. No shop seems to have it, and she needs it before the Sabbath. I step aside. This shop doesn't have it either. The pharmacist rings me up quickly then starts to help the woman find it elsewhere.

On my way out, I see that they have standard surgical masks in a stylish black. I'm out of the purple ones and tired of the blue. The cashier tells me that they just came in, and that they look good. I get a pack of them.

I head back up the far side of the street. A shop that I hadn't seen before sells tempting devices for making coffee. I go in and look around but don't get anything.

Further up, I get clementines, persimmons, baking pans, challah, a single donut, and a sabich and soda for lunch. I sit down with them on a bench back in the city square. The same men are playing the same game at the table. I watch them and the cats, and listen to the birds and traffic, as I eat.

Saturday, December 12th, 2020

The ice cream joint is just opening as I walk by. It's dark already. The Sabbath is over. It's too chilly to eat ice cream outdoors, so I ask for a sahlab again.

"OK, but it will be a few minutes. You can come back, or sit over here." I sit down.

The worker continues setting out the sherbets and gelatos in their bins. The case on the left has two rows of nine bins. The case on the right has two rows of twelve, though the two bins on the far end of each row are divided in half. Those and the four bins nearest them hold frozen fruit. The rest of the bins on that side hold gelatos.

Several customers come in while I'm waiting. From the conversations, I can tell that they're regulars. Each is getting kilos of gelato to go. Most of the kilos contain multiple flavors. He puts them in side by side, like Neapolitan ice cream.

He finally gets around to me when they're gone. It's OK. I'm not in a hurry. He takes a liter of milk from the refrigerator and pours some into a metal cup. He steams that from the cappuccino maker, then pours the milk from the metal cup into a paper one. He spoons in a large amount of one white powder, possibly a starch, and a smaller amount of another. He steams the mix again in the paper cup and hands it to me.

"Coconut, peanuts, and cinnamon are over there. You know what to do." I take a plastic spoon from a dispenser, go over to the small table, and put the toppings on.

I go to a bench outside to eat it. More people pass by. Cars honk at each other. Across the street, another eatery opens, with food to go. The workers wait for customers to come in.

Sunday, December 13th, 2020

The bosses tag me to light the candles at the office tonight. They ask me if I want to practice the blessings. No one is ever quite sure how much I know of Jewish practice and rituals. It's more than many Americans but less, I think, than even many secular people here. I'm OK with these prayers.

I start in a lower key than I did last year. I couldn't hit the high notes then, and my voice cracked. This time it's right in range. I have a bit of trouble lighting the first candle. Eventually I get it.

At the end of each blessing, the rest of the staff do a choral "A-a-men." They sound great.

I blank on the melody of one of the obligatory songs, but others start in with it and I follow. The other one, I could sing in my sleep. We don't do the hymn that I arranged for my mother's orchestra a few years back, but that's OK.

The bosses hand out cookies afterward. We get back to work. When I get home, I set up the candles for lighting, but realize that I've already done it for today. I put one more candle in the menorah. It's all set for tomorrow.

Monday, December 14th, 2020

I almost miss tonight's candle lighting at the office.

As I head to the restroom, the boss is just starting to set the menorah up. I figure that I have plenty of time.

When I get back, the lighting is already in progress. One of the programmers, another immigrant, is slowly working his way through the first of the blessings. He still has trouble reading Hebrew text, although he speaks it pretty fluently. Another programmer, with whom he works closely, guides him when he gets stuck.

A few minutes later, the boss spaces out on a word in another paragraph that he always recites. We remind him, in unison. The harmonies are better than ever on the hymn that everybody knows.

Afterward, the bosses' son distributes donuts. I see that there's a trick to having the powdered sugar stay on them: it actually comes in separate packets, and is sprinkled on the donuts just before we eat them.

I take mine back to my desk. I have spent the day figuring out a bug in a process that we use to put screen images in manuals. I write a couple of pages of code to test possibilities. As I work things out, the code gets shorter. The solution fits on a single line. I show it to my boss. He has to head out. We'll implement it tomorrow.

I leave a little later. The candles have completely burned down. The donut box is still on the receptionist's desk. I look inside. It's empty. Freed from temptation, I put my mask on, clock out, and leave.

Tuesday, December 15th, 2020

Two strange sculptures appear in the city square. At least, I think they're sculptures. Smooth white tubes rise a meter or so from the pavement, then split into four limbs each, ending in points. It's as if a pair of artificial squid have crash-landed head first amidst the benches, or a pair of giant albino jesters have lost their hats.

Coming back through the square after work, I intend to look more closely at them, but they're gone. There is no sign that they had ever been there. I wonder briefly if they had actually been part of my vivid dreams last night, crawling into my sleeping mind along with triangular slugs and the trains that I rode, both inside and on their roofs.

Nothing seems out of place in the square. The caregivers and elders aren't around. They tend not to show up on evenings when there might be rain. A family stands and sits where they usually are, taking each other's pictures with their phones. The box from a selfie stand rests next to them, with a pole that holds a ring light and arms for phones and tablets. I got one myself a few months ago. I haven't yet used it. I thought it would come in handy for part of my film project. That image has fallen away.

I think of getting some pizza or a falafel, but decide against it. I have what to eat at home, and I don't want to risk the rain. I'll put some dinner together there, light the candles, get some writing done, and finally watch a movie that has been sitting on my drive. If it rains and the power doesn't go out, I'll listen to it and read.

Wednesday, December 16th, 2020

I head to work later than usual today. I eat breakfast while I'm on the phone doing tech support for my family. I can hear it raining, almost as hard as it did a few weeks ago, when a full year's worth fell in a single day. The news online tells me that somewhere in my city, people have had to be rescued from a flood. This all adds up to a perfect storm of excuses for procrastinating.

When I finally get outside, it's not as bad as I'd feared. There's heavy rain, as I expected, but I have my good hooded rain jacket and a baseball cap. The top half of me, at least, remains dry.

I have to dodge a minefield of snails on the pedestrian street. The sidewalks are littered with fallen citrus. I kick them out of my way. I have to take two detours, on streets that are flooded where I usually cross them.

By the time I get to the office, my shoes and jeans are soaked. I take off my shoes and put them under my desk, next to the blue balloon that drifted into my cube several weeks ago. I don't take off my jeans. There's probably a company policy against that.

The rain continues all day. It lets up somewhat during the afternoon prayers. One of the guests opens a window onto the atrium. It helps to keep the hallway from getting too stuffy. The prayers are a little longer than usual. Today is both Chanukah and the night of the new moon.

Just after sunset, we light the candles again. The bosses, once again, hand out cookies. I finish my work and head home a while later. It's still raining. I don't mind, but I'm glad to get home and finally change out of my jeans.

Thursday, December 17th, 2020

As I head to bed, I see an odd shape in the middle of the kitchen floor. I look at it more closely. It's a long slug, about five inches from antennae to tail, making a sharp left turn, heading back to the door. It's moving relatively quickly. I don't think I'd seen it there when I was in the kitchen a few minutes before.

Before I turn out the light, I note where it is and where it's going. I make sure that I avoid that area when I go from my bed to the bathroom during the night. I don't want to step on it.

In the morning, it's gone. Good.

When I head out to work, it isn't raining, but it starts when I'm halfway there.

For lunch, the bosses order hummus plates. It's another programmer's birthday. On the bed of hummus, each has tahini, chickpeas, a sliced egg, paprika, and other substances that I don't recognize. The pita is darker and denser than usual. It all is still warm when we get it.

When I go into the kitchen later to get more coffee, add-ons for the hummus are still out on the counter: raw onion, garlic, olives, what looks like jalapeños, and what I think is chili paste. My boss points it out. He says it's dessert. I think he's kidding.

After dark, we light the final night's candles. The worker who does it isn't sure of the melodies. We all sing them in unison, followed by the hymns with the now-familiar harmonies. The bosses hand out cookies again. People take pictures.

After work, in the city square, I think of getting one last donut. The bakeries don't have them anymore. I'm surprised. I get some pizza and a soda and eat it at a chess table.

A man with a shaggy beard and a worn motorcycle jacket comes over. He wishes me a *bon appétit*, sits down with his back to me, and chats with his friends at the table next to ours.

It starts to rain again as I finish eating. I'm under a canopy, so I have time to put everything together before I head out. I carefully step around more snails and slugs on the pedestrian street as I hurry home.

Friday, December 18th, 2020

An unofficial picnic has sprouted on the lawn outside the mall. The café inside is open, but with no seating. People have brought their food outdoors. They are sitting on the grass, as well as on what looks like bright plastic children's furniture that has mysteriously appeared.

A tall metal fence surrounds the lawn's perimeter, but one space is open so people coming from the bus stop can get in. The nearest entrance to the mall is functioning again. I don't need to go around to the other side anymore.

When I get in, I go directly to the supermarket, to be sure to get what I need from there before it closes for the Sabbath. It's busy, but not badly so. Produce there is cheaper than elsewhere, and quite good. Clementines are finally in season, somewhat late, shades of orange rather than green.

They have just about everything I'm looking for. The endcap with flavored syrups for my seltzer maker is gone. I suspect that the syrups are elsewhere, but they aren't anywhere that I look. The challah from the bakery is still hot. I have to take it off the rack carefully, grasping it with a plastic bag and wriggling it loose from where the bottom has stuck to the baking paper.

I shop efficiently. When I get in line to check out, the person in front of me tells me, in English, that she is going to take a while, but that the lane next to mine is almost empty. It is. I thank her and move over.

I head back through the mall and stop at the café. I think of getting coffee and something to eat. I don't know how much of the regular menu that they have, though. What I usually get wouldn't work well to go. My bag of groceries is heavy, and I'm not sure that I would find a good spot to eat outdoors. I continue on outside and catch the next bus home.

Saturday, December 19th, 2020

The Sabbath café is open, though only for coffee and pastries and only for take-out. I spot the open doors as I walk past. I wander in.

At first, I don't see anyone there. A young woman comes out from the back. She's wearing a white t-shirt and jeans, not the usual uniform. She steps behind the counter to the coffee machine.

"What would you like?" Coffee and a pastry.

"Large or small coffee?" Large.

She makes a large cappuccino. That's the default if you just order coffee.

"Which pastry?" There are two left in the case. I get the almond danish.

"Heated?" Yes.

She steps back out and goes to the register. It's at the far side of the room. Another man comes in as she's ringing up the check. He peppers her with questions. "Are you open?" Yes. "Do you have sandwiches?" No, just coffee. "Salads?" No, just coffee. "Smoothies?" No.

He walks away. She comes over to me with the check. It's twenty-five shekels, twice what I would pay elsewhere. But they're the only place open, and their food is good.

I pay cash. She goes back to the register and gets my change.

I put sweetener in my coffee and find a lid that fits. I cross the street to the city square and sit down. It's quiet. A couple of families bicycle past. I can relax. I have time. The cleaner won't be at my house for a few more hours.

From one of the open windows above the square, I can hear a family singing the traditional hymns sung at Sabbath lunch. They're out of tune. It doesn't matter. They sing. I eat. It isn't raining. It's a good afternoon.

Sunday, December 20th, 2020

I don't get very far before the elevator opens again. A teenage boy approaches, sees me inside, and stops. He steps forward, then back, then forward, and stops again. I nod to him. Two unrelated people are allowed on an elevator at once.

A young girl walks toward him, then an older man. The man raises his hand. It's OK. They're together. They'll wait.

On the ground floor, at the coffee shop to one side of our doors, people sit outside with their drinks. The moveable furniture still isn't there, but the yellow police tape that had blocked the built-in benches has come down.

I get my usual snack at the supermarket. The woman in front of me in the express line has what I see at first as two cereal boxes. Looking more closely, I see that they're the kind of slipcases that might hold art books. They have branding from vodka. Maybe there are two bottles in each, or something in addition to the vodka. She takes a long time to count out the cash to pay and then to put them in her shopping bag.

When I get on the elevator again, so does one of my bosses. Once again, the doors open on the next floor. Someone approaches. My boss holds up two fingers and sternly shakes her head. The door closes. She lowers her hand. "I only use my hands. I don't talk. When you don't talk, they can't argue." We ride the rest of the way in silence.

Monday, December 21st, 2020

I get three items rather than the usual two at the supermarket. The cashier asks me if I need a bag. I say I do not. I use the wrong form of "not."

The cashier corrects me. What she says makes sense in Hebrew, but would translate to "Not 'Not.' 'Not.' Not 'Not.' " I understand what she means.

After work, as I cross into the city square, I hear Christmas songs. That's unusual. The caregivers and elders are in their usual spot at the front of the square. The music is playing from a speaker attached to a caregiver's phone. Most of them are from outside the country. They're unlikely to be Jewish.

I head off to their left, to the store with the odd sandwiches and good sahlab. I see that they still have burekas left. I get one.

The teenaged worker takes it out of the warming cart. With a metal spatula, he cuts it into eight pieces, once the long way and three times the short way. He shells the egg that had rested on top of it in the cart and slices it up.

I take a grapefruit juice from the refrigerator. The burekas and juice come to thirty shekels.

I hand him a hundred, fresh from the ATM. He hands me thirty back. I put the change in my wallet. We realize at the same time that there's been a mistake. I take the change back out. He hands me another two twenties.

I take the bag with the burekas to a chess table and reach inside. There's no fork. I think of going back and getting one, but decide against it. I put my headphones back on and bring it all home.

Tuesday, December 22nd, 2020

In a lull at work, I see an emailed announcement of a book that I can't resist. I order the book from a site in England.

An almost immediate automated response says that they won't be able to send it for a while. As of today, all shipping from England to here has been shut down due to the new virus mutation. At least they sent me the ebook as a freebie.

Downstairs in the supermarket, another customer asks me something. I think it's about the container of yogurt he's holding. I can tell he's speaking Hebrew, but his unfamiliar accent makes it completely unintelligible.

I end up in the checkout line behind him. He answers his phone in English. He's from somewhere in the southern US, with a drawl so thick that he could probably talk to alligators. Had I known that, I probably could have understood and helped him.

After work, in the pizzeria on the city square, a woman raises a ruckus about something in her order. People scurry around behind the counter. I wait.

When they finally get to me, I just want one of the slices of Sicilian pizza that's on display. After all that hassle, they seem thrown off balance by an order that's so easy.

The cashier blanks on how to ring up a single slice. Another worker explains it to him in English. They put the slice on the cardboard carrier facing the wrong way. I have to do some tricky juggling until I find a free table and sit down.

Wednesday, December 23rd, 2020

The coffee shop around the corner from the Sabbath café has a full takeaway menu. I'm only there for a hot drink, but I notice the menu on the counter. I ask about it, but fumble the Hebrew.

The worker answers in English. "Yes, we have sandwiches, salads, other things. We have a menu in English if you want to see." I don't, but it's good to know. That chain has a good inexpensive Israeli breakfast, but it wouldn't really work as takeaway.

I get a coffee and sit in a sort of park on the other side of the shop from the city square. It isn't much. Wide brick sidewalks, with chairs and two picnic tables, run around the north and west edges of a parking lot. A planter runs down the middle of the northern leg. Beyond that, a low fence with an open gate separates it from another similar park, down a few steps, around another parking lot.

I remember the coffee shop building, or another similar building in the same spot, from a visit here a decade or so ago. I shot video of graffiti on its walls. One set, in flowing black handwriting in Hebrew on cement, says "Life's what you make of it." Another wall, or perhaps the same one but a distance away, says in English "This is not a rebellious statement." I think the same person wrote both. All that is gone now. And I may be completely wrong about where the graffiti was.

I look over at the coffee shop again and think of getting something to go. I don't. I have food that I should eat at home.

This place is in the same chain as the one at the mall. They probably have a full takeaway menu, too. I may get something there on Friday and join the picnic on the lawn.

Thursday, December 24th, 2020

I throw on my hoodie and head off to work. When I'm halfway up the stairs, it starts to rain. I head back inside and switch into my raincoat. As I head up the stairs again, the rain stops. I keep going.

I spend the day at work on a tedious task. I have to keep opening files, fixing them, closing them, and going on to the next. There are dozens, perhaps hundreds, of files. I occasionally lose my place. Sometimes the repetitive process makes me zone out completely. I lose time as I stare blankly at the screen. My mind goes someplace else entirely. Fortunately, sound from the environment brings me back. The programmer across the aisle sneezes frequently. That works.

After I leave, I stop at the burger joint. Another lockdown starts on Sunday. I don't know when I'll get to have another mushroom burger. The cashier appears to be one that I've spoken with in the past, who is fluent in English. I start to order in English. It isn't the same cashier. The two look identical behind the masks.

She turns and calls for the boss to translate. He's busy. I end up doing most of the order in Hebrew, though she tries to speak to me with what English she has. The loud music makes it more difficult. I could understand her better if I could hear her. Commercial rap-metal from decades ago is taking up the whole sound spectrum. The shop suddenly becomes busy. Flocks of teenagers enter. The phone rings with large orders.

I finally get my supper. I carry it home. I'm a little too warm in my raincoat, but I can't effectively take it off. When I get inside, I take it off and hang it up. As I close the door, the rain starts up again.

Friday, December 25th, 2020

The queuing machine spits out a piece of paper. I'm number 163 in line for the pharmacy. They're now helping customer 128. This will be a while. I think of coming back another time. It's always busy on Fridays.

I'm on a mission, though, picking up prescriptions for my family who live at the House of a Hundred Grandmothers.

I'd visited them earlier, sitting on a bench in the park outside it. They handed me a Ziploc bag with their prescription printed out and health plan membership card. They didn't have to pay anything for them today. As I understand it, many medicines are "in the basket," covered by the plans. For some others, once you hit the payment limit for them, refills for the rest of the year are free.

The numbers in the pharmacy line go by relatively quickly. Many people still give up and leave. The numbers count through from 132 to 140 without anyone coming to the counter.

Some of the people who leave without being served place their numbers in a neat pile on top of a display of masks near the queuing machine. People riffle through the pile. If they find a number that's sufficiently far ahead, they take it and leave their own.

I'm ready when called. I tell the pharmacist that I have two separate orders. He fills my family's first, then my own. I bag them up separately and head out. I still have to run the rest of my Friday errands before the stores close for the Sabbath.

Saturday, December 26th, 2020

An alert tells me that the dance center is livestreaming. I open a window to watch. So do a couple of dozen other people.

The screen shows an unmoving image of one of the walkways. The image is vertical. It's probably coming from someone's phone.

Eventually the image moves. The person with the camera wanders through the walkway, turns around, and sets it down. We watch the walkway from the other side. Someone walks past the camera. People in the chat stream ask what is going on. The website says that nothing is scheduled.

The camera goes back through the walkway and across the plaza. Several large equipment cases sit evenly spaced across the plaza in a straight line. Phones set up on two of them also show live images. People sit on the low stone walls. Some talk. Some drink coffee. A dog runs through. People off-screen discuss something in French. I don't speak enough French to understand.

After almost an hour, someone picks up the camera and shuts the stream down. A new lockdown starts tomorrow. That is as close as I'll get to spending quiet time outside the dance center. It's been a pleasant hour.

Later, someone official tells the chatstream that it was part of a world-wide demonstration by shut-down cultural centers. Oh. I go back to the page and pop it open to full screen. While I do other things, I let it play again.

Sunday, December 27th, 2020

We're celebrating one of the bosses' birthdays.
They've both come to work early, but they head out again to get their vaccinations. We have to wait a longer time for appointments. I'll be getting mine a week from Wednesday. The bosses have a way of getting things to happen on demand. I don't yet know the magic phrases that the locals yell at each other. They seem to work.

Lunch arrives soon after the bosses get back. To celebrate the birth-day, they've ordered in sushi and a kind of Chinese noodles with veg-etables. Both are delicious. That we're having Chinese food on the first working day after Christmas is completely coincidental.

As with other celebrations this year, we don't crowd into the confer-ence room to eat. A worker puts the meals together and hands them to us as we stand in the hall.

After lunch and the afternoon prayers, they unveil a cake. We stand outside the conference room, almost appropriately distanced. Blowing out candles on cakes is no longer allowed. Someone hands the boss two leftover Chanukah candles and lights them. She turns away from us, blows them out, turns back, and bows.

We all sing "Today is your birthday! Today is your birthday!" She hollers "No! No! It was yesterday!" We switch to "Yesterday was your birthday!" without skipping a beat.

The cake is wonderful, with a layer of caramel and what tastes like cannoli filling. People chatter in the hallway in Hebrew. Someone asks me how much I understand. Ten percent? Fifteen? In this conversation, I understand about forty percent. Another worker says that when he was my age, he understood Hebrew perfectly. Right. He's two years younger than I am. And he's been here for over thirty years.

People sing that the boss should live to one hundred and twenty. If I live that long, I may catch on.

Monday, December 28th, 2020

I stand, puzzled, in the space in the supermarket downstairs where people queue for the cashiers. Most of the lanes appear busy. Customers have left several carts there. Two have children in them.

I head over toward the line for people with ten items or fewer. My arms are full of groceries, but I think I still qualify. When I pass the lane before it, the cashier slaps her hand on the counter and points to me. She doesn't have a customer at the moment. I step around a cart and a child and drop my items on the conveyor belt.

She rings me up quickly. I hand her my debit card. "Joseph," she says. What? "Oh," she says in English. "I thought that I remembered your name. I saw your card when you were here before. I see your card now. I was right."

They've changed the card reading mechanism to an electronic sensor. The customer usually holds the card up to it. She already has my card. She does it. She types something on a screen that I can't see.

An error appears on the sensor. "I shall try again." It fails again.

I reach for my other card. "No, we do not need that. This card will work."

She tries it a third time. Right when it beeps for the scan, she types a code. "We have success! Sometimes we have to type very fast."

I put my groceries in my bag. When the receipt prints out, she hands it and the card to me. "There you are. Have a nice –" She looks out the window. "Evening. Have a nice evening, Joseph." I think I will.

Tuesday, December 29th, 2020

Early in the morning, toward the front of the city square, older people sit and read their newspapers. Many of the papers are in Hebrew. Many appear to be in Russian. A man hawking free newspapers tries to hand me one. I decline.

Despite the lockdown, most shops are open. The clothing stores are closed. My favorite hummus joint is taking the opportunity to do renovations. Their menu had covered its front wall below the counter. It's gone. The wall now has attractive wood-like paneling.

The shop with the odd sandwiches and good sahlab is open. I get a coffee and a cheese burekas. I had a routine blood test at my health plan's clinic this morning. I fasted overnight. I'm famished.

I take my breakfast to a chess table and eat it there. When I'm done, I head to work.

On the street my office is on, I pass a kindergarten. Over a fence just shorter than my eye level, I see a woman standing alone. She wears a gray cable-knit sweater and a black skirt. She shivers as if cold. Her cigarette has burned down close to the filter. She is staring into her phone. She may be crying. The loudspeaker over her head plays a never-ending version of "Old MacDonald Had a Farm."

Wednesday, December 30th, 2020

The sandwich shop is already closed by the time I get to the city square. On the plaza next to the Great Synagogue, one door of the ice cream shop is open. People are standing outside. As I approach, I see that two of them are handing money to the third. He ducks inside and brings out cones for them. He sees me standing there.

"Can I help you?" Can I have a sahlab?

"Large or small?" Large.

We had been speaking Hebrew. He switches to English. "Yes. One moment. You must stand outside the door or police come."

He goes inside and mixes it up while I dig out coins to pay him. He comes out and hands me the sahlab, with all the toppings on it. I hand him exact change and head over to a bench to eat.

My family is doing an international text chat. I have to keep putting the cup down to tap my screen.

Behind me, an ambulance is set up as a bloodmobile. Its lights spin silently. Reflections of the red beacons swoop across my phone.

When I'm done, I throw out my cup and head home. I have walked this path hundreds of times. I miss a turn somewhere. I get lost. I know roughly where I am, but not where the streets go. I follow the one I'm on. I figure that I'm headed northeast. I'm headed south.

The road ends on the street with the ice cream shop, about a block away. I know where I am now.

I head home again. This time, I get it right.

Thursday, December 31st, 2020

My direct boss asks me what I'm looking for in the kitchen cabinets. I'm looking for a coffee mug. I need coffee. "I thought perhaps you were looking for happiness." That too, but happiness is best appreciated when awake.

When I get to my desk, I see that part of our computer system has stopped working. I need to use it to do screenshots for the manual I'm finishing today.

The boss isn't in the office. Many of us are standing around. I overhear some coworkers, speaking in Spanish, mentioning the chant, "The people united will never be defeated." I don't know what they're saying about it. I know the song. It gets stuck in my head for hours.

When I go downstairs to the supermarket, I see a woman slip some envelopes into a tall red box. I couldn't identify it before. So that's what mailboxes look like here. Knowing that, the sign about pickup times on it makes sense. I had thought the box held some kind of meter. The only times that I've mailed letters here, other people have handled it for me.

When I get back upstairs, the computer is working again. No one is sure what had happened. I finish my manual on time. Many workers leave for the weekend a bit early. As I head out, I think of wishing our Spanish and Russian speakers a "Feliz Novy God," but no one left in the office would get it.

January 2021

Friday, January 1st, 2021

I scan my groceries in the supermarket at the Heart of the City. A young worker pitches me their club card. It's sort of like the ones in US supermarkets, except that it's a real credit card. I had turned it down before. The buses have changed. Other supermarkets are less accessible. Now it makes sense.

Partway into the pitch, his high-speed Hebrew loses me. I say I don't understand. He switches to English. I would like to sign up, but didn't they just say that the store is closing right now for the Sabbath? "No problem. It will only take a moment." Management probably judges him on how many signups he gets. I've been there.

The signup kiosk is about a meter from where I'm checking out. He takes my government ID and types in my number. He asks if I have another credit card. I hand him the one from the mall supermarket. "Wonderful. We work the same way. This has almost all the information we need."

He also asks me for my phone number and address. We have to try the address a few times. It turns out he can't quite hear me over the noise. We eventually get it right.

Since I'm signing up for the card, I get fifty shekels off this purchase. That would be good, but I'm only buying thirty shekels worth of groceries. The discount won't work. "Do you see twenty shekels of more things you want? They will be free." I don't want to roam through the closing store.

I see some sliced cheese in a case nearby. I get it. It still comes to too little. The worker disappears, then shows up again with another package of the same cheese. OK.

I need to sign some forms on the kiosk screen. I step over to it. To sign, I have to block the path from the checkout lanes to the exit. A woman comes up to me and asks me to let her by. I do.

The worker watches her leave. "A customer asked you quietly. That never happens."

I have to shift over a couple of more times while I sign everything. When I step back to my checkout station, I see that the screen has locked. A manager has to come over and type a code.

The worker hands me a confirmation page. I scan a bar code on it to get the discount. I only have to pay a few remaining shekels for everything. We thank each other.

I bag my groceries and try to leave. A guard has to unlock the exit to let me out. I step outside and check my phone. I should still have time to get a challah at the bakery and some lunch at the sandwich shop before heading home.

Saturday, January 2nd, 2021

Two empty cups of noodles sit on the chess table with the best light. They've been there a while. After I throw them in the trash, I brush away the noodles that had spilled on the table then dried. I sit down with a book and my coffee.

The Sabbath café is open, with just the one worker. She sits at a table with her laptop until I come in. The shops seem to have made a tacit agreement with the lockdown authorities. They're OK with one masked person at a time coming into the shop and leaving with what they get. Tables and chairs are set up on the patio, but I go to the city square.

Men with dogs and children walk by. I see a lot of scooters and terriers. A young girl is learning to ride a bike. I never have. Each time I've tried, I've ended up stopping the bike by brushing the ground with my face.

In front of the sandwich shop, a man is doing something loud with a truck and a metal cart. I can't see what it is. It involves a lot of banging.

At the taxi stand, burly men with shorts and sweatshirts wait for riders to come by or call.

As I read a music book, I get an idea for how to improve some visuals in my film project. I want them to work more effectively on smaller screens.

I stand and throw away my coffee cup. As I leave the square, the streetlights come on, one by one.

Sunday, January 3rd, 2021

The door to the burger joint is ajar. I stick my head in and ask if I can order takeaway.

The cashier says something about a telephone. I don't quite hear it. Another worker, standing behind me, taps on the outside of the window. "Call here."

I back out of the doorway and look. A sign shows the shop's phone number. I call it. The cashier answers. We wave at each other through the window. I order on the phone. It feels like the way that prison visits are depicted on TV. The cashier and I are talking both with our hands and on the phone.

I do it all in Hebrew, though I get jumbled once. I remember that they call sweet potatoes "*batata*" and fries "*chips*." Thrown by using one English word, I ask for "*batata chips*" rather than the proper "*chips batata*." After a second try, the cashier understands. She says to wait outside for a few minutes.

Another worker comes out with the bag and calls my name. I take the bag and hand him my card. He rings me up and returns the card. I duck around two scooters from the delivery company and continue on home.

Monday, January 4th, 2021

The shortcut to the mall is dark. A few pale, yellowed lamps glow above the path around the playing fields, but no light shines on the larger road that runs past the club and the roller skating pen. To my left, I hear recorded music and people playing basketball. I can't see them in the shadows. I wonder if they can play strictly by sound.

I start to walk down the road. We're a few nights past the full moon. The moonlight is enough. Still, I recall that months ago, when I last walked here, construction blocked the far end. That sent me off course, even in the daylight.

I take a path out to the parking lot and head to the street. I hear traffic. No cars go past. The sound must be from the freeway, far from here. I only see one other person on the street.

At the entrance to the mall, the few customers each hold a hand up to a mounted thermometer. It proclaims "Normal temperature" in English.

The guard lets us enter. He doesn't bother to check most people's bags. Out of habit, I have mine open. He glances at it and waves me in.

Inside, the lights are dim. A handful of people stand around. I see the bright lights of the supermarket at the end of the hall. That's all I need.

Tuesday, January 5th, 2021

My phone pings soon after I wake up. It's a text from my health plan. My doctor will be calling at 8:40 AM. They had told me a few days ago that she would be calling today, but I didn't know at what time. I was worried that I wouldn't be able to answer the phone when she chose to call. Now I know.

She calls precisely on time. She has the results of my blood tests. They have sent them to me, too, but I didn't know what they mean. Arcane Hebrew acronyms label sliding scales with numbers that I can't understand.

It turns out that I did pretty well. My B12 is low. She says I'm not eating enough meat. I'll start taking tablets for it. My glucose is good. "You don't have diabetes … yet." I haven't yet made some specialist appointments that she says that I need. I haven't been measuring my weight and blood pressure.

She says to make an in-person appointment. "I will measure these and tell you again how important it is to look after your health."

I make the appointment before I can procrastinate on it. On Monday morning, she will yell at me gently. Things will get done.

Wednesday, January 6th, 2021

Bright slogans cover the outside of the vaccination hut, one block inland from the seashore. I miss the entrance and go in through the wrong door. I find my way to the front from inside.

The space feels warm and cheerful. The workers seem excited to help. They scan my health plan card and give me a number.

The numbers go past quickly. When the automated voice calls mine, I am welcomed into a smaller area with booths separated by drapes. A nurse waves me in to one and peppers me with questions. We start in Hebrew, but I quickly ask for English. I don't want to guess what medical questions mean.

Do I have any allergies? Have I had any shots in the past two weeks? Do I have a fever? Do I have the virus? She whispers the virus's name, as if she doesn't want to summon demons. Right or left? I don't know what she means. She mimes writing. I do, too. I see that I'm writing with my right hand. Right and left confuse me. She gives me the shot in my other arm. After the initial pinprick, I feel nothing.

She says to wait in the main area for fifteen minutes. I do. I read the wall in front of me, painted with wishes: That we might return to loving. That we might hug Grandma and Grandpa. That we might travel the world. That we might go back to doing what we love.

When it's time to go, I pick up a bottle of water and a fortune cookie: "Soon we will see our team win on the field."

A text message from the health plan tells us that anyone eligible who hasn't been vaccinated yet should just show up here anytime in the next two days. I hear a worker say that they'll be open 24/7.

I walk along the beach as the sun sets. I carefully skirt the edge of the surf. A raven runs beside me, cawing in sets of threes. A tiny blond girl hops on one foot, pausing and balancing to pick up shells.

One small puddle turns out to be deep. I get soaked up to my knees. After that, stepping in more water doesn't matter.

Thursday, January 7th, 2021

Three boys on foot-powered scooters zoom around the center of the plaza outside the Great Synagogue. It's a safe, bounded area. Three shallow steps lead down to it on the street side. Higher walls bound it on two. The fourth has what is now a large square of dirt. It may have been tilled for new planting. I can't picture what had been there before.

The same girls as before sit on the ground, up against the far wall. Families cluster around a row of chairs under roofs that would shade them from the sun, were the sun still out.

I sit at one end of the plaza, far enough from everyone else to be comfortable taking my mask down and eating my sahlab. I may not be able to get another for a while. A new lockdown starts at midnight. Announcements warn us that it will be enforced more strictly than the current one.

I listen on my headphones to reports of the chaos at the US Capitol, collected into podcasts after the fact. A car with markings from the lottery agency drifts slowly past. A woman's recorded voice booming from it announces the latest winning numbers. Maybe someone within earshot got lucky. Nobody appears to react. The winner must be elsewhere. The car travels on.

Friday, January 8th, 2021

The small park behind the coffee shop on the city square has become a de facto outdoor café.

After my Friday shopping, I see that the shop's front counter is open. I approach. They tell me to order around back. I go there and look around. People are sitting at the picnic tables, on plastic chairs, and on milk crates.

A worker emerges from a nondescript door. "Do you want to order?" I ask her for a large coffee granita. I hand her money. She returns after a while with the drink and my change.

I sit on a low wall, a couple of meters from the trash can. Most of the seats are either taken or too close to other clusters of people.

A tighter lockdown has been in effect since midnight. I don't see much sign of it. Only the book and clothing stores are closed. All the falafel joints but one are open for orders. People stand around, a proper distance from their doors.

Before I get my coffee, I order a cheese burekas from the sandwich shop and eat it at a chess table. The usual Friday backgammon game is in progress. The owner of the hummus joint sits at a table in front of his shop. He takes to-go orders on the phone and from passersby. They stand back near where the tables used to be. He brings the completed orders to them.

In the brick-lined park, sitting on the wall, I start to drink my granita quickly. I get a brain freeze, lower than usual, by the side of my nose. It eventually passes. I drink the rest more slowly.

When I'm done, I get up, take my groceries, and leave. A man, walking with two small daughters and their bicycles, comes and sits on the wall where I had been.

Saturday, January 9th, 2021

Even the Sabbath café is closed for the lockdown. An ice cream joint around the corner has its door open as usual, but an array of tables blocks the entrance. Plastic menus on several tables show the available flavors. Workers talk inside. None notice me looking at the menus.

A small store a few doors down is open. It carries liquor and some food. A handful of men usually sit outside, talking in something like Arabic, but they aren't there today.

I see an ice cream freezer out front. I pick out a cone and go to the counter. There's a coffee machine behind it. I ask for an espresso. "Short or long?" As many times as people have explained the difference to me, I can never remember what it means when I need to. I ask for the long.

I head back to the city square with the cone and coffee. I sit at the best-lit chess table. The cone is very good: vanilla, but with a layer of a harder butter-flavored candy on top and a chocolate coating. I hear birds in the tree above me. I put the paper top from the cone over the coffee cup just in case.

There's enough light for me to read more of the book on music composition I've been carrying around. A woman wearing what looks like a sari comes past me, smiles, and says *"Bon appétit."*

Children roll past me on bicycles. One heads straight for the street, yelling, unable to stop. A grown man at the curb grabs the boy and the bike, spinning with the momentum. The man continues to hold him as he cries.

A couple runs over. The man gently hands the boy over to them and stands the bike up against a lamp post. He nods to them and walks away. The streetlight comes on, casting the family in a vague halo as the sun continues to set.

Sunday, January 10th, 2021

Nine of us wait for a tenth man to appear for the afternoon prayers. The boss looks around. "I know it's been hard for people to get here through the ice and snow." It's seventy degrees Fahrenheit and sunny.

Lockdown roadblocks had slowed some people coming in to work. Cars were being stopped on the major roads. Most of us have forms showing that we are essential workers. We support hospital computer systems. Of those who have showed up on my side of the office, only one drives to work. The rest of us walk, bike, or take buses or trains.

I stand in my usual place, leaning up against a pillar between two windows. The boss looks at me. "You should step into the sun. You are too pale." OK. I get enough sun when I walk to work.

The boss starts off the first prayer slowly. We don't need the ten men for that one. He takes his time, enunciating each word rather than plowing through in the usual high-speed murmur.

A tenth man shows up just as the boss gets to the end. He takes a spot near the office door. I don't know if he's actually praying, but his attentive presence is enough.

Monday, January 11th, 2021

The crowd outside the pharmacy is confused. As I approach, I see a few people step up to the doors, which open for them. Some are let in. Some aren't. I get to the doors as they open again.

I hear the guard explain what's going on. It sounds like he's done this a lot. "If you are here for prescriptions, only five people can come in at a time. If you are here for any other part of the store, you can come in now." The official limit for the store as a whole is seventy customers. I guess they're nowhere near that.

I'm here for a prescription. I have to wait. The next time the door opens, the guard lets the five people in front of me in. I'm number six.

Other people crowd behind me. Some ask me in Hebrew what's happening. I can't put the words together. Some speak to me in Russian. I can't answer them either.

After a while, five more of us are let in. The man behind me barrels ahead and gets to the queuing machine first. The machine spits out a number. He takes it and hands it to me, since I was waiting before him. He then takes a number for himself. His courtesy surprises me.

I'm number 372. When they call 371, no one answers quickly, so they call me. Just as I get to the counter, a woman zooms over from the cosmetics racks, yelling that she is 371. Another pharmacist appears at the next counter. "Sir, 372, I can assist you here."

I'm there for the vitamin B-12. He gets it for me. There's no discount for getting it as a prescription from my health plan, but at about fifteen dollars for a three-month supply, that's OK. I'm to take one a day, under my tongue. I'm not sure when.

When I get up in the morning, I take the first pill of the day. I have to wait half an hour before eating. I slip the B-12 tablet under my tongue. It's small and fits there comfortably. It tastes of artificial cherries. It dissolves after about twenty minutes. That's OK.

I catch up on email, get breakfast, and head off to see my doctor, in person this time.

Tuesday, January 12th, 2021

The tag in one of the bins of gelato is wrong. In Hebrew, it correctly shows the contents as strawberry sherbet. In English letters, it says

"Dulce de Leche." The bin behind it really is *dulce de leche* and has been tagged correctly. Perhaps the person making the tags got lost in the list of flavors. They also might not have known what flavor *dulce de leche* really is, or what it means in whatever language that is. I'm not sure if it's Spanish, Italian, or something else.

I spot the tag as I stand outside the shop waiting for a sahlab. Officially, they shouldn't be serving people, but, even with the tighter lockdown, standing outside seems OK.

I think of telling the worker that the sign is wrong, but there's little point to it. I don't know how I'd tell him, and he probably wouldn't be able to fix it. He's on the phone, anyway. He can't find one of the ingredients and is asking someone else where it is.

When I get the sahlab, I sit on my usual bench. People drift past me and around the plaza. A young girl in a yellow dress runs back and forth under the roof over the chairs. Occasionally, she jumps in the air and stomps down on one of the colored lights set in the ground.

A man in a torn parka walks along the curb, shrieking quietly every few seconds. A delivery person stops his scooter and calls a name. A man dressed in traditional black and white, with a matching black and white mask, takes bags from the delivery person, walks to the plaza steps, and sits down with his family to eat.

A teenager walks along another edge of the plaza as if on a tightrope. Halfway along, she loses her balance and starts to fall. She turns slightly, bends her knees, and launches herself into the air. She spins, lands safely, and bows. Her friends applaud.

I finish my sahlab. I pick up the cup, spoon, and napkins, as well as the trash that had been on the bench when I got there. I put my mask back on and continue on home.

Wednesday, January 13th, 2021

In the twenty-shekel store, some things cost twenty shekels. Some things cost less. Some things aren't worth as much as they're charging.

Twenty shekels equals a bit over six dollars now. A few weeks ago, it was about five dollars. The papers say that our money is worth more now, because we are doing well on vaccinations.

A few people are waiting in line outside when I get there. The line moves quickly. They've designed the store to get people in and out efficiently. There's little space to pause and calculate whether things are worth their price. Customers spot things, get them, and think later.

The one glitch is right at the door. When we enter, we wave our hands in front of a temperature scanner. It isn't working well. The sensor is more directional than I've seen elsewhere. I have to try it a few times before it lets me in.

I'm looking for shoelaces. Both of mine have broken. I'm told that shoemakers carry them, but the one in the neighborhood is never open when I go past. Retail shoe stores don't have them. Drugstores don't either. I still think in terms of US stores, where you can get just about anything anywhere.

I look for the shoelaces here in the twenty-shekel store. I don't see them. I start to ask a worker. I forget the word, though I used to know it. I lift my foot and pull on one of them. The worker shakes her head. "Shoelaces," she says in English. "No. We don't have them. Sorry."

I thank her and wind my way through the store and out. The remnants of my current laces will hold for a few more days. I'll try two shoemakers on Friday morning. They have to have them somewhere.

Thursday, January 14th, 2021

A hand comes into view and presses something hard against my forehead. A finger pulls the trigger. It beeps. The voice of our usual guest announces, "You are clear to come to pray."

I look up. He has swiped the scanning thermometer from the reception desk. He goes around doing this to several of us. He skips the boss, whose desk is too large for him to reach across.

We shamble over to the hallway. It's colder than usual there. Several weeks ago, a full year's worth of rain fell in one day. It's been dry and warmer since then. Now it's raining again. The guest opens a window, then closes it.

A tenth man shows up. The boss's son calls out the first line of the opening psalm, starting the prayers.

My mind wanders. Someone had asked me a question about music production at lunchtime. My answer to him had rambled. I talked about Frank Zappa, Peter Gabriel, and Taylor Swift. I think I got the point across, but I want to research more.

The leader calls out another line in the midst of the silent prayer. Today is the new moon, so we add a paragraph. His voice brings me back to the present. I continue with the prayers, listening to the other men murmuring and shuffling, and to the rain.

Friday, January 15th, 2021

The store-bought sahlab comes in a lidded cup, much like the yogurt with add-ins that I get each afternoon. I've never seen it before.

I'm in a small supermarket off the city square, finishing up my Friday shopping. I'd been going to the larger supermarket in the Heart of the City, but that's gotten complicated.

I had signed up for their club card. It arrived in the mail a few days ago. It said to text a word to a phone number to get my PIN code. It took me a while to figure out how to send a text from my phone to a nameless number rather than to a contact. One of the jungle of apps on my phone can do it, but the field to enter the number is mislabeled in the interface.

I think I figured it out, and sent the code, but never got a response. It should have happened instantly. If I go to the usual supermarket, they'll badger me to get the card. I can show them that I already have it, but don't have the code. I don't feel like being looked at like an idiot again, so I'm at the other store today.

The sahlab is in their dairy case. I get one, on a whim. When I get home and want a snack, I look at the package. Normally, things packed like that are eaten cold. Sahlab is better hot.

The lid contains the usual mix-ins: ground peanuts, coconuts, and spice. The cup has the sahlab itself.

I put it in the microwave for about a minute. I stare carefully as it turns and heats. I don't know if this kind of plastic will melt or catch fire. It doesn't.

I take it out, peel the covering from the lid, and dump the flavorings on top. It's pretty good. It doesn't quite have the same flavor or texture as what I get in the shops, but it could serve as a stopgap. I'll have to remember it. I may stock up on more.

Saturday, January 16th, 2021

I have to zip up my hoodie for the first time this season. I have trouble finding the slider and fear that it may have broken off sometime. I carefully run my fingers up that side of the zipper. I find it at the top, nestled against the collar.

The city square is chilly. I probably should have worn warm socks with my sandals, too. I'm sitting with an espresso from the corner shop with the ice cream freezers out front.

I'm working my way through another chapter of the music text. It's a quick read, but I keep stopping to think.

Fewer people than usual are out now. It may be too cold for many. Dogs and their humans go past occasionally. Last week, it was mostly terriers. Today, I see a lot of what I think are Labrador retrievers.

In the quiet of the afternoon, I spot things I hadn't seen before. A sign says that the city's first bus station was here, next to the square. Or maybe the square itself used to be the bus station.

A box that I think controls traffic lights has what looks like an abandoned monitor on top of it. That turns out to be a solar panel.

I don't stay downtown for long. It's too chilly. I make myself a new heuristic: when the temperature drops below 15 C, wear socks.

Sunday, January 17th, 2021

The thunderstorm starts while I'm in the supermarket downstairs from the office. I hadn't figured on that. I'm not dressed for it.

While checking out, I wonder what to do. I have a long time to think. The person before me is paying for some of his purchase with a paper bag full of change. The cashier doesn't complain. She pours it out onto a newspaper, separates the coins, and counts them.

I know that my apple and yogurt will cost between six and eight shekels, depending on the weight of the apple. I have my ten-shekel piece ready.

I head out and stand under the canopy at the exit. I'd rather not deal with the rain. It doesn't look like it will be stopping soon.

A corridor near the courtesy desk heads out of the store. I'm not sure where it goes. I double back into the store and follow it. It dead-ends at an elevator down to the parking deck. I figure that I can go down, then take another elevator up to the office.

This elevator only makes two stops: here, on the ground floor (Level Zero) and Level Minus-2. I get off there. I figure that I'm within a few meters of the other elevator. I circle the outside of the one that I came down in. I don't see it. I circle again, looking at the surrounding walls. Still nothing.

I give up, head back to the store, go out again, and run to the door of the office building itself. I get wet, but not too wet.

It's still raining at the end of the day. My bosses give me a ride home. They tell me that there is a way to get from one elevator to the other on Minus-2. Someday they'll show me.

Monday, January 18th, 2021

Only one checkout line is open at the supermarket at the Heart of the City. As I approach it, the cashier walks away. He's in the midst of ringing someone up.

A man stands between the checkout and me. He doesn't have a bag or basket. His arms are full of groceries. While we wait, several more people get in line behind me. Some change their minds and go over to the self-scanners. I would use them, but I have some meat that I'm not sure how to scan.

This weekend will be a good time to make a cholent. I want to try out my new card. The text message with the link to the PIN code finally arrived yesterday. The instantaneous can take a while here.

The man in front of me drops his groceries on the floor. Nothing breaks. He stomps out of the store, shouting in what might be Vietnamese.

I move up to where he was. I start placing my groceries on the conveyor belt. The cashier eventually returns. He speaks to the customer whose purchase was in progress. "So you want to cancel all this?" She nods.

He moves her groceries to the aisle behind him and rings me up. He scans my card when he's done. He never asks for the PIN. Since it's my first purchase with the new card, I get seventy-five shekels off. That's good.

I pack up my groceries and leave. Looking back, I see several customers waiting. No one has picked up what the shouting man dropped. No other lines have opened. The customers don't look happy.

Tuesday, January 19th, 2021

It's raining again as I head down to the supermarket. I try to get there underground.

The elevator from the supermarket only goes to one other floor, Minus-2. The elevator from the office building goes there, too. I head out of the office and take the elevator to Minus-2. I go to an exit door to the parking deck itself. It's locked. So is the other one.

I see an open staircase. I take it down to Minus-3. When I get there, I realize that it's useless for this. There's no way up to the supermarket from there. Departing cars spiral up a corkscrew path, but there's no space to walk along it.

I get on the office elevator, take it back to the ground floor, and run outside to the supermarket. It isn't raining too hard.

I stop by the guard to get my temperature scanned. He doesn't look up from his phone. He points. They've put up a scanner on a tripod mount. I scan my hand. 36.5 degrees. OK.

I go inside to shop. I grab an apple and yogurt and stand in line. I look in my wallet. I don't have a ten-shekel coin or a small bill, just a hundred and a pile of change. My purchase comes to 7.6 shekels.

I count out coins, mostly half-shekel pieces, and hand them to the cashier. I've counted wrong. She needs another 1.4 shekels. The customer behind me asks, in a pitying tone, if she can help. No.

I dig out the remaining amount and hand it to the cashier, then go back outside. I take a breath and prepare to run back through the rain.

Wednesday, January 20th, 2021

I pull up the hood of my sweatshirt as more rain starts to fall. The hood's enough for now.

The weather report said that we would only have a 20 percent chance of rain today. The rain now is only falling about 20 percent as hard as it was. It's a vague dripping drizzle rather than a torrent. I guess they were right. The cats still wander about. The snails haven't come out yet.

Around lunchtime, a volley of thunder shakes the building. I'm immediately alert. When I last worked around here, in the Eighties, the sound of an explosion like that would put everyone on edge. Now, few react.

Another similar clap of thunder a few hours later summons a hailstorm. It falls straight down, not at an angle like the rain. I finally have the opportunity to text my local family: "Gang! Gang! The hail's all here!" It ends quickly.

At the afternoon prayers, the building manager tells us that he had seen hail today the size of a falafel ball. Somehow, the floor of the atrium appears dry.

I leave work early. I want to be home to watch the American inauguration. I walk through more moments of drizzle.

Once I'm home, I see that the power glitched during the day. Some things have reset. Some haven't.

As I turn on the TV, I hear one more, smaller thunderclap and a few seconds of further rain. The clouds quickly give up and drift away.

Thursday, January 21st, 2021

It's cold outside, but not too cold, damp but not raining. I get to work at about the usual time and continue with what I usually do.

I'm rewriting a manual from several years ago. Not much in the program has changed, but the manual needs a complete overhaul. After I first read it last week, I had to ask my boss what the program actually is for and what it does. The website didn't help much either. The overly technical writing assumes that you were already familiar with the obscure quirks of the operating system. If you don't, as I wasn't, it's effectively technobabble.

I mostly work on fixing the formatting of what I have. Once that's done, I can start to rewrite it. I also shoot images of the program's few screens.

Just as I'm about to head out, the boss calls me into his office. He finally demos the program for me. When I note some oddities in the screen menus, he changes them on the spot. They're better, but I now have to reshoot them for the manual.

I miss the bus that I wanted to take, as well as the one after that. I could certainly walk, but the bosses give me a ride home.

An alert on my phone tells me that the government will be changing the bus rates soon. Most will be reduced. The article says, with a straight face, that local fares around here will be lowered from 5.9 shekels to 6. I close my eyes for a moment and look again. Yes, that's what it says. I put my phone back in my pocket. I'll find out the new fare when it happens, but probably not before.

Friday, January 22nd, 2021

Ten or more men are gathered around the weekly backgammon match in the city square. There are enough of them that they could burst into prayer if they wanted to. I doubt that they would.

I'm out earlier than usual for my Friday shopping. I was too tired last night to start up a fresh pot of cold brew, so I don't have coffee ready at home.

I head out relatively soon after waking. The sun is straight ahead as I walk through the square. It shouldn't be. I'm walking south. Everything ahead of me that I can see at all is in silhouette.

I stop into the sandwich shop and get a large cappuccino. It's hotter than I expect. Drinking it takes longer than I want.

There's a line outside the pharmacy, as usual. This time, they aren't distinguishing between those there for prescriptions and general shoppers.

A docile dog waits a few meters away, chained to a post. A toddler, still practicing how to walk, crashes into it. It yelps once, then quietly sits back down.

The line moves quickly. When I get inside, only one person is ahead of me in line. I get the one medication that I need and leave. Elsewhere on the street, I get my groceries, a challah, and another espresso, then head back home.

Saturday, January 23rd, 2021

This cholent is more ad-hoc than those I've made before. Usually, I use a recipe and measure things carefully. I've been told repeatedly that measuring cups are just for Americans. OK, then.

This time, I dump into the crock pot one package of white barley, one package of bulgur, one can of white beans, one can of garbanzo beans, the thawed-out leftover gravy-like stuff from the previous beef stew, a couple of teaspoons of baharat spice, and two kilograms of cubed-up flanken. The flanken says on the package "Asada Flanken #9." So I guess that's what *carne asada* is. I should look up the seasonings for it.

I pour in water to cover, stir it all up, and leave the crock pot on Auto for about fifteen hours. The result is pretty good. It's much more dense than usual. What I'd been making before was too thin, so this is better. It's kind of like oatmeal (without the strong oatmeal flavor) with beans and chunks of meat in it. If it weren't for the heavy meat, it might be good for breakfasts. I'll have to remember that.

There isn't a lot of flavor. The taste of the meat kind of gets lost. I may spice it further when I reheat future meals.

What's left after lunch fills ten of my serving-sized freezer containers, the container that had held the gravy, and another larger container that I had gotten with some meat-based to-go food a long time ago.

Some remnants of the cholent are still caked in the crock pot. I leave them to soak overnight.

Late in the evening, I realize that I haven't eaten any supper. I'm still full from lunch. I should eat something, though, so I don't wake up hungry in the middle of the night.

I won't have to worry about what to make for Sabbath lunches for the next few months. By that time, it should be getting hot again. If I make anything in bulk then, it will be something more suited to the season.

Sunday, January 24th, 2021

The office kitchen is crowded. Three people are talking inside. They tell me that I look tired and wonder if I'm still staying up late to celebrate the inauguration. Some of them have taken to calling me President Joe.

I pour myself a cup of coffee from the water boiler near the door and back out while talking to them. I'm telling them excitedly about some music I'm working on.

I forget that at the far end of the entrance to the kitchen, a pillar juts out from the adjoining wall. I crash into it. My coffee spills onto my belly and onto the floor. I go back into the kitchen, get paper towels, and kneel on the floor to wipe up the spill.

When I have gotten up what the paper towels will hold, I try to stand. My left foot is on a wet spot. It slides out from under me. I flatten out on the floor. I get back up on my hands and knees, crawl to a pillar, and pull myself up to stand.

I see that the belly of my shirt is soaked. It's a dark army green. It should dry quickly. It won't show much of a stain. My skin is slightly burnt, but not badly so.

I head back into the kitchen, pick up my cup with what coffee remains in it, and return to my desk. It's going to be a long day.

Monday, January 25th, 2021

Through eavesdropping and conversation, I pick up some new words. I had known that "to compile" is, in Hebrew, "*l'kampeyl.*" Today, I hear some programmers using the word "*l'kanfeyg.*" I figure out, from context, that that's "to configure." I mention it to my family. They add that "to replicate" is "*l'rapleyk.*"

Apparently, all these terms use the same grammatical structure. They cut the root off at four letters. I don't know offhand of Hebrew verbs that use more than that. Some may exist.

A while back, I wondered online if "to put things in freezer bags" might be "*l'zapleyk.*" I haven't actually heard anyone say that. Yet.

The day is generally quiet, without thrills or further spills. I plow ahead on the manual I'm rewriting. I'm supposed to have it done by the end of the week, and I'm taking Wednesday off.

I work later than usual, but get a ride home from a coworker. I planned to walk home, but my boss announces that the programmer, who is leaving at the same time, will "give me a *tramp.*" I know that he means he will give me a ride. Another word made the jump from English, or maybe German, long ago. I think of declining, but I accept. The boss has commanded it. His will is done.

Tuesday, January 26th, 2021

I only write checks once a year. That's how rent is handled: the tenant writes a full year's worth of checks in advance and hands them to the landlord. Luckily, I paid attention to where I put the checkbook last year.

I know that the amount won't change. When I first got the lease, it said that the landlady could raise the amount by a little each year. I knew of a lawyer who would look over leases for free for immigrants in their first year. He suggested that I ask that they raise it by less. I did. The landlady wrote on the lease that they won't raise the rent at all. Um, OK. The lawyer kept a copy of the lease as a model. He said that it was one of the best he'd ever seen.

As of mid-February, I will have been in this apartment for three years. It's time for the next set of checks. My landlady reminds me in a text message.

She also lets me know how much I owe on the electricity bill. That's a little over a hundred dollars for two months. Not bad. One advantage of living in a basement apartment: it doesn't tend to get too hot or too cold. I've put the heat on a half dozen times or so this winter, only for about half an hour each time.

On the way home from work, I get money from the ATM to pay the bill. I give the landlady exact change as usual. I write out the checks. I have exactly twelve checks in my checkbook. I'll have to get another one before this time next year.

Wednesday, January 27th, 2021

The vaccination tent is more crowded than it was last time. We've had heavy rain since my first shot. People now wait in line inside. They've shifted some walls for this.

I have an appointment, but that doesn't seem to matter. It looks like they're vaccinating anyone who comes in. Some people get to jump the line. By law, people over eighty don't have to wait. They seem to be escorting in anyone with a white beard. Maybe I shouldn't have shaved mine a few years ago.

I have my health plan ID ready when I get to the front of the line. They don't look at it. They just ask for my government ID code. They hand me a number in the queue for shots, but tell me to ignore it and just go to where they're doing the vaccinations.

When I step through that doorway, they ask me which health plan I'm with. I tell them. Mine has priority. The worker turns to a woman in a white coat who is stepping out of a booth. "I know you're about to go on break, but can you do one more?" Of course.

She confirms my ID number and that this is the second vaccination. She's tired. She tosses a cotton ball into a trash bin, but misses it twice. I'm not worried. The target area on my arm is pretty large.

The shot takes an instant. I'm surprised. Last time it took longer. She tapes another cotton ball to the spot. "That's it. Go out and sit for ten minutes. Relax. Get some water."

A text message tells me that I can print out a temporary confirmation of my vaccination on the health plan website. The official "green passport" will come later.

I sit down in the waiting area and check the news on my phone. A government official is saying that we may have to take booster shots each year. So be it. If it's as simple as this and the flu shot, it will be worthwhile.

Thursday, January 28th, 2021

Plates of fruit cover one end of the conference table. One plate has cut up fresh fruit: apples, persimmons, clementines, kiwis, mangoes, bananas, and some I can't identify. Another has dried fruit: pineapple, raisins, and cranberries. Most are local. I didn't know that we grew bananas here, but Google tells me that we do.

Today is one of the most minor holidays, Tu Bishvat, the New Year for the Trees. There's a tradition of a sort of seder for it, but much more casual than for Passover. People mostly just eat fruit and, if they remember, say the blessings for them.

Decades ago, I wrote the liturgy for a Tu Bishvat seder that my congregation in Austin used. I left space in it for people to interject their own thoughts or songs. They did. I was surprised when someone I didn't know recited something from my first book, which had just come out.

Here, we're gathered more casually. We're clustered more closely together than usual, so most of us are wearing masks while we wait. The boss brings wine, but we don't have a corkscrew anywhere. He goes downstairs to the supermarket to buy one. He returns after a while with a small corkscrew, as well as two containers of cookies.

He pours wine for each of us. I expect him to say a blessing, perhaps one tailored to the holiday, but he just says "*L'chaim.*" We drink. We eat. We talk. After a while, we get back to work.

Friday, January 29th, 2021

The bakery has set out a vat of stuffed grape leaves. I've never seen anything that wasn't baked there before.

I ask for a small container of them. They only have one size. They sell them by weight. The cashier puts some into a container for me, one at a time. I tell him to stop after five. He puts six in. OK.

I buy them, along with a challah. I've already gotten most of my groceries at the Heart of the City supermarket. The chicken livers that I get are much cheaper than other meat. I hadn't noticed that before.

My favorite hummus joint is open on the city square. Customers line up at a table several doors down. A worker shuttles back and forth, taking and delivering orders. Delivery people have a different line, and apparently have priority.

I get my usual hummus with tahini and a couple of pita to go. The price has gone up. It's now 25 shekels rather than 22.

I don't have any coffee ready at home. I double back to the sandwich shop and get a large cappuccino. Two half-full bottles of ouzo sit on the counter next to cartons of regular, skim, and soy milk.

I sit at a chess table and drink the coffee. The seat is a bit wet, but that's OK.

I eat the hummus when I get home. Even though I had a small breakfast, I'm full after half the order. I put the rest in the refrigerator to finish someday soon.

Saturday, January 30th, 2021

Few other people are in the city square. It's late. The streetlights have come on.

I recognize many of the people who pass me: the father with two young girls, one on a scooter, one on a bike; the woman from the Sabbath café, huddled in a puffy coat against what she feels as cold; the much older woman, pulling a cart from one trash bin to the next, collecting bottles to redeem.

I'm sitting at a chess table, reading a book on postmodern dance. On the way here, I stopped at a small food store that is open on the Sabbath. I'm eating Bamba with caramel filling and drinking a small cappuccino.

I notice two purple tags stuck to the table. I realize that I'm at the same table at which I sat yesterday.

A man on a bench far from me is speaking loudly in English on his phone. He's trying to make some sort of business deal. He stops frequently and repeats more slowly what he has just said.

My phone beeps to tell me that the Sabbath will be over in ten minutes. I close my eyes for a moment to rest them from reading in the now-dim light, pack up and discard my trash, and go home.

Sunday, January 31st, 2021

My work glasses fall apart as I take them off before lunch. Most of the frame stays in my left hand. The right temple lands on my desk.

The glasses were cheap in the States. Five identical pairs cost something like seven or twelve dollars. I have several more pairs at home. I may even know where. But this is the pair that I keep at work, to use when looking at computer screens.

One section of my trifocals is right for that, but it's too narrow for me to see an entire monitor through it. I put the broken pair on to read screens during lunch and afterward, but they are off-kilter and slide off easily.

At one point, I look at the break through my good glasses. The plastic around the screw that connects the temple to the frame has worn out. I try sliding the pieces together, but there isn't enough plastic there to hold them in place.

When I go down to the supermarket for a late-afternoon snack, I pick up some super-glue. At my desk, I carefully apply it to the hinge where the glasses broke. I fit the pieces together as precisely as I can and hold them in place for a minute or so. Some of the glue oozes out and bonds my thumb to my pointer finger.

I put my glasses down and carefully pull my fingers apart, scraping the glue from between them. They detach from each other. Most of the glue comes off. The rest will wear away sometime during the week.

I pick up the glasses and wiggle the connection. It'll hold, though the hinge no longer bends. That isn't a problem. The glasses never leave my desk. I give them one good tug to make sure the glue will hold, put them on, and get back to work.

February 2021

Monday, February 1st, 2021

This bus driver flies over speed bumps. He slides around turns like a BMX biker playing bumper cars.

I'm standing at the center of the bus, desperately hanging on to one of those handholds that replaced the strap hangers' straps. Plenty of seats are available. I can't get to them. Every time I try to move, gravity shifts in another direction. I'm holding my phone in one hand. I would put it in my pocket, so I could use both hands to navigate the handholds and poles, but my pockets never seem to be where my hand and phone hit my body.

The driver slows slightly as he approaches bus stops, but not enough to make walking possible. He doesn't actually stop at any of them. The overhead announcements call out their names, but it's set wrong. It's naming the stops in reverse order, as it would on a return trip. It's good that I know where I'm going.

The bus finally stops at the Heart of the City. I stumble off and walk on sea legs one block east to the gelato shop. I settle onto a bench with a hot sahlab to steady my nerves before heading on home.

Tuesday, February 2nd, 2021

My dietitian suggests that I change my afternoon snacks. I shouldn't get the yogurt with the peanuts in the lid anymore. I'm to switch to low-fat, low-sugar yogurt, get the peanuts separately, and mix exactly twelve peanuts in with the yogurt. OK.

At the supermarket downstairs, I get a container of "American peanuts." I try them with the yogurt. They're odd, with a sort of crunchy outer layer. I look at the packaging. It has warnings for high salt and high sugar. Apparently that layer is a sort of candy shell. I wouldn't have known it from the taste.

Today, I get a container of something with a name very much like the English word "almonds." I know the Hebrew word for almonds, and this isn't it. Still I'm curious. When I look inside, I find fairly raw peanuts, along with other things that aren't nuts. At least it doesn't have the warning stickers.

I have yet to find dry roasted peanuts, like you find everywhere in the States. I already know that I can't find fresh ground peanut butter, though I've heard rumors that a shop three towns over might have it. They're another lost delicacy from the Old Country. I make do with what I can find.

Wednesday, February 3rd, 2021

This screen doesn't tell me anything that I can use. It's an "About" page, but it doesn't show me what I want to know about this.

There's a form to fill out to learn more. I would do that, but the "send" button is obscured by a banner at the bottom of the screen talking about cookies. I would dismiss that, but the button at the end of the banner is covered by a hovering blob that wants to chat with me.

I don't want to chat with them. I don't appear to have a choice. I click on the blob. A message tells me that they aren't around right now, but I can contact them with the form that I was going to use in the first place. Charming.

I hit the back button to get out of there. A window pops up asking if I would answer a brief survey about their site. I'm tempted, but I decline, though I might appreciate the challenge of writing a sentence entirely made up of four-letter words.

I go back to the page from which I got to this one. I've lost interest in the item that the "About" page supposedly was about. I try to retrace the train of thought that led me there. I've forgotten. If it's important enough, I'll remember later. I have other things to do.

Thursday, February 4th, 2021

According to the automatic translator, the text message from the Medical Center says "The cockroising lapheasure at its peak and the amount of the daily verb remains high!" Um, OK.

Someone else who got the message says that the translator is telling her "The corona plague is at its peak and the daily verified number remains high!" That makes more sense. Apparently I'm the only one who got Finnegan's wake-up call.

The rest of the message says that they're opening up vaccines to anyone over 16, so everyone should click a link for an appointment. "You are at the disposal as you need."

It's been a week since my second vaccination, so I should be immune – except they're worrying about mutations. The game of molecular whack-a-mole goes on.

Several of my office mates have gotten both their shots. Several had the virus a while ago, none seriously, so they're supposed to be immune.

The numbers for the country are pretty good, but not good enough to let down our guard. Cases among people over sixty are half of what they once were, but cases among children have gone way up.

We don't know what's going to happen next with the lockdown. All I can do is wear my mask, watch the news, and, apparently, keep away from the cockroising lapheasure.

Friday, February 5th, 2021

The package on the counter at the sandwich shop is labeled "Grandma's Hair." I pick it up and take a closer look. It's cotton candy.

The bottle of ouzo behind the glass has more in it than last week. Either they've added in the contents of the other bottle, or it's a fresh bottle of the same brand.

The worker is sitting under a canopy with friends, drinking from paper coffee cups. He trots back into the shop when he sees me enter.

I get a sandwich and an espresso at the cheap coffee chain in the Heart of the City. The sandwich is labeled "bagel toast" but it doesn't resemble what Americans would call either a bagel or toast. It's a large, round seeded bun with cheese and other things inside. The worker puts it in a press and heats it for a few minutes.

I drink the espresso while I wait, lifting my mask to sip from it. I put the sandwich, in its paper wrapper, in the bag with my groceries.

I stop at the bakery to get a challah. The vat of grape leaves is there again. I still have some left from last week, so I don't get more. The ones I've had are wonderful, though, sweet and solid, without the edge of bitterness that I sometimes taste in the leaves.

At the shop with the cotton candy, I get the sahlab. It's as good as before, too dense to drink. I sit at a chess table and eat it slowly with a spoon. Most of the men are gone from the Friday backgammon session. Only the two players remain, staring at the board and drinking Tuborg.

The clothing stores here on the city square are closed. The hummus joint is open. The coffee shops are serving people, but everything's to go.

Officially, things should change when the lockdown ends on Sunday. I suspect that they won't. Everything will look the same as it does now.

Saturday, February 6th, 2021

I finally get outside well after dark. The street is silent, except for a group of children screeching and playing about a block to my right. I turn left and walk down the pedestrian street. I can still hear them about two blocks further away.

It hasn't rained since yesterday morning. The snails have retreated to wherever they go when it's dry. One empty shell remains by the edge of the path.

I greet the cats that I pass. One, lying in the middle of the sidewalk near the city square, doesn't respond. It doesn't move, even when I walk right up to it. It appears to be lying comfortably, but I think it may have died. I would call the appropriate authorities, but I don't know whom. The sidewalk is brightly lit, so there's little chance that anyone will trip over it.

The main street is quiet, though some stores have reopened after the Sabbath. I get a sahlab from the gelato joint. The worker asks me something that I don't catch. I look puzzled. A man at the far end of the shop calls out, "Complete? Complete?" He pronounces it as in French. I repeat the word and nod.

On the way home, I see that the cat is gone. I hope it walked away on its own.

Sunday, February 7th, 2021

The mirror has been on the porch for close to a month now. It leans against a wall, across from the cardboard boxes where the cats stay at night. I imagine that they use it for grooming, checking that their whiskers are straight, and each hair is perfectly in place.

In the backyard, the landlord has taken down the rusted swing set. A long wooden box rests on the ground where it was. It took him about a week to build the box, cutting down long planks retrieved from the spot across the road where the community puts its trimmed branches and large trash.

As I head to work, I see a wheelbarrow filled with dirt near the top of my stairs. He may use it to fill in the box for planting. A contraption in the front yard may once have been a futon frame. I think he's turning it into a table. He hasn't touched it in a while. The pink tarp that covers it will probably stay there until the rains end.

As I head out of the gate, a kitten runs in. It has been trying to jump over it, but can't quite get that high. It seems annoyed that it had to wait for a human.

It trots down the path and onto the porch. It stops at the mirror. It may be surprised to see itself. It darts away quickly, runs down the steps, and finds a comfortable place inside the wooden box.

Monday, February 8th, 2021

I have to tap in a lot of data to use the café's app for the first time.

I started to do so last night, but I was too tired and hungry. I just went home. Tonight, I have more energy. I give it another shot. I sit down at the other end of the city square and take out my phone.

First, I have to select my home branch. Fortunately, it's the nearest one. I then select what I want to eat from the menu. It's smaller than their usual menu, without some of the items I'd hoped they'd have. I go for the vegetarian Mexican Bowl. This branch has no meat dishes.

Once that's done, I have to register as a user. They need my first and last name, phone number, email, birthdate, and a password, twice. Then I log my credit card. I take it out of my wallet to enter the data: government ID number, card number, that three-digit thing on the back, and its expiration date.

They send a code to the phone, so I can confirm that it's me. I don't entirely trust the code. I suppose that one out of every ten thousand people might get "9999", but I wonder if it's a glitch. I enter it anyway. I have to click to agree to several things I vaguely understand.

I look across the square at the café. I know the worker at the window from before. She speaks English, but is grumpy. I just click "agree" on everything.

I finish the order and walk to the window. I ask the worker if I would pick the order up there or in back, as we did during the lockdown. She is confused. No app orders have come in. I start to worry.

A device on the counter buzzes and prints the order. I got to the café faster than it did. I'm to wait at the window. I handle almost all the conversation in Hebrew. I get stuck on one word, when she asks me if I want cutlery. I had been told the word several years ago. I remembered that it was an acronym, but had forgotten the word itself, since I hadn't used it.

I get my order fairly quickly. I start to head home, but double back after half a block and return to the city square. I get a soda at a shop there and sit down at a chess table to eat. A cat jumps on the table and sniffs at the bowl. It jumps back down. I guess it doesn't like vegetables.

I eat the Mexican bowl as I watch people pass. It's pretty good. But it would be better in Texas.

Tuesday, February 9th, 2021

I haven't sat at this stone table before. Most of the tables have chess boards built into the stone. This has a backgammon board. The Friday players don't gather here. They bring their own board and set it up on a chess table. I suspect that they chose the table nearest to the shop where they get their beer.

I'm at the far end of the city square, near the café. I'm ordering from them again. I don't plan to make a habit of getting dinner here too often. That could get expensive.

I want to see if ordering the second time is easier. My phone or their server remembers the needed information. I order a grilled salmon sandwich.

This time, I get the soda at the other shop on the way to the café. I stash it in my hoodie's right pocket. I get to the café after my order has reached it.

The worker at the front window sees me approach.

"App?" Yes.

"Yosef?" Yes.

"Just a few minutes."

I shift to the side and wait. To my left, other customers order coffees to go from the cashier. To my right, a young girl repeatedly crashes her tricycle into the wall, laughing.

A dog in the distance barks every few seconds. The sound bounces off of several buildings. They refract and filter it. A lower bark reaches me a few milliseconds before one a perfect fourth higher.

My sandwich is done quickly. I go to the nearest table, the one with the backgammon inlay, and eat the sandwich. It is warm and delicious. Yesterday's cat isn't around. I suspect that it would be much more interested tonight.

Wednesday, February 10th, 2021

Lunch appears in a bag from a general Asian restaurant near here. The bosses have ordered in. It's a coworker's birthday.

My egg roll is pretty good. It comes with a slightly spicy duck sauce. The salmon, however, is disappointing. It consists of little bits of salmon in blobs of dough. I think they're supposed to be light and fluffy. They aren't.

Most of the bowl is filled with salad. Most of the salad is dry chopped cabbage. It comes with a salad dressing that seems to be a mishmash of miso and mayonnaise. I eat the salad. I suppose it has good fiber.

The boss comes around and asks how it is. I tell him. He knows that I tend to tell the truth, but that I also tend to like things. His lunch was similar. The chicken ranged between barely cooked and burnt, without ever hitting the right point in between.

The coworker across the aisle says that you just can't get real Japanese food here. His son lives in Japan and has tried to find their food when he has come to visit. What there is here doesn't work.

The bosses have ordered good food before. The usual shawarma is excellent. The best was roasted chicken with a lot of roast vegetables. We got that once. I will always remember it.

When I go down to the supermarket later in the afternoon, I pick up a package of chopsticks to keep in my desk. None came with lunch. I won't be caught without them again.

Thursday, February 11th, 2021

In the office kitchen, a coworker goes on an extended rant about Americans, vaccination, and capitalism. I don't know a lot of the words he uses. I smile and nod vaguely as I make my coffee. I'd probably agree with what he's saying, but I can't be sure.

After the afternoon prayers, several of us get into a discussion of the word "beyond." One coworker thinks it means the same thing as "behind." Another thinks that something beyond you is always in front of you. I demonstrate that that isn't so by trying to reach an object that's off to my left, more than an arm's length away. And then I talk about how "beyond" isn't always in terms of physical distance. I reference Buzz Lightyear. It helps.

On the way home, I pass a spot on the sidewalk where a mirror shattered last week. The glass still glistens ominously. I wonder if someone gets seven more years of bad luck if their foot further crushes a shard. I don't take a chance. I walk in the street.

Friday, February 12th, 2021

I'm at the only empty table on the city square. I can smell why it's empty.

I'm downwind from the Friday backgammon players. One of them is smoking a cigar. I like it. It reminds me of the pipe tobacco that I smoked forty-odd years ago. In college, during blizzards, we would all hang out in a dorm room, smoking pipes and listening to Bruckner. We would drink lots of tea – Earl Grey, I believe, long before Captain Picard made it trendy.

Once, when we ran out of mugs, I tried to make the tea in a glass beer mug. It exploded. The hot water fell in my lap. Those who were there said that that was the fastest anyone had seen me move.

I've gotten lunch today from my favorite hummus joint. Their normal window is open, but all orders are still to go. I get the usual hummus with tahini and two large pitas. I've gotten reasonably adept at scooping up the hummus with a shred of the pita.

When I'm done, I go into the sandwich shop to get a large coffee. The bottle of ouzo is on the counter, behind the plastic barrier. Three clear shot glasses form a perfect line from the bottle to the credit card scanner.

When I return to the table, the players are gone. The backgammon set is still on their table, closed and unguarded. After several minutes, one of them returns and sits next to it, drinking another beer.

The music from the café shifts to something quiet. I can hear the sounds of the square through it: birds, traffic, children shrieking and laughing, and, far in the distance, the street corner violin. I finish reading an article on my phone, then pick up my bag of groceries, put on a podcast, and wander home.

Saturday, February 13th, 2021

Fringed, colored banners on wires zigzag above the city square. The cadence repeats: white, blue, yellow, red, orange; white, blue, yellow, red, orange. At first glance, some stretches look like they run in reverse. After a moment, I realize that I'm seeing the sequence from the other side. They cross the road and run along the main street at least as far as the Great Synagogue. I can't see any further from here.

The Sabbath café is closed, even for takeout. Last week, when the lockdown was tighter, it was open. I have to go to a different shop to get coffee.

When the worker hands it to me without a lid, I try to ask for one, but can't remember the word. I try a gesture, covering the cup with my hand. He thinks, for some reason, that I want a receipt. He prints one out. I try again, using the English word "lid."

"Oh," he mumbles, followed by a Hebrew word I can't quite hear. "We don't have –" he mumbles what I think is the same word.

I take my coffee and carry it carefully to the city square. I step around dogs and obstacles, and trace the path of banners: orange, red, yellow, blue, white; orange, red, yellow, blue, white.

Sunday, February 14th, 2021

I face a challenge this morning, getting up the stairs.

As I come outside, I see a watering hose stretching from the outdoor faucet across to a point out of sight. I climb almost to the top. I have enough clearance.

I raise my right foot above the hose. My left foot slips off the wet step it's on. That's OK. I've figured that that might happen, and planned for how the foot would land on the step below without injury.

I'm holding tight onto the banister. My left foot hits the step below. My knee flexes. I shift my weight onto my hands. My right leg is now pointing straight out, still above the hose.

Once I'm balanced on my left foot again, I move my balance to my hands. I hop right and forward onto the step above, where I had slipped. I land securely.

I tilt and bend my right knee until my foot touches the ground on the far side of the hose. I move my hands and my center of gravity toward that leg, then swing my left leg over the hose.

My foot hits the ground as it should. I stand.

My landlord comes running over, apologizing profusely. He hadn't thought I was still at home. It's OK. I'm OK.

He shifts the hose, so it doesn't form such an obstacle. I hope he remembers to do so next time.

Monday, February 15th, 2021

The barber emerges from the back of his shop. His arms are full of towels. I ask him how things have been, now that the lockdown has eased.

"Last week was crazy. I booked everybody. I was too busy. This week, I'm easier on myself. I even let myself wash the towels in the middle of the day."

He stuffs the towels into his washing machine and turns the knob. He gestures at the hair-washing chair. "Please."

I sit down in it and take off my glasses.

"I haven't been working much for the past year. Toward the end, I told the partner of my life that I love her and the kids, but I just want to get out of the house and go to work. I never said that before."

He massages the lather into my scalp. I'm quite aware that, apart from unintended collisions in hallways, these haircuts are the only touch that I've experienced from another person in close to a year.

He wraps a towel around my head and guides me to the barber chair. "You want something not too long, not too short, that you won't have to care for too much." He knows.

The speakers overhead play 70s funk, heavy on the horns. He hums along and dances as he cuts.

"Are you still using that DJI device when you film? I have to get one sometime." I haven't been filming much. But I should be doing a lot more this year.

When he's done, I hand him my customer card and the money. He hands the money back.

"Look at the card. Everything is punched. This one is free." He tears the card up and trashes it. "Say hello to your family for me. I will see you again."

Tuesday, February 16th, 2021

A truck is blocking the sidewalk on the way to work. I have to cross to the other side.

Looking back, I see another truck behind it. Something like a ladder leads from one truck up to the balcony of an apartment, five or six stories above us. Plastic bins that look like trash cans slide down it. A giant claw, rising from the other truck, picks up larger items from the balcony and carries them down to the ground, like a cat carrying kittens by the scruff of the neck. They're gutting the apartment, tearing out everything, including the kitchen sink.

Across the street, someone has finally swept up the mirror that shattered there last week.

A block further on, four women sit on benches in a schoolyard. The school should be opening again next week. They may be teachers preparing for the onslaught of kids, or may just be neighbors, gathering there while it's quiet.

We've been told to expect rain, but I haven't seen it yet. It waits until I'm in the supermarket, getting my afternoon snack. The downpour starts and stops abruptly. What I hear as continuing rain as I prepare to run back around to work turns out to be the sound of cars' tires rolling through fresh puddles.

I walk back inside. I have my hoodie upstairs. As long as it doesn't rain too hard on the way home, I'm ready.

Wednesday, February 17th, 2021

I finally get the courage to ask the boss where I can buy a belt around here. What I've seen in stores so far don't fit me. He's round, too. He would know.

"You should just do what I do. Pick them up when you're in Thailand." He isn't entirely kidding. He tells me a long story about how he got the belt that he is now wearing, and how he found out later that it was made of elephant hide.

"But more quickly, there's a shop on the main street where I get these things. It's one very old man." He gives me the name and address of the store. I had known that there was a place like that on that street, but had forgotten exactly where it was or what its sign would say.

"I will be near there later today. I have to stop at a place next door. I have to get lices." I look confused.

"For my shoes." He raises his foot and points. Oh. Laces.

"It is hard to find those here." I know.

"There is another place that you can get a belt made for you, next to the Grand Synagogue, down a corridor to the left. They make them there. But it will cost twice as much and take twice as long, and may not be better."

After work, I think of going to the shop he suggested. When I get off the bus and start to head toward it, the rain starts up again. I go home. My current belt should last at least until Friday.

Thursday, February 18th, 2021

Our youngest programmer, the only woman on the team, is leaving the company today. I understand that it was a mutual parting of the ways. I think she's headed to another job, though I'm not sure.

She has brought in an immense amount of munchies to celebrate. I've never seen a departing worker do that before. They are arrayed on the counter of the office kitchen: chocolate bars, hamantaschen, crembo, cookies and cakes, plates of cashews and dried cranberries, and other items that I can't name. I eat too much of them. I intentionally don't keep any of that stuff, other than the nuts and dried fruit, in my house. That's why.

The boss gathers us in the corridor between the cubes and gives a grand speech, praising her and wishing her well.

I get more things than usual done today. In the morning, I rewrite a blurb to be sent to our partners about new ways of working together. The boss and my direct boss have written it, so it has some peculiar wording. English seems to use singulars and plurals differently than some other languages. I have to figure out what they meant and sort it out.

In the afternoon, I incorporate fixes from a technical review into a manual I have almost finished. I enjoy working with the programmer who made them. All his comments are precise, understandable, and keyed to the exact line in the document that needs to be fixed.

The fixes are punctuated by trips to the kitchen for more coffee and sweets. It's a good thing that we tend to retain our workers, and don't have these celebrations often.

Friday, February 19th, 2021

I almost miss the clothing shop as I go past. It's raining. Hard. I was going to wait it out, but it hadn't let up by noon. I'm not sure when this place closes for the Sabbath.

The shop is tiny, and right next door to another store with a similar name. I spot it just in time. I stop.

The owner is standing at the doorway, behind a table that blocks customers from coming in. Due to virus restrictions, only two of us could have fit in there. Blocking the door is probably easier.

I step up to him. An awning keeps the rain away. I start to tell him what I want, but I forget the word. I unzip my jacket and tug on my belt. He says the word. I recognize it. I nod.

"What color?" Black. Black always works.

He pulls one off the rack. "Try this. There are larger ones, too." I try it. It's too small.

"OK, one moment." He flips through the rack and pulls out another one. He hands it to me. I try it. Perfect.

"I have other clothes for you, too. Trousers. Jeans. Sweaters. Hoodies that zip up." I tell him that I'll remember this place. I will.

I pay him and head off to do other shopping. I'm tempted to stop, take off my current belt, discard it, and put the new one on. I'm carrying other things, though, and I don't want to put them down on anything in the rain. Odds are good that, if I try to juggle everything, my pants will fall down. I guess I can wait until I get home.

Saturday, February 20th, 2021

I sit on a bench outside the House of a Hundred Grandmothers. Finding my vaccination certificate in my shoulder bag takes a while. It is, of course, where I put things that I can't misplace. I need to have everything organized.

This is the first time in months that family members have been able to visit residents. I make sure my mask is on correctly and head to the guard's desk.

I present my certificate. "Who are you visiting?" I tell him. "And you are?" I tell him.

He pulls out a log book and writes the information down. He gets my name wrong, but it'll be clear who it was.

He brandishes another form and asks me something. I don't understand him. "OK. You may go to the apartment."

The rules are strict. I must go directly there. I can't pause in the halls. I must avoid residents other than my family. I can't take an elevator with anyone else in it.

I head straight there. I notice a few changes on the way. The big fish tank is gone. They've cleared out some clutter in the atrium with the trees. The lights seem brighter.

I get up to the apartment and knock with my usual rhythm. They know it's me anyway, but the pattern is a habit. I go in. My family is there.

Normally, I get a glass of water when I get there, but family members are now not allowed to eat and drink while visiting. Our masks must stay on. We sit and talk for a couple of hours. It's good to be back.

Sunday, February 21st, 2021

The afternoon prayers should start at ten minutes to two. The boss has decreed that. They almost never do.

The agent comes through at about that time, proceeding down the corridors and summoning us. He usually sings. On Thursdays, he sings a song to beckon the Sabbath to come to us. On Sundays, he sings a song to Elijah, welcoming the mundane week.

When he passes me, I change my glasses and head to the hallway. I'm often the first one there. Others respond less rapidly. The boss is generally among the last, making a grand entrance.

When there are ten of us, the prayers start. Sometimes someone has to go back in to round up stragglers.

Today, the best singer among us leads the prayers. It's the anniversary of a relative's passing, so he recites the Mourner's Kaddish at the end. The agent has been saying it every day, since one of his relatives passed away a few months ago. He usually speaks the text plainly, in a consistent rhythm. Today, the prayer leader chants it. The agent chants with him, with the same cadence and melody.

When we're done, we head back into the office. A coworker and I stop by the receptionist's desk and talk about our weekends. As usual, he ran a personal marathon to the beach and back. I got a lot done on the film project.

The conversation quickly runs down. His smartwatch rings with an incoming call. He heads to his desk. I make more coffee, then get back to work.

Monday, February 22nd, 2021

A Russian programmer is asking me something I can't quite follow about volleyball. I eventually realize that he is saying "variable."

It takes me a similar number of repetitions to figure out that the word that the French manager is saying, "Eyarshi," is "hierarchy."

Later, I overhear someone speaking in English on his phone: "Tell me, in America do they make you sign forms with contracts stating that the work is not being done by slaves?"

At work, we get word that the father of a worker passed away last night. Normally, people from the office would go to the funeral. Because of the virus, only family attends the ceremony this afternoon. The worker sends a group text thanking us for our condolences. Because of the virus, we can't come over for the usual shiva calls.

After work, I get a sahlab at the sandwich shop on the city square. As usual, the owner is sitting in the tent outside with other people, each with a coffee cup. Three full ouzo bottles are behind the counter.

I see a teenage girl taking photographs with a real camera, not a phone. She is watching a gap in a fence where kittens live. A woman walks over with an open can and scoops food onto the cement. The kittens and one larger cat come over and eat. It looks like they know the woman well.

The beagle that wanders around the square without a leash walks over to me and sniffs my shoes. They don't tell him anything interesting. He walks away.

Tuesday, February 23rd, 2021

Clusters of people sit outside the coffee shop at the entrance to my office building. Some sit on the benches permanently built into the patio walls. Others sit in yellow plastic chairs. The city has placed these chairs around town, including in the city square. Signs on them invite people to sit.

As I understand it, we're officially not supposed to be sitting at a coffee shop, just getting the coffee and leaving. Maybe it's OK because there aren't any tables.

I'm meeting a relative there. She's getting her second vaccination today. I come down after the afternoon prayers. We haven't seen each other in months. We both have new haircuts, from the same barber. She introduced me to him.

We talk about what we've been up to. I don't have much new to tell. She reads these posts, so she's pretty well caught up. She does say that I make the city sound somewhat nicer than it actually looks.

I fill her in on some details of the film project and of the crowdfunding campaign I'm planning for it. The weather turns colder as we sit there.

I return to work after half an hour. When I come back downstairs a few hours later, it's raining again.

Wednesday, February 24th, 2021

The boss is wearing a fake nose and mustache and a floppy hat. "I cannot live like this!" he bellows in English. "We have no mirrors!" I'm about to suggest that he use his phone, but he has zoomed away from my cube.

We're celebrating Purim today. It's actually on Friday, but we don't work that day, and much of the staff will be fasting tomorrow.

Someone asks who my costume is. I don't have one. I improvise. I put on my sweatshirt and flip the hood up. I'm now Elliot from *Mr. Robot*. The boss hands me a fake nose, mustache, and eyeglasses. "No one may attend the afternoon prayers without these." OK. The temples on the eyeglasses barely fit on my big head. With my mask and real glasses, the space around my ears is crowded.

Several people take pictures before the prayers. During the service, people coming down the hall do a double-take, seeing us worshiping in goofy costumes.

Afterward, the bosses hand out the traditional gift bags of goodies: I get a small bottle of berry liqueur, a couple of hamantaschen, candy bars, cookies, Bamba, and one of those noisemakers that rolls out like Pinocchio's nose when you blow into it.

I hope to attend the online Purim service from my mother's synagogue on Friday. It will come in handy then.

Thursday, February 25th, 2021

A truck rolls slowly past our office building, blasting holiday music. We're four stories up, behind closed windows. The music is too loud for me to work. I stop and listen. The melody is something like "Pick a Bale of Cotton." The lyrics are probably in Hebrew, but may be Yiddish. There's a good jazz piano solo in the midst of it, which sounds like someone I used to know in Brooklyn thirty years ago. Otherwise, the song rumbles and thumps.

I hear the music again as I wait outside the burger joint for my order. The van comes gradually into view. At first, I think it's a gaudy garbage truck. It's about that size. The door to the back is open. Inside, I see a wall of black speakers, two meters tall and wide. Someone I can't see is talking over the music, ignoring its rhythm. He may be in the cab. If he's also driving, it might be good that the truck is that slow.

Many of the other people outside are walking their dogs. An all-night curfew starts in less than an hour. There will be fines for being more than a kilometer from one's house or for visiting anyone. People usually party en masse on Purim. Not this year, or at least not tonight.

The curfew lifts at dawn. There will no doubt be parties during the day in religious enclaves, illegal but too big to shut down.

The burger shop owner calls my name. I hear him through the open door. I go in and pick up my supper. He and I wish each other a happy holiday.

I wander home, listening to a podcast about the recent storms in Texas. Here, for now, it's reasonably warm and dry.

Friday, February 26th, 2021

The angel looks down on the crowd in the city square. Three meters tall on stilts, she could look eye-to-eye at the pirate or either of the clowns, but they are focused on their balance and their juggling.

A gold hula-hoop escapes the grip of one of the acrobats and hits the angel on the leg. It doesn't change her stance. The acrobat catches it again on the rebound.

The musicians at the inner edge of the circle surround them. Two drummers, one with one drum, one with two, maintain a complex rhythm. An alto sax, sousaphone, and two trumpets play repeating riffs, occasionally breaking into contrasting bebop-like phrases.

One acrobat leads the crowd in clapping on the beat. She moves among us, yelling at us to clap, then returns to the inner circle, hops up on a bench and tries to conduct an end to the performance. The drummers aren't watching her. It takes them some time to notice.

The crowd applauds. The performers shout their thanks. The music starts up again. Led by the angel, they cross the street, still playing and juggling. We follow.

They make a right turn. I'm headed straight. I wait for them to pass. The last drummer curves around me and follows the rest down the street.

I walk away. There's still time to finish the rest of my Friday shopping.

Saturday, February 27th, 2021

Fresh flowers are blooming in the park on the way to the House of a Hundred Grandmothers. The city redoes the display occasionally. The plot was barren last I looked, but it isn't now. I don't know what kind of flowers they are. They're all the same, but in different colors.

People and dogs sit or roam around the park. A religious family comes in when I do. The father is wearing black and white. The mother wears more colors, all muted. Neither wears a mask.

Three small children run circles around them. The father pulls an even smaller boy in a contraption somewhere between a classic little red wagon and a portable crib. One girl abruptly runs backward into my path. I stop. We don't collide. An older boy darts out of the bushes, chasing a soccer ball. He catches up with it, kicks it, and chases it back to where he emerged. I guess that only the bushes, or perhaps a broken fence, separate the park from the yard of the house just west of it.

Up a few steps, a circle surrounded by benches is strewn with dirt and drying leaves. No one has swept there in a while. Up more steps, I see more pods in the giraffe trees. It isn't time yet for them to fall.

I check the trash area at the exit for anything worth salvaging. Nothing catches my eye. I continue on.

Sunday, February 28th, 2021

The storefront for the transit pass is crowded. Two people are sitting near the door. A worker is helping a third at the desk.

I'm not sure if there's room for a fourth person under the virus restrictions. There's no sign. I go in.

My monthly pass is about to expire. I'm supposed to be able to recharge it with my phone, but the sensor in the phone doesn't work. I hope to recharge the pass at a kiosk inside.

It looks like the customer at the desk, with her back to me, is getting a pass for the first time. The worker is being careful taking her picture. She holds the webcam at a precise angle and gets an image.

The customer goes behind the worker's desk and looks at the picture. She doesn't like it. One of the women waiting gets up and joins her. She's her mother. She doesn't like it either.

The worker has an idea. "Pick up your chair and sit here, against the wall. The light is better, and your hair will look good against the beige."

She does. I can now see her face. She is strikingly beautiful, with perfect hair and precisely artful makeup. I understand why she's particular about the photo.

The other woman sitting by the door calls out suggestions. I ask if I can just go ahead and use the machine. I can't. Its network connection is down.

The worker types in some data, puts a card into a machine, and turns to me. "That will take a minute. Do you have your pass and a credit card?"

I have them ready. I tell her that I want the same monthly pass that I've been getting.

She puts my pass on a sensor, and types a lot of information into the credit card machine. She slaps my card down next to it. "And now we pray."

After a moment, something makes a disappointing sound: bee-doop. "I'm sorry. The credit card network is broken. We can try cash, or you can come back tomorrow."

I have to be near there in the morning anyway. I'll try again then.

(the start of) March 2021

Monday, March 1st, 2021

A line of white-haired men waits outside the transit pass storefront in the early morning. It's the first of the month, and time for them to get new monthly passes. I'm on my way to work. I decide to come back yet again in the evening.

The owner of the sandwich shop on the city square sits in a tent across from it, along with about eight other people. Nothing is going on. They're just sitting.

Outside the bakery, a man with an amplified tenor recorder plays "My Way" with a karaoke backing.

The manager of the burger joint rolls a shopping cart filled with gallon jars of pickle slices toward his shop.

After work, on the bus back to the Heart of the City, I find that my transit pass is completely empty. The driver waves me on anyway.

I stop at the ATM when I get off the bus. If the network at the shop is still down, I'll be ready.

When I get back to the storefront, no one is waiting. I pay cash. I also put another fifty shekels on the card. If I don't renew the monthly pass in time in the future, I can still pay for rides.

For another five shekels, I buy a doohickey that can read the card and recharge it from my computer. The worker asks me something. I don't understand.

She tries again, more simply. "Do you know how to connect this? It's USB." I think I can handle that. I now have all the transit bases covered, just in case.

Tuesday, March 2nd, 2021

The new programmer starts talking to me in Russian. I don't know what he's saying. He can tell. He quickly switches to Hebrew. I still don't understand him. He pauses. "English?" I nod.

His English is quite good. We talk for a couple of minutes. He asks if I'm from England. Nope, the US.

"Really? I have never met an American who speaks as clearly as you do." I tell him that I used to be on the radio.

Across the aisle from me, a long-time programmer digs into system code. He repeatedly shakes his head, tsks, and repeats the name of the programmer who died last year, who had worked at that same desk. He was a good person, but left a trail of bugs in his wake.

Another programmer, who retired at about the same time, has come back to work for a few days. He and the boss are hollering at each other behind closed doors. They work well together and are quite close, but you wouldn't know that from listening to them.

The sales person whose father passed away last week has returned. He would sometimes participate in the afternoon prayers. I figure that he will join us to say the Mourner's Kaddish. He doesn't. He can join if he wants. There's no pressure to do so.

Toward the end of the day, we get a new rule about ordering lunches. Some of us have waited each morning for the group text nudging us to order, since sometimes the bosses would order something different for us. Now we're told to order every day that we want to. If the bosses want to override that, they can. But if they don't, orders must be in by a certain time, with or without the prompt.

They send out a Google Invite for every workday starting now, so our calendars will automatically remind us. That will work, too.

Wednesday, March 3rd, 2021

The boss stands in the aisle and makes a grand announcement. I don't understand it. He repeats it for me in English.

"In the kitchen, we now have ten empty Nescafé jars on the counter. They should go away. They could be good for making – what do people make with cucumbers?" Pickles? "Yes, they could be good for making pickles."

Purim has passed. Passover is coming quickly. The bosses have sent out an email that they'll be ordering supplies for the office and the kitchen. If we want anything, we should let them know.

In the afternoon, I get an email from my family. We're doing the Passover seder together with a relative out of town. We'll be there for two days.

I'm in charge of getting disposable dishes, to make that part of the setup easier. They send me a comprehensive text message with what to get: tablecloths, dinner plates, forks, knives, serving platters, all disposable. It's daunting. I know that I can get most of it at the Heart of the City, where there's a full aisle of that stuff. But I'll have to see if I do better.

It's in about three weeks. Time to get working on it.

Thursday, March 4th, 2021

I get all the way to my office building before I realize that I've forgotten my mask. I usually remember to wear one. When I forget, I'm reminded by seeing someone else with one.

There are usually other people walking on my street: with dogs, to their cars, or to the trash heap. I see them when I step through the gate. It's raining today. I walk all the way to work before I see anybody else.

I'm self-conscious as I go through the lobby and up to my office with a naked face. No one else seems to notice.

Once at my desk, I dig into my shoulder bag. I keep a spare stash of masks in it just in case this happens. It hasn't before.

When I put one on later to go down the hall to the men's room, I feel that it's tighter than the ones that I have been wearing. My first thought is that it doesn't fit as well. My second is that it fits better. Less air might escape. The tip of my nose is squished. but I can live with that.

I don't care for the generic pale blue. It reminds me of commercials for diapers and other absorbent things. I usually wear purple. But this mask will suffice for today.

Friday, March 5th, 2021

I hear music booming in the distance as I approach the city square. When I round the bend past the café, I see a DJ setup with massive speakers. It's standing alone on the traffic island that I cross to the square itself. No one is near it. No one appears to be in charge. The music does a skillful segue between songs. It may be a prerecorded playlist. Someone may be mixing remotely. I don't hear an announcer.

The square and the main street are mobbed. The whole city seems to be shopping and hanging out there. The weather is perfect. Some of us are wearing sweatshirts. Many people are not. It isn't raining.

I make my usual stops in the supermarket and the bakery. I get a sabich in the shop a few doors down.

Most of the tables in the square are taken. I find one near where I usually sit, a little further from the Friday backgammon players. I eat my lunch there.

When I'm done, I get an espresso at the café. I stand and drink it off to the side. The music is still booming, with no one guarding it. In other cities where I've lived, the setup might have been stolen or smashed by now.

As I throw my espresso cup away, I realize that I've forgotten one purchase. My imperious cleaning person should finally appear tomorrow after several lockdown delays. She has commanded me to get more floor cleaner. Yes, Ma'am. I stop into the tiny supermarket across from the café and get it.

On my way home, three young men walking in front of me stop, put their packages down, climb a wall, and pick kumquats from a tree in someone's yard. Apparently, the kumquats are delicious. Some fall to the ground. The cats enjoy them, too.

Saturday, March 6th, 2021

I drop in on family at the House of a Hundred Grandmothers at the usual time this afternoon. We talk about how we're doing, the future of this Facebook project, getting my life organized financially, and other such things.

I don't stay as long as usual. The cleaner is coming after three months away. That's good. The fruit flies in the kitchen have been complaining about conditions in there.

I get a message that the Cinematheque is opening on Tuesday. They're showing a film of a Nick Cave concert. I don't know his music, though I'm told that I should. I immediately buy a ticket. I'll be there.

Looking further, I see that the dance center is opening up again. My favorite troupe will be there in April. Done. The ticket prices are higher than before, but I can handle that, It makes sense. The audience is limited, and they have to catch up on close to a year without revenue from shows.

I have my Green Pass, showing that I've been vaccinated, right on the home screen of my phone. I'll have to have that or the paper vaccination certificate to get into the theatre. I'm ready. I'm not about to binge on entertainment, but it will be good to get out among people again.

Sunday, March 7th, 2021

I haven't eaten indoors at the Sabbath café before. I also don't think I've been there when it isn't the Sabbath. I think I started going there when the House of Hundred Grandmothers first went on lockdown last year and I couldn't visit family.

The restaurants are open as of today. I've been craving shakshuka all afternoon. I head there straight from work. I stop in the doorway.

A server sees me. "Do you want to eat inside? You'll need your Green Pass." I show it to her on my phone. I tell her that it's the first time I've used it. She responds with a Hebrew word that doesn't translate, sort of like "*Bon Appétit,*" but usually used when you see someone wearing new clothes.

I sit down at a table for one in the corner. A few parties are at other tables, which are spaced further from each other than before.

I order the shakshuka. It's as good as I remember and less expensive. It comes with a salad, two large rolls, a ramekin of tahini and one of olives.

The order comes quickly. The server makes a mistake putting it down on the table. The handle of the burning-hot pan points right at my chest. That's happened before. I use my fork and knife to rotate it gingerly to where it isn't a danger.

I eat everything. Later in the evening, I feel like I may have eaten too much. But it's worth it.

Monday, March 8th, 2021

I invite someone on Facebook to our afternoon prayers. He has been looking for people doing them in the area. He doesn't show. That's OK. I think some of the other invitations were closer to him.

During the Mourner's Kaddish, a soldier walks through twice in the same direction. I guess that he's lost and in a loop. Someone we don't know shows up at the back at the same time. He hasn't come for the prayers, but doesn't want to disrupt them. He knows that we're about a minute from the end. He stands quietly until it's over.

The power goes out in the building about an hour later. I lose about twenty minutes of work, but I can easily recreate it. The boss comes out of his office singing wedding music. He announces that the bride and groom are about to come down the aisle. This must refer to some tradition that I don't know.

As we stand around, a new worker asks me what kind of music I make. I try to describe the soundtrack that I'm working on now, with the layers of algorithmic improvisations and mixes of scrambled speech and found sounds. He says that he's into the Rolling Stones. I surprise him by singing a bit of one of their more obscure songs, which I don't think has ever been on an album.

Later, he gets to talking with a programmer about Peter Hammill's music. They're both fans, but of different parts of his career. I only know one of his songs, though I knew what he sang on a Robert Fripp album. We talk about music for a while.

When the lights come back on, we return to work.

Tuesday, March 9th, 2021

"Please be patient. The technology has been sleeping for a year." The woman at the front of the hall turns and looks at two men behind her. One turns knobs and pushes buttons. The other shrugs.

I have gotten to the theatre early. I'm one of the first audience members. They haven't quite sorted out the ritual of entering.

I need to show them my Green Pass, so they know that I've been vaccinated. Or maybe I don't. There's a disagreement over that.

I do need to show my ticket, which is on my phone. They try to scan it a few times before it works.

I have to wave my hand in front of the thermometer, which shouts "Normal temperature!" in English. Apparently there's no volume control.

And I have to show them my government ID.

I finally get to sit down and watch workers fumble with the setup up front. A laptop is playing videos via VLC on the big screen, but there's no sound. Eventually someone changes a setting, then changes it back to how it was. The sound returns.

I count 24 people in the hall. The maximum, when seats aren't blocked off, is 158. The food counter is closed. I doubt that they're making any money tonight, even with tickets priced at 50 percent more than they were when the theatre was last open a year ago, but it's a test.

About fifteen minutes after the start time, a man without a mask picks up a microphone and talks to us. He's a local DJ and author. I understand about half of what he's saying. He seems to be going on for a long time, but he's enthusiastic and most of the audience enjoys it. I keep watching the computer clock on the screen. I wouldn't feel time passing so keenly if it weren't there.

After half an hour, he thanks us and puts down the mic. People applaud. The lights go down. The movie finally begins.

Wednesday, March 10th, 2021

A year ago yesterday, I posted here about seeing people with masks on a bus for the first time. I posted the next day and the next, keeping to a set of writing guidelines that I had made for myself. I have kept going every day since then, posting (since I started counting) 200-500 words a day.

Now, 365 daily posts later, I think I'm done. We've had a bit of a return to some of how things were. I'm frankly running out of things to say. Rather than stretch on like a TV series whose network insists that it continue after it's run out of gas, I feel that it's time to stop.

epilogue

September 2021

Monday, September 6th, 2021

Rosh Hashanah eve at the House of a Hundred Grandmothers: I get there a little earlier than planned. I'm wearing a new white shirt and a generic tan baseball cap above my usual jeans and sandals. Both my boss and my family have nudged me into trimming my goatee.

I go upstairs and meet my family, then come back down with them. We head over to the Nursing Unit. As has become a tradition at the House, I'm saying the prayer over wine, the Kiddush, while other family members say the other prayers (this time, over apples and honey).

The staff greet me like I'm some sort of celebrity. It helps that my family are unofficial spiritual leaders there. My voice sounds good while I sing the prayer. After some mistakes in previous visits, I know to start low in my range, allowing room for the high notes. I lose the melody at one point, but improvise something that fits the words until I get back to where I know what I'm doing.

The second prayer, the Shehechiyanu, isn't as easy. It's shorter, and I know the text, so I look up and around at the residents gathered there. I hear my voice start to choke up and break as I sing "... that you have kept us alive, sustained us, and brought us to this season." The prayer gets to me. While some in the room have been in the Nursing Unit for years, some who were here for the last holiday are no longer with us, and some who are here now may not make it to the next.

We leave that room and wait outside the dining hall for it to open. Other family members join us, having come in from out of town. There's a bit of a traffic jam in the hallway, as wheelchairs and walkers jostle to get past one another.

When we are let in, my family, all seven of us, sit at the head table. Another family member, as, again, is the tradition, says the Kiddush for all assembled, and gives the ritual explanation for other items on the table (pomegranates, dates, fish heads, apples and honey).

The top staff of the House join the usual workers in serving dinner. There's a lot of food: chicken soup with a sort of wonton in it, salad, chopped liver, gefilte fish, roasted goose, potatoes, carrots, and rice, with a dessert of peach strudel with non-dairy ice cream and a drizzle of chocolate.

The head of the family says the prayer after meals as people disperse. Many come by our table to wish us a happy new year and to coo at the three-year-old at the far end of the table. The Hundred Grandmothers do what grandmothers do best.

I head back upstairs with my family, then return downstairs and go home. I take the long way, around the park rather than through it, in case my end of it is locked.

My landlords aren't home. I guess that they're off with their many children and grandchildren. I come inside my apartment, upload the photo, and start writing.

About the Author

Joseph Zitt is an author, composer, filmmaker, and multimedia artist. After spending most of his life in various cities around the USA, he now lives in Israel. *www.josephzitt.com*

Selected Works

Books

- *The Book of Voices*
- *Surprise Me With Beauty: The Music of Human Systems*
- *19th Nervous Breakdown: Making Human Connections in the Landscape of Commerce*

Music

- *Comma: (voices)*
- *Moses (for speaker and Orchestra)*
- *Jerusaklyn*

Films

- *How Beautiful: the Transformation of Sacred Space*
- *Mandala Shores*

Performance

- *Shekhinah: the Presence*
- *Minyan: after Chagall*

www.ingramcontent.com/pod-product-compliance
Lightning Source LLC
Chambersburg PA
CBHW051304130726
47987CB00004B/1658